The
Princeton
Review®

WITHDRAWN

SAT®

ADVANCED

The Staff of The Princeton Review

PrincetonReview.com

Penguin
Random
House

The Princeton Review
110 East 42nd St, 7th Floor
New York, NY 10017

Published in the United States by Penguin Random House,
LLC, New York, and in Canada by Random House of Canada,
division of Penguin Random House Ltd., Toronto.

Terms of Service: The Princeton Review Online Companion
Tools ("Student Tools") for retail books are available for only
the two most recent editions of that book. Student Tools may
be activated only once per eligible book purchased for a total
of 24 months of access. Activation of Student Tools more than
once per book is in direct violation of these Terms of Service
and may result in discontinuation of access to Student Tools
Services.

SAT is a registered trademark of the College Board, which
does not sponsor or endorse this product.

The Princeton Review is not affiliated with Princeton
University.

ISBN: 978-0-525-57170-4
eBook ISBN: 978-0-525-57184-1
ISSN: 2767-7265

The material in this book is up-to-date at the time of
publication. However, changes may have been instituted by
the testing body in the test after this book was published.

If there are any important late-breaking developments,
changes, or corrections to the materials in this book, we will
post that information online in the Student Tools. Register
your book and check your Student Tools to see if there are any
updates posted there.

Editor: Eleanor Green
Production Editor: Sarah Litt and Liz Dacey
Production Artist: Jennifer Chapman

Printed in the United States of America.

10 9 8 7 6 5 4 3 2 1

Editorial

Rob Franek, Editor-in-Chief
David Soto, Director of Content Development
Stephen Koch, Student Survey Manager
Deborah Weber, Director of Production
Gabriel Berlin, Production Design Manager
Selena Coppock, Director of Editorial
Aaron Riccio, Senior Editor
Meave Shelton, Senior Editor
Anna Goodlett, Editor
Chris Chimera, Editor
Eleanor Green, Editor
Orion McBean, Editor
Patricia Murphy, Editorial Assistant

Penguin Random House Publishing Team

Tom Russell, VP, Publisher
Alison Stoltzfus, Publishing Director
Brett Wright, Senior Editor
Amanda Yee, Associate Managing Editor
Ellen Reed, Production Manager
Suzanne Lee, Designer
Eugenia Lo, Publishing Assistant

For customer service, please contact
editorialsupport@review.com,
and be sure to include:

- full title of the book

- ISBN

- page number

Acknowledgments

Authors
Sara Kuperstein
Amy Minster
Cynthia Ward

Contributors
Anne Bader
Brian Becker
Gabby Budzon
Brad Kelly
Dave MacKenzie
Kathryn Menafee
Elizabeth Owens
Danielle Perrini
Jess Thomas

National Content Director, High School Programs
Amy Minster

Contents

Get More
(Free) Content
at PrincetonReview.com/prep

As easy as **1•2•3**

1 Go to PrincetonReview.com/prep
or scan the **QR code**
and enter the following
ISBN for your book:
9780525571704

2 Answer a few simple questions
to set up an exclusive
Princeton Review account.
*(If you already have one,
you can just log in.)*

3 Enjoy access to
your **FREE** content!

Once you've registered, you can...

- Access and print out extra SAT practice drills, as well as corresponding answers and explanations

- Take a full-length SAT and/or ACT

- Get valuable advice about the college application process, including tips for writing a great essay and where to apply for financial aid

- If you're still choosing between colleges, use our searchable rankings of *The Best 387 Colleges* to find out more information about your dream school

- Check to see if there have been any corrections or updates to this edition

Need to report a potential **content** issue?

Contact **EditorialSupport@review.com** and include:

- full title of the book
- ISBN
- page number

Need to report a **technical** issue?

Contact **TPRStudentTech@review.com** and provide:

- your full name
- email address used to register the book
- full book title and ISBN
- Operating system (Mac/PC) and browser (Firefox, Safari, etc.)

Part I
Orientation

Chapter 1
Introduction to the SAT

The pursuit of a perfect or near-perfect SAT score is an impressive goal. Achieving that goal requires a thorough command of the material and strategies specific to the SAT. To begin your quest, learn everything you can about the test. This chapter presents an overview of the SAT, advice about when to take it, and a guide to reporting your scores.

WELCOME

So you think you can score a 1450 or better? We're all for it. The Princeton Review supports all students who want to do their best. We've written this book specifically for students who are in a position to score at the very highest levels. We believe that to achieve a perfect or near-perfect score, you have to know as much as possible about the test itself and, more importantly, know yourself.

You may know all of the basic facts about the SAT already, but even if you think you do, we encourage you to read through this chapter to be sure you know every single thing you can about the test you're going to conquer.

FUN FACTS ABOUT THE SAT

All of the content review and strategies we teach in the following lessons are based on the specific structure and format of the SAT. Before you can beat the test, you have to know how it's built.

Structure

The SAT consists of three main sections: Reading, Writing and Language, and Math. The Math is broken into two sub-sections, the first of which must be completed without the use of a calculator.

Reading	Writing and Language	Math (No Calculator)	Math (Calculator)
65 minutes	35 minutes	25 minutes	55 minutes
52 questions	44 questions	20 questions	38 questions

Prior to June 2021, the SAT also included an "optional" essay, but that has been eliminated. Without that section, you're looking at about three hours of test-taking. That takes some stamina!

Scoring

The Reading and Writing and Language sections are scored together on a scale from 200–800, and added to the total from the two Math sections (also on a scale from 200–800) for a total score between 400 to 1600. There are also a series of sub-scores that point out how you did on specific types of questions, such as math problems that require data analysis or reading questions that focus on understanding words in context. All that really matters, however, is the overall score, which has a maximum of 1600.

Content

In Parts II–IV, we'll thoroughly review the content and strategies you need for each of the three main sections. Here is a brief overview of each section.

Reading

The Reading section contains five passages, for which there will be 52 multiple-choice questions (10 or 11 per passage). These passages can be anywhere from 500 to 750 words, may include associated data to be interpreted along with the text, and range from literature to social studies and science. One of the five passages will actually have two shorter, paired passages. Passage-based questions are *never* presented in order of difficulty; the order of questions tends to be chronological.

Writing and Language

The Writing and Language section consists of four passages, each with 11 associated questions, for a total of 44 multiple-choice questions. These tend to be shorter passages, somewhere between 400 and 450 words, but otherwise cover the same topics as the Reading section, as well as some career-oriented topics.

Math

The Math section features 58 questions, split between a no-calculator section (20 questions) and a calculator section (38 questions). Both Math sections are made up of mostly multiple-choice questions, and both sections feature grid-in questions at the end (5 and 8, respectively). Within the multiple-choice portion, there is a loose order of difficulty, which resets with the start of the grid-in questions. Even though the first few grid-ins are "easier," some students find the lack of multiple-choice options to be tricky.

Content on the Math section is drawn from arithmetic, pre-algebra, elementary algebra, intermediate algebra, plane geometry, and coordinate geometry. Some advanced topics, such as trigonometric ratios and radian measure, are tested, but they make up only a small percentage of all questions.

THE SAT SCHEDULE

In the United States, the SAT is offered seven times a year: August, October, November, December, March, May, and June. The March test is not offered in international locations.

Take the SAT when your schedule best allows. Many high-scorers take their first SAT in the fall of their junior year. If you have more commitments in the fall from sports, plays, or clubs, then plan to take your first SAT in the winter or spring.

Many high school counselors advise waiting to take the SAT until spring because students may be unfamiliar with some of the more difficult material before then. Students on an honors track, however, will have covered all of the content by the end of sophomore year at the latest. Even if you aren't in an honors program, there are relatively few concepts that will be unfamiliar to you.

Most students end up taking the SAT two or three times. We recommend that you find a 3–4 month window in your schedule that covers at least two SAT tests. Prep first, take a test, then continue prepping as needed for a second or third test. This way, you can be done with the SAT in a relatively short period of time.

REGISTERING FOR THE SAT

Go to collegeboard.org and create a student account. At collegeboard.org, you can view test dates, fees, and registration deadlines. You can research the requirements and processes to apply for extended time or other accommodations, register for the test, view your scores, and order score reports.

You can contact College Board customer service by phone at 866-756-7346 (or +1 212-713-7789 for international callers), but you cannot sign up for the test by phone if you are taking it for the first time.

Test Security

As part of the registration process, you have to upload or mail a photograph that will be printed on your admissions ticket. On test day, you have to take the ticket and acceptable photo identification with you.

Registration Tips

You have options for obtaining SAT score reports, copies of your test, and cancellation. We have recommendations on each.

Score Reports

When you register, do not supply the codes for any schools on your application list. Wait until you are happy with your score and no longer plan to take the SAT before you choose the scores to send to your schools. Any extra fees are worth this flexibility.

Test Information Release

If you take your first SAT in October, March, or May, we recommend you sign up for the Question and Answer Service when you register. Six to eight weeks after the test, you'll receive a copy of the test and your answers. This service costs an additional fee and is available only for the dates above. You can order the Question and Answer Service up to five months after the test date, but it's easier to order at the time you register. It's a great tool to help you prepare for your next SAT.

How Many Times Should You Take the SAT?

We will be thrilled if you review the content in this book, take the SAT for the first time, and earn the score you seek. If you don't hit your target score the first time, take it again. In fact, we recommend that you enter the process planning to take the SAT two or three times. Nerves and anxiety can be unpredictable catalysts, and for many students, the first experience can seem harder than what you've seen in practice. Perception is reality, so we won't waste your time explaining that it only *seems* harder and different. That's why we recommend taking your first SAT as soon as you think you may be ready. Get that first experience with a real test over with as soon as possible, and leave yourself enough time to take the test again. Subsequent administrations won't seem nearly as hard and daunting as the first.

While no one wants to take the SAT more than three times, it's not out of the question if you haven't reached the score you need. Just make sure you consider what you will do differently before taking the test again. Dedicate yourself to trying new strategies that you initially thought you wouldn't need.

Score Choice

College Board allows you to choose which scores you want to send to colleges. If you take the test multiple times, make sure to wait until you get the score you want. Then you can send just that score to the schools on your list. However, keep in mind that some colleges and scholarship programs may ask you to send all your SAT scores.

Score Cancellation

You have the option to cancel your scores, either immediately (at the testing center) or soon after the exam. Usually, you should use this option only under extreme circumstances—you were violently ill, there was a punk band rehearsing in the next classroom, or something equally dramatic. Don't cancel your scores just because you feel like you had a bad day; you can always take the test again, and it's good to have a starting point to compare subsequent tests to. If you *really* feel you must cancel your scores, you have until 11:59 P.M. (EST) on the Wednesday after the exam. See the College Board website for more information.

HOW TO PREPARE FOR THE SAT

The following lessons cover the content and strategies for the Math, Reading, and Writing and Language sections. Review all lessons, even in the subjects that you think you already have targeted as your strengths. We want to make sure you're thoroughly prepared, and we'll risk boring you a tad to cover content you may know. But we won't waste your time. All of the content and strategies we cover are necessary.

As we noted above, the easiest path to your best score is to maximize your strengths. Earn every point that you can from your strengths even as you acquire new skills and strategies to improve your weaknesses.

Practice, Practice, Practice

To achieve a great SAT score, you have to practice a lot! We recommend that you practice with both real SAT tests and Princeton Review practice tests.

You can also pick up a copy of the College Board's *The Official SAT Study Guide*, which contains real practice tests, answer explanations, and scoring guides. That said, this same content can also be printed out for free from the College Board website at collegereadiness.collegeboard.org/sat/practice/full-length-practice-tests.

For more practice materials, The Princeton Review publishes *SAT Premium Prep* and *10 Practice Tests for the SAT*. In addition, we recommend contacting your local Princeton Review office to investigate free practice test dates and follow-up sessions. Visit princetonreview.com for more information, including a comprehensive list of all other available titles.

TEST-TAKER, KNOW THYSELF

As we said at the beginning of this chapter, to earn a perfect or near-perfect score on the SAT, it's not enough to know everything about the test. You also need to know yourself. Identify your own strengths and weaknesses. Don't try to make yourself something you're not. You do not need to be a master of every subject to earn a top score on the SAT. You do need to be a master test-taker. Stop the part of your brain that wants to do the question the *right* way. *How* you get the question right doesn't matter. All that matters is that you get it right. So don't waste time trying to make yourself into the math or reading genius you thought you needed to be.

Read more in the next chapter about the overall strategies, and read through all the lessons in individual subjects that follow. Be willing to tweak what you already do well, and be willing to try entirely new approaches for what you don't do well.

Summary

- ○ Knowing the structure of the SAT is the first step to mastering the test.

- ○ Set aside a few months in your schedule to allow for consistent SAT prep until you get your goal score.

- ○ Order the Question and Answer Service if it's available for your test date.

- ○ Plan to take the SAT 2–3 times.

- ○ Take the SAT again if you do not achieve the best score you've hit in practice.

- ○ Know your options about score reporting and cancellation.

- ○ Practice on real SATs as much as possible.

- ○ Use Princeton Review practice materials to supplement your preparation.

Chapter 2
Strategy, Pacing, and Scoring

To earn a perfect or near-perfect SAT score, you need strategies specific to the SAT. In this chapter, we'll provide an overview of the universal strategies. Each section of the SAT demands a specific approach, and even the most universal strategies vary in their applications. In Parts II–IV, we'll discuss these strategies in greater detail customized to the Writing and Language, Math, and Reading sections.

THE BASIC APPROACH

The SAT is different from the tests you take in school, and, therefore, you need to approach the SAT differently. The Princeton Review's strategies are not arbitrary. To be effective, strategies have to be based on the SAT and not just any old test.

Enemy #1: Time

Consider the structure of each section. On the Reading Test, for example. you'll have 65 minutes to answer 52 questions. Depending on how long it takes you to read the passages, which is why we encourage skimming and actively reading, that's not much more than a minute per question. Time is your enemy on the SAT, and you have to use it wisely and be aware of how that time pressure can bring out your worst instincts as a test-taker.

Enemy #2: Yourself

There is something particularly evil about tests like the SAT. The skills you've been rewarded for throughout your academic career can easily work against you. You've been taught since you started school to follow directions, go in order, and finish everything. But treating the SAT the same way you would a school test won't necessarily earn you a perfect or near-perfect score.

On the other hand, treating the SAT as a scary, alien beast can leave your brain blank and can lead to irrational, self-defeating behavior. When you pick up a #2 pencil, you tend to leave your common sense at the door. Test nerves and anxieties can make you misread a question, commit a careless error, see something that isn't there, blind you to what is there, talk you into a bad answer, and worst of all, convince you to spend good time after bad.

Work Smarter, Not Harder

When you're already answering most questions correctly, it can be difficult to change your approach. But to answer nearly *every* question correctly, you have to do something different. You can't just work harder. Instead, you have to work smarter. Realize what isn't working. Be open-minded about changing your approach. Know what to tweak and what to replace entirely. Determine when to abandon one approach and try another.

The following is an introduction to the general strategies to use on the SAT. In Parts II–IV we'll discuss how these strategies are customized for each section on the SAT.

SAT STRATEGIES

Pacing

The biggest mistake many high scorers make is to spend too *little* time on the easy and medium questions, and too *much* time on the hard ones. That might seem backward—the hard questions are hard (duh), so you need to spend as much time as possible on them, right?

The problem with this approach is that if you rush through the easy and medium questions, you are almost certain to make a few careless mistakes, which will have a devastating impact on your score. If you want to score in the high 700s on a section, you can't afford *any* careless mistakes. So here's the first step toward improving your score: *slow down* and spend enough time (but not a minute more) on the easy and medium questions to get *every* one of them right. With practice, you should have enough time for the hard questions as well, but you've got to get the easy and medium questions right first.

Personal Order of Difficulty (POOD)

Because the questions on the SAT aren't presented in order of difficulty, you'll want to create your own Personal Order of Difficulty (POOD). Don't be a slave to the order of the test. If you're stumped by a question, circle it and come back later. Do all the questions that are easy and medium *for you*, and save the hardest ones for last.

Process of Elimination (POE)

Multiple-choice questions offer one great advantage: they provide the correct answer right there on the page. Of course, they hide the correct answer amidst three incorrect answers. However, it's often easier to spot the wrong answers than it is to identify the right ones, particularly when you apply a smart Process of Elimination (POE).

The Best Way to Bubble In

Work a page at a time, circling your answers right in the booklet. Transfer all the answers from a single page to the bubble sheet at once. It's better to stay focused on working questions than to disrupt your concentration to find where you left off on the scantron. This will also help you remember to leave blanks for questions that you plan on coming back to. If you do this, you'll become more accurate at both tasks.

POE is a powerful strategy on the SAT. For some question types, you'll always use POE rather than wasting time trying to figure out the answer on your own. For other questions, you'll use POE when you're stuck. The SAT hides the correct answer behind wrong ones, but when you cross off just one or two wrong answers, the correct answer can become more obvious, sometimes jumping right off the page.

POOD, Pacing, and POE all work together to help you get as many questions right as possible.

Use Your Pencil
You own the test booklet, and you should write where and when it helps you. Use your pencil to literally cross off wrong answers on the page.

SCORING

There are two types of scores on the SAT: raw and scaled. Your raw score on the SAT is the number of questions you got right, period. Every time you answer an SAT question correctly, you get 1 raw point, regardless of the difficulty or type.

Because the questions on the SAT are constantly changing, the College Board scales the scores as it converts from the raw number of correct answers to your final 400–1600 score. However, these deviations tend to be minor, so you should be able to use the following conversion table, based on recently released data, to get an idea of how many questions you'll have to get right to reach your target score.

RAW SCORE CONVERSION TABLE 1 SECTION AND TEST SCORES

Raw Score (# of correct answers)	Math Section Score	Reading Test Score	Writing and Language Test Score	Raw Score (# of correct answers)	Math Section Score	Reading Test Score	Writing and Language Test Score
0	200	10	10	30	530	28	29
1	200	10	10	31	540	28	30
2	210	10	10	32	550	29	30
3	230	11	10	33	560	29	31
4	240	12	11	34	560	30	32
5	260	13	12	35	570	30	32
6	280	14	13	36	580	31	33
7	290	15	13	37	590	31	34
8	310	15	14	38	600	32	34
9	320	16	15	39	600	32	35
10	330	17	16	40	610	33	36
11	340	17	16	41	620	33	37
12	360	18	17	42	630	34	38
13	370	19	18	43	640	35	39
14	380	19	19	44	650	35	40
15	390	20	19	45	660	36	
16	410	20	20	46	670	37	
17	420	21	21	47	670	37	
18	430	21	21	48	680	38	
19	440	22	22	49	690	38	
20	450	22	23	50	700	39	
21	460	23	23	51	710	40	
22	470	23	24	52	730	40	
23	480	24	25	53	740		
24	480	24	25	54	750		
25	490	25	26	55	760		
26	500	25	26	56	780		
27	510	26	27	57	790		
28	520	26	28	58	800		
29	520	27	28				

CONVERSION EQUATION 1 SECTION AND TEST SCORES

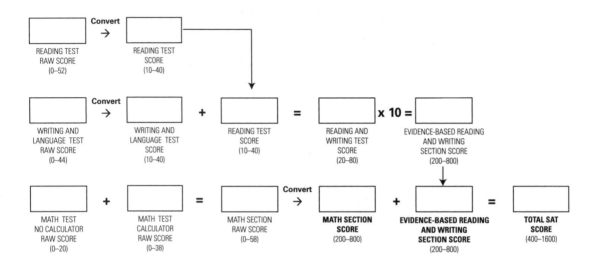

Should You Guess?

There is no penalty for guessing, so think of this question another way: should you leave a question blank and have a 100% chance of getting it wrong, or guess and have at least a 25% chance of getting it right? Obviously you should fill something in. It can only help your score. Ideally, you'll have the time to make an educated guess, using POE to increase your odds, but if you've only got a minute or two left, pick a letter and bubble it in for all of the remaining choices. This letter will be your letter of the day (LOTD).

BE RUTHLESS

The worst mistake a test-taker can make is to throw good time after bad. You read a question, don't understand it, so you read it again. And again. If you stare at it really hard, you know you're going to just *see* it. And you can't move on, because really, after spending all that time it would be a waste not to keep at it, right?

Wrong. You can't let one tough question drag you down, and you can't let your worst instincts tempt you into self-defeating behavior. Instead, the surest way to earn a great SAT score is to follow our advice.

- Use the techniques and strategies in the lessons to work efficiently and *accurately* through the questions. Set a goal right now of zero careless mistakes.
- Know when to move on. If you're stuck, come back later.

In Parts II–IV, you'll learn how POOD, Pacing, and POE work in each section.

SAT HIGH-SCORER MYTHS, BUSTED

At the Princeton Review, we've worked with thousands of students who are aiming for a top SAT score, so we've witnessed all the mistakes they've made in their prep. Let's look at how the typical high-scoring student approaches the quest for a near-perfect SAT score.

This student goes through the test quickly and in the order the questions are given. After all, it's pretty easy! The student doesn't write much on the test, since most math problems can be done only on the calculator or using mental math, and for the rest of the test you can just look at the answers and choose the correct one, right? Then, this student makes a bunch of careless mistakes, but the student dismisses them because, after all, those questions should have been easy. The student takes a full practice test every day for a week, thinking that more time spent doing SAT questions will result in a higher score. However, the student doesn't take the time to learn SAT-specific strategies (instead, doing everything the way it is taught in school) or to review why the student missed the questions that were incorrect. This student might eventually see some progress, but probably not before running out of practice materials!

This student has a completely wrong idea about how to effectively and efficiently boost their score. Let's bust some myths that this example illustrates:

MYTH: If I need to answer all or almost all the questions on the test to get my goal score, it doesn't matter if I make the effort to find and answer the easier questions first.

BUSTED: It is always worth the small amount of time it takes to find easier questions to answer first. Say you are working the Reading section and you often miss a couple of questions on the first passage, which is fiction, but never on the science passages. By starting with the science passages, you will build up points and confidence right away. When you get to the fiction passage later on (probably working it last), you will not only have a good sense of how you are doing, but you will also know exactly how much time you have left for the passage that is hardest for you. If you don't have much time left, you can be sure to work only the easiest questions on the final passage and use your LOTD on any you don't get to. If, however, you have plenty of time, you can really work that last passage, confident that you've already completed all the other questions in the section.

MYTH: If I move quickly through a section, I can save a few minutes at the end to check my work.

> **POOD!**
> Using your Personal Order of Difficulty (POOD) means skipping questions that are harder or more time-consuming *for you*, at least initially. For more on this topic, see page 13.

BUSTED: This is not a smart strategy. If you hurry through the section, you are likely to make careless errors on some questions you know how to do. Also, once you get to the end, you've already chosen an answer for the questions, so it will be difficult to identify ones that you got wrong. It is much better to work through the section at a steady pace to avoid careless errors. If you do hit a question you aren't sure about, skip it initially and come back to it if there is time. You can take timed tests or test sections to determine a good pace at which to work through a section without making careless mistakes.

MYTH: If I am only missing a handful of questions, I should work to learn the content I am weak on and not worry about the mistakes I made on questions covering the content I know.

BUSTED: High-scoring students do well on these tests because they know the content. Yes, you may not be an ace at reordering sentences or on equations for exponential growth, but you still know most of what you need for this test. And the SAT (unlike school) doesn't give partial points for work—if you get the question wrong, regardless of why you got it wrong, you get no points at all. So, if ANY of your incorrect answers on a practice test or drill came from being careless, that is something to work on immediately. Study your errors to determine where your mistake is occurring—is it misreading the question or passage, is it falling for trap answers, is it making sloppy calculations? Whatever the error is, do drills on that type of question until you stamp out that error. After that, you can worry about a topic like exponential growth, which does not even get tested on every SAT.

MYTH: I am smart and a good student, so I don't really need to write much down in my test booklet or on practice questions.

BUSTED: One way to avoid those careless errors we just talked about—writing stuff down! Many students tend to think they can and should do a lot of work in their heads, be it keeping track of Reading answers or doing mental math. These are surefire ways of making a mistake, and you are less likely to notice it because you can't *see* the mistake written down. Use your pencil to underline key words, take notes, eliminate answers, and do calculations. Unless you are not making a single careless error, you are likely to benefit from taking the time to use your pencil as a key part of your test-taking process. In addition, having work on the page is crucial when you practice: it's difficult to know why you missed a question on a practice drill or test if you don't have any physical record of how you chose your answer. Finally, writing your work down on the page can, ironically, *save* you time—you won't have to redo work if you need to double-check something or if your concentration is broken by something, which will keep you continuously working towards more answers.

> **Pencils only!**
> You may be the sort of student who prefers to use pens and/or highlighters over pencils. However, the SAT doesn't allow those tools on the test. So practice with a pencil on all your SAT work. (And we recommend using a wooden number 2 pencil rather than mechanical—mechanical pencils are also disallowed!)

MYTH: Doing as much practice as I can is the best way to improve my SAT score.

BUSTED (KIND OF): Yes, practice is good, but *how* you practice is very important. Just doing drill after drill aiming to get all the questions right is not going to guarantee a perfect score on the real SAT. In fact, just practicing over and over without reflection will reinforce any bad test-taking habits you have. Instead, review your work after each drill. Don't just score it—read the explanations, even for the ones you got right. For the ones you missed, you should be tracking if you made any careless errors. Aside from carelessness, if you get any wrong that you thought were right, keep track of why you were drawn to that wrong answer. Again, try to identify patterns so you can work on that issue. Also, review your work to see if there were any questions on which you could have used a better or faster approach, often indicated in the explanations. The biggest improvements come from thoughtful review, not from simply doing practice sections. Lastly, note that it is fine to take practice tests and do drills multiple times. If you take the same practice test a second time and don't get 100% on it, then you didn't truly learn from the review you did, did you? Ideally, if you have reviewed a question with its explanation, if you see that exact same question in the future, you'll get it right—and your odds of getting a *similar* question right are greatly improved.

Summary

- o Don't let your own worst instincts work against you on the SAT. Work Smarter, Not Harder.

- o Identify your own Personal Order of Difficulty (POOD). Don't be a slave to the order of the test.

- o Pace yourself. Don't rush through easy and medium questions only to make careless errors.

- o Use Process of Elimination (POE) to save time, when you're stuck, or when you're out of time.

- o If time does run out, make sure that you've at least guessed something for every multiple-choice question. This is a good time to use your Letter of the Day (LOTD).

- o Be ruthless. If one strategy isn't working, switch immediately to another.

Part II
Reading

Chapter 3
Introduction to
SAT Reading

INTRODUCTION

When you read a book or watch a movie, you're typically able to make a choice. The questions you may typically ask yourself when checking the bookstore shelves or the movie listings may not only be "What would I like to see or read?" but also, whether you realize it or not, "How would I like to see or read?"

You are actually reading all the time, and how you read can take a tremendous number of forms. The basics are always the same: the letters combine to make words, and those words make sentences and paragraphs. Somehow, in the middle of all of it, meaning is dumped into your brain. However, it's not quite that simple because ultimately *what* you read determines *how* you read.

Let's take an obvious example. What do you do differently when you read these two pieces of text?

1. *Tomorrow, and tomorrow, and tomorrow,*
   Creeps in this petty pace from day to day
   To the last syllable of recorded time,
   And all our yesterdays have lighted fools
   The way to dusty death. Out, out, brief candle!

2. *I saw Lisa the other day lol she told me the funniest thing oh and what are you doing this Fri?*

It's safe to say that we're looking at two very different things, so how we approach those two things will also be very different. (The first comes from Shakespeare's *Macbeth*, and the second comes from a text message.)

One big difference in your approach to these two texts is that you'll probably read the first example more carefully if you're reading and writing about it for an English class. Its language is unfamiliar, so understanding it is the first basic hurdle. Once you get through to a basic understanding of the words, there's the question of meaning. You might look at the repetition of the word "tomorrow" or try to find the referents for "this petty pace" or "brief candle." You could spend a lifetime reading these lines, as many scholars have, and find something new or newly meaningful each time.

You'll use a much different skill set on the other text. There's no reason to look at how the language is used here. The weird non-grammar of the passage isn't really worthy of attention either. This text message is all content, and all the basic information you need to receive from it is right there. You'll never have a reason to read it again.

Neither approach is better. They are just different.

Now how about the Shakespeare passage in different contexts? How, for example, would it change the way you read if

1. You read the "Tomorrow, and tomorrow, and tomorrow" speech in a class
2. You read the "Tomorrow, and tomorrow, and tomorrow" speech on an English test

We've already thought about how you'd read in the first instance. Now, in the second, you're reading the same speech, but this time you have to read it on a test.

There are a number of things you'd have to do differently this time. For one, you'll probably have to answer some questions about the text: you may be asked to analyze the language or literary devices, you may be asked to identify the speaker (Macbeth!), or you may be asked to tie the passage to some theme or larger question you discussed in class. The point, though, is that you're asked to be a more active participant in your reading than you were initially, and that's going to change how you read. There's also the fact that you'll have to read on a timed test, that you'll probably already be familiar with the passage, and that you're much more likely to assess than to understand.

You often apply these different styles of reading without even realizing it. One of the keys to success on the most difficult passages of the SAT is to be aware of what you do when you read. When you read a passage about a topic that's not of particular interest to you, you might skim, make assumptions, match words in the passage and the answer choices, and spend far too much time along the way. The best way to beat the SAT at its own game, to really crack the SAT, is to understand the peculiarities of SAT Reading and how it differs from other reading you do in school and out. The students who knock the SAT out of the park are those who have the self-awareness necessary to avoid the SAT's traps.

GENRES OF READING

We are all familiar with the genres of writing—romance, horror, and sci-fi are just three of the most popular. However, becoming a good, self-conscious reader is about realizing that there are genres of reading as well. What you're trained to do in your English classes is something we could call the genre of Literary Reading.

If you like to read, or if you do particularly well in your English classes, then you're probably already very proficient at Literary Reading. Above all, this genre is characterized by sophisticated interpretations. The papers that you write in high school or college

English classes require creative but convincing readings of the meanings of particular texts. There are some basic aspects on which everyone has to agree—plot, characters, narrative voice—but beyond that, the rein is relatively free. In many classes, you are actually encouraged to come up with your own interpretation, and you are evaluated on your ability to interpret a text in a personal way. This is why some people love to read novels in their spare time. Two people may read the same novel but have totally different reactions to it because literary reading is rooted in a kind of personalization. The students who do best in English classes, and those who go on to become English majors, are those who forge the closest personal connections to the material that they read, and are not necessarily those who understand the text in the most "correct" way. The best English students, in other words, are those who have mastered the genre of Literary Reading.

The Genre of SAT Reading

There's a simple reason that the best readers in an English class are not necessarily the best readers on the SAT: Literary Reading and SAT Reading are two different genres of reading. They require different skill sets.

It helps to remember what a standardized test is. Essentially, the College Board needs to be able to promise that everyone—regardless of race, gender, region, or family income—can read a question and have an equal shot at getting the correct answer. If the SAT were testing Literary Reading, everyone would come up with a different answer, and the test would be impossible to score because it would no longer be standardized.

As a result, SAT Reading can be better characterized by *understanding* than by *interpretation*. Interpretation is personal to the reader. Understanding is all about what the text says. This is good news because it means that everything you'll need to answer the questions will be right in front of you in the text, but it also means that you have to stop approaching it the same way you've been trained to approach reading in your English classes all along.

Reading for understanding is tough! Let's take a paragraph from an SAT passage about the studio recording device Auto-Tune:

> The first major hit to popularize Auto-Tune was Cher's "Believe," which was released in 1998. Since that time, the vocal pitch corrector has become almost a staple of
> Line popular music. A 2011 study said that 95% of Top 40
> 5 radio hits that year had used Auto-Tune to one degree or another. The technology is clearly here to stay, though its effects on the present and future of popular music are hotly debated. While some have argued that the new technology has opened up new possibilities for popular
> 10 music, others have responded that the technology has ripped music from its roots, creating an industry built on computer enhancement rather than musical talent.

This is part of a larger essay, but let's think for a moment about how we might answer a question about it on the SAT.

1

In this paragraph, what is the author's main point about Auto-Tune?

A) The technology was useful in the late 1990s, but it is no longer useful.

B) The technology has changed popular music for the worse.

C) Popular music is now dominated by poor singers whose voices are modified.

D) Popular music has been influenced by the introduction of Auto-Tune technology.

While this question seems fairly straightforward, it can actually be very difficult if you apply your Literary Reading skills. In Literary Reading, the major question is typically, "What does the author *mean*?" or "What is the author suggesting?" You can take those questions in a number of directions.

You could say, for example, that (A) is the correct answer because the author singles out Cher's "Believe," thus implying that this was an innovative use of Auto-Tune technology. The later discussion of the widespread use of the technology could also be said to imply that the author believes that Cher's use of Auto-Tune inspired many imitators and that popular music is now watered-down and dull.

But does the author actually *say* any of this?

How about (B)? The author clearly suggests that Auto-Tune is changing popular music, and he cites some critics who suggest that it is ruining music. We might say that the author is implying his own critique of Auto-Tune in giving more space to Auto-Tune's detractors than to its supporters.

But, again, even with all these smart reasons, can we actually choose this as our correct answer?

As for (C), the author does cite a statistic (the 2011 study) that indicates that popular music is now dominated by Auto-Tune. Because Auto-Tune does modify the voices of singers, couldn't we say that these singers must be poor? Seems logical, but is it definitely true?

In the end, however, only (D) is actually *stated* in the passage, so it is the only possible correct answer. We can even point to the lines that make it correct (*A 2011 study said that 95% of Top 40 radio hits that year had used Auto-Tune to one degree or another. The technology is clearly here to stay*). No intense thinking or reasoning is required.

This demonstrates the cornerstone of the genre of SAT Reading: correct answers are always rooted firmly in the text and are based on what the author *actually says*, not what the author *could be perceived to say*. There will always be a word or phrase that offers direct, irrefutable support for the correct answer. If you find yourself *reasoning* rather than *identifying*, be careful!

So here's the thing that the administrators of the SAT will never admit but that is absolutely true, particularly for students like you who do well in school and are shooting for Verbal scores in the 700s:

> Thinking is not rewarded on the SAT.

We could debate the merits of this approach all day long. Ultimately, though, whether the test is better, worse, or equal to what you learn in school doesn't change the basic fact: SAT Reading is a genre of reading that will not change, but you can learn and perfect the skills necessary to master it.

So the rule of the SAT Reading genre is as follows:

> Read to understand, not to assess. Read for information, not interpretation.

Answer Support and Selective Close Reading

As you will see in the next chapter, it's not a good idea to read every word of an SAT passage. It's best to let the questions guide you through the passage. You don't get points for reading the text—you get points for answering the questions. Read the parts of the text that will get you the points. Who cares about the rest?

When you do read, even though you'll be reading smaller chunks of text, make sure you are reading carefully. Every answer on this test will have specific support within the passage, and sometimes that support can hide in particular words or phrases. If you're skimming rather than reading carefully, you may miss these words or phrases altogether.

Take this selection from a recent PSAT.

Daddy was seeing an awful lot of his new friend.
One of the rooms in his house was all of a sudden full
of her stuff; neither Sarah nor her brother was allowed
Line in there anymore. It had started with a few dinners and
5 shopping trips, and now it seemed that their father's friend
basically lived in the house and was shifting around some
furniture that had been in place for as long as Sarah could
remember.

34

The phrases "an awful lot" and "all of a sudden" serve to emphasize Sarah's

A) disapproval of her father's new girlfriend

B) wish that things could be as they once were

C) unwillingness to accept a new person into her life

D) surprise at a new development in her father's home

This question asks you to do exactly the kind of close reading that you should always do. Another way of asking the question would be, *Why does the author use the phrases "an awful lot" and "all of a sudden"?* One way to test the effectiveness of language is to take the word or phrase in question out of the passage.

So the first two lines would change to the following:

> *Daddy was seeing a lot of his new friend. One of the rooms in his house was full of her stuff.*

Now compare that to what it actually says.

> *Daddy was seeing an awful lot of his new friend. One of the rooms in his house was all of a sudden full of her stuff.*

Notice how the original lines add Sarah's voice to the third-person narration. Phrases like *an awful lot* and *all of a sudden*, in other words, come from Sarah herself, and they help to emphasize her surprise at how quickly things are moving between her father and his "new friend." Of the answer choices listed, (D) best captures the use of these terms.

Let's try a slightly more difficult passage.

To take one example, the name "Iraq" is not quite as applicable to all its citizens as the names "France," "Portugal," or "The United States" are in their own
Line regions. For many Westerners, nationality is a given and
5 ultimately trumps the more local identifications of town, city, or state. In Iraq, as the Bush administration learned, religious distinctions are more meaningful than national similarities. Approximately 65% of those living in Iraq are Shia Muslims, but does this make it a Shia country?
10 To an extent, maybe, but Sunni Muslims represent a powerful and vocal minority, and the northern regions of Iraq comprise a semi-autonomous region of a third group, the Kurds. The Western notions of nation-above-all and religious coexistence don't hold up in countries like
15 this because the value systems of these countries have developed so independently of Western notions.

12

What does the first sentence suggest about the name of the nation of Iraq?

A) The name of the country comes from the region in which the majority of Shias live.

B) The name of the country has less significance in Iraq than it does in other countries.

C) The name of the country does not apply to most citizens, who therefore frequently disregard the name.

D) The name of the country refers to an area that does not include the region of Kurdistan.

In this sentence, notice the difference that the words "quite as" make. Without them, the sentence would read as follows: *To take one example, the name "Iraq" is not applicable to all citizens....* Without the "quite as," therefore, this sentence is much more extreme, and the answer might be (C) or (D). As it is, though, the only answer that can work is (B).

Let's try another.

13

According to the author, how do Westerners identify with the towns, cities, or state in which they live?

A) These local identifications play some role, but the idea of belonging to a nation is more important.

B) These local identifications hold some importance but are trumped by religious identifications.

C) These local identifications are most important in European countries such as France and Portugal.

D) These local identifications are less important than both religious and national identifications.

The correct answer here is (A), but (B), (C), and (D) all contain some compelling parts, particularly if you have not read the passage closely. Choices (B) and (D) contain the words *religious identification,* and (C) contains the countries *France and Portugal.* Although all of these words may have appeared in the initial passage, the answer choices rearrange the words to say things that the passage doesn't say. Use the context clues if you're not sure what terms like *trumps* and *given* mean in this particular context. The sentences surrounding this one define those words specifically. Again, these passages can't really presume any outside knowledge at all, so anything that seems especially difficult or complicated will be defined in the passage itself. When you read, do so carefully, and make sure that you've read enough to know what the passage is saying.

In future chapters, we will discuss our particular approach to reading passages, but if you're looking for the very highest scores on this test, remember that SAT Reading is a genre of reading with its own particular set of rules.

Play to Your Strengths

You will get all five of the Reading passages at once. There is no reason that you have to do them in order! Remember, you will have one World Literature and two each of Science and History/Social Studies. Pick and choose your order! First do the passages where you're most likely to get points. If you love reading novels, Literature might be a great place to start. If you love data, see if you've got a Science passage with graphs.

To get a top score, you'll have to do all five passages, but starting with the passage you like the most will help you to be efficient right off the bat. In turn, this will help you build momentum much more effectively than starting with a more challenging passage.

The following are some things to consider:

- **Type of passage**: There's always one Literature passage and two each of Science and History/Social Studies, but not necessarily in that order. One of the five will be a dual-reading passage.

- **Topic of passage:** The blurb will give you some basic information about the passage. If it makes you the least bit curious, that may help you decide whether to do the passage or skip it.

- **Types of questions**: You may find some question types easier than others, so skim those to see if there are a lot of line references and lead words. In general, those two question types help you to find what you're looking for relatively quickly, whereas other big-idea questions may require you to spend more time wading through the passage to find what you want.

READING INTRODUCTION EXERCISE

Questions 1–6 are based on the following passage.

The following passage is an excerpt from the memoir of a well-known African American singer and community leader. It is set in New York and Philadelphia in the 1920s.

I now had what amounted to a complex about music. Hopes had been raised too high, and when they crashed too low, I
Line could not be objective. Perhaps I had not
5 admitted it to myself, but Town Hall in New York had represented the mainstream of American musical life, and I had plunged into it hoping to become one of the fortunate swimmers.
10   I kept rehashing the concert in my mind, lingering on some points and thrusting others so thoroughly aside that I do not remember to this day which dress I wore, whether it was the one
15 Mrs. Patterson had made over for me or a special one. I don't remember what financial arrangements were made with the young man who managed the event, but I do know that I received nothing and that
20 he must have lost money. I thought then, and still do, that I might have done better if I had not been told that auditorium was full. If you are sensitive, and I was perhaps too sensitive, a misrepresentation like that
25 can throw you off balance, particularly if you feel that you have a great deal at stake.
    I stopped going regularly to Mr. Boghetti's studio. I appeared once in a while, and things must have gone very
30 indifferently. He realized how much the fiasco had shaken me, and he did not make an issue of my irregular attendance.
    Mother and I talked about the whole thing, and with her patience and
35 understanding she helped me out of my trouble. I knew that the criticism was right and that I should not have given the critics the opportunity to write as they did. I kept reiterating that I had wanted so very much
40 to sing well enough to please everybody.
    "Listen my child," Mother said. "Whatever you do in this world, no matter how good it is, you will never be able to please everybody. All you can strive for is
45 to do the best it is humanly possible for you to do."
    As the months went by I was able again to consider singing as a career. "Think about it for a while," Mother advised, "and
50 think of other things you might like to do."
    I thought about it. It took a long time before I could confront singing again with enthusiasm, before the old conviction returned that nothing in life could be as
55 important as music.

1

The passage as a whole best supports which explanation of the narrator's "complex about music" (lines 1–2) ?

A) A critical review of a performance caused her to change careers.

B) Becoming an accomplished singer was not her primary ambition.

C) A formidable experience led her to question her aspirations.

D) Performing in Town Hall was the pinnacle of her early musical career.

2

In line 9, "fortunate swimmers" refers to the author's

A) obsession with music.

B) desire to be a popular singer.

C) respect for other famous singers.

D) rapid change of fortune.

3

The use of the phrase "thrusting . . . aside" (line 12) conveys a sense of the narrator's

A) distress.

B) resentment.

C) instability.

D) perseverance.

4

According to the passage, "misrepresentation" (line 24) refers to a discrepancy between

A) the narrator's actual proficiency at singing and her performance at the Town Hall.

B) the stated number of people in attendance and the actual number.

C) the reaction of the audience to the Town Hall performance and the reviews of it.

D) the narrator's desire to please everybody and her inability to do so.

5

The third paragraph (lines 27–32) primarily focuses on

A) the importance of rehearsals.

B) the kindness of strangers.

C) a return to a musical career.

D) the consequences of a performance.

6

In lines 37–38, the narrator's comment about having "given critics the opportunity" suggests that she

A) acknowledged that the unfavorable reviews were warranted.

B) intended to switch careers from music to journalism.

C) doubted that the critics who reviewed her did so objectively.

D) recognized the influence critics exert on a singer's career.

Summary

- o   SAT Reading is not the same as English class reading.
- o   Read to understand, not to assess.
- o   Read for information, not interpretation.
- o   Read only what you need, but read it carefully.
- o   Use the structure of the test to your advantage.

Chapter 4
SAT Reading: The Basic Approach and Beyond

In the Introduction, we talked about the genre of SAT Reading. In this chapter, we'll discuss The Princeton Review's Basic Approach for attacking this peculiar genre.

Even for skilled readers, SAT Reading can be tough:

- There's not enough time to read the passage and work the questions.
- The passages are long, so it's easy to lose your focus.
- You end up reading a ton of stuff you don't need.
- The questions are written in a confusing way.
- It often seems like more than one answer could work.

We know what makes the SAT Reading section tough. Our Basic Approach is designed to address every single one of these issues!

This section is a time-crunch for everyone, so here's our most important piece of advice.

Don't read the passage until you know what you're looking for.

Think about it. Typically, you'll read the whole passage, promptly forget everything you just read, and have to re-read the whole passage while you work the questions. Why not cut out that first read-through? After all, you aren't scored on your ability to read quickly or to understand every aspect of the passage, as you might be in an English class. On SAT Reading, you get points for answering questions, so you'll want to get to those questions as quickly as possible and let them frame how you read.

Do the following:

1. **Read the Blurb.**
   The blurb may be only a sentence or two, but it will help you identify the type of passage and tell you briefly what the passage is about.

2. **Select and Understand a Question.**
   Save the general questions for later, and start with the first specific question. Restate the question to make sure you know what you are looking for.

3. **Read What You Need.**
   Most answers are found within a 10- to 12-line window of text. Find that window and read it carefully. Read it with the question in mind, which will help with efficiency.

4. **Predict the Answer.**
   Find something in the text that answers the question. Underline it. Do not try to analyze or paraphrase. Stick with what's actually stated in the text.

5. **POE.**
   Find the answer by eliminating three bad answers. "Bad answers" are either inconsistent with your prediction or contain one of the College Board's common traps.

> **Note:**
> Because this book has smaller pages than the SAT test booklet does, the sample passages take up more lines than they will on the SAT. Therefore, the usual 10- to 12-line window will appear longer in this book. Often, the appropriate window is about one paragraph long, so you can use that as a guide as you work the examples.

FIND WHAT YOU NEED

In order to Read What You Need (Step 3 of the Basic Approach), you will have to efficiently find the information you need within the passage. Try these strategies:

- **Line and paragraph references.** Some questions include line or paragraph references, and these have the obvious advantage of directing you to the part of the passage that you need.

- **Lead words.** Some questions that lack line references include lead words—words that will "lead" you back to particular parts of the passage. Look, in particular, for proper nouns, italics, numbers, or words in quotations—basically, anything you can easily scan for in the passage.

- **Question sequence.** The specific questions roughly follow the order of the passage. If you do the questions in order, you will work through the passage in order, and you can use the line references from the previous or subsequent question to help you find the answer to a question that lacks a line reference.

POE Criteria

The SAT can throw you a few curveballs, so be on the lookout for four common kinds of trap answers.

To learn about the SAT Reading Basic Approach in more detail, check out these other Princeton Review titles: *SAT Prep, SAT Premium Prep*, and *Reading and Writing Workout for the SAT.*

- **Mostly Right, Slightly Wrong**. These answer choices look just about perfect, but even one word can make an answer choice wrong. Use your pencil to break longer answer choices into shorter, more easily examined pieces, and look for pieces that don't match the text. Note extreme words like "all " or "only," as they often indicate that an answer choice goes beyond the scope of the text.

- **Could Be True**. These answer choices might initially look good because they seem to fit logically with the text, or because you know they are true based on your outside knowledge. You might be able to argue for these answers in an essay or a discussion, but they lack concrete support from the passage. Remember: don't rely on your own interpretations. Make sure to do Step 4 and underline a prediction of the correct answer *in the text.*

- **Right Words, Wrong Meaning**. The SAT will give you answer choices that recycle words from the passage but don't match what the passage actually says. Read the window and the answer choices carefully. Don't just match words.

- **Right Answer, Wrong Question**. The SAT will give you answer choices that are actually stated in the passage, but that don't answer the question that was asked. Rephrase the question for yourself in Step 2 so that you know exactly what you are looking for.

Try the Basic Approach out on a few questions in the following passage. For now, just work questions 14, 16, and 17, then check your answers on the following page. (We'll discuss the other question types later in this chapter.) You may want to mark the passage pages for ease of use.

Skimming or Skipping: What's the Skinny?

Some people can benefit from a very quick skim of the passage between Steps 1 and 2. We have found that most students score higher *without* skimming the passage, but if you can use your skimming time wisely (that is, you can finish in a few minutes and get a sense of the main idea and structure of the passage), go for it. Just remember that you don't get points for reading the passage. You get points for answering the questions, so that's where you should be spending most of your time.

Questions 12–21 are based on the following passage.

This passage is from Helen Keller, *The Story of My Life*. Originally published in 1902. Helen Keller was stricken with an illness that left her deaf and blind as a young child.

I guessed vaguely from my mother's signs and from the hurrying to and fro in the house that something unusual was
Line about to happen, so I went to the door
5 and waited on the steps. The afternoon sun penetrated the mass of honeysuckle that covered the porch, and fell on my upturned face. My fingers lingered almost unconsciously on the familiar leaves and
10 blossoms which had just come forth to greet the sweet southern spring. I did not know what the future held of marvel or surprise for me. Anger and bitterness had preyed upon me continually for weeks
15 and a deep languor had succeeded this passionate struggle.

Have you ever been at sea in a dense fog, when it seemed as if a tangible white darkness shut you in, and the great ship,
20 tense and anxious, groped her way toward the shore with plummet and sounding-line, and you waited with beating heart for something to happen? I was like that ship before my education began, only I
25 was without compass or sounding-line, and had no way of knowing how near the harbour was. "Light! Give me light!" was the wordless cry of my soul, and the light of love shone on me in that very hour.
30 I felt approaching footsteps, I stretched out my hand as I supposed to my mother. Someone took it, and I was caught up and held close in the arms of her who had come to reveal all things to me, and, more
35 than all things else, to love me.

The morning after my teacher came she led me into her room and gave me a doll. When I had played with it a little while, Miss Sullivan slowly spelled into my hand

40 the word "d-o-l-l." I was at once interested in this finger play and tried to imitate it. When I finally succeeded in making the letters correctly I was flushed with childish pleasure and pride. Running downstairs to
45 my mother I held up my hand and made the letters for doll. I did not know that I was spelling a word or even that words existed; I was simply making my fingers go in monkeylike imitation. But my teacher
50 had been with me several weeks before I understood that everything has a name.

One day, while I was playing with my new doll, Miss Sullivan put my big rag doll into my lap also, spelled "d-o-l-l" and
55 tried to make me understand that "d-o-l-l" applied to both. Earlier in the day we had a tussle over the words "m-u-g" and "w-a-t-e-r." Miss Sullivan had tried to impress it upon me that "m-u-g" is mug and that
60 "w-a-t-e-r" is water, but I persisted in confounding the two. In despair she had dropped the subject for the time, only to renew it at the first opportunity. I became impatient at her repeated attempts and,
65 seizing the new doll, I dashed it upon the floor. I was keenly delighted when I felt the fragments of the broken doll at my feet. Neither sorrow nor regret followed my passionate outburst. I had not loved
70 the doll. In the still, dark world in which I lived there was no strong sentiment or tenderness.

We walked down the path to the well-house, attracted by the fragrance of the
75 honeysuckle with which it was covered. Someone was pumping water and my teacher placed my hand under the spout. As the cool stream gushed over one hand she spelled into the other the word
80 water, first slowly, then rapidly. I stood still, my whole attention fixed upon the motions of her fingers. Suddenly I felt

a misty consciousness as of something forgotten—a thrill of returning thought;
85 and somehow the mystery of language was revealed to me. I knew then that "w-a-t-e-r" meant the wonderful cool something that was flowing over my hand. That living word awakened my soul, gave it light,
90 hope, joy, set it free! There were barriers still, it is true, but barriers that could in time be swept away.

I left the well-house eager to learn. Everything had a name, and each name
95 gave birth to a new thought. As we returned to the house every object which I touched seemed to quiver with life. That was because I saw everything with the strange, new sight that had come to me.
100 On entering the door I remembered the doll I had broken. I felt my way to the hearth and picked up the pieces. I tried vainly to put them together. Then my eyes filled with tears; for I realized what
105 I had done, and for the first time I felt repentance and sorrow.

12

The passage as a whole suggests that the author views language as

A) a necessary but frustrating part of life.

B) the key to her appreciation of the world around her.

C) a phenomenon that remains mysterious.

D) the only method she can use to express her feelings.

13

Which choice best describes the developmental pattern of the passage?

A) A personal account of a transformative experience

B) An objective evaluation of a new teaching method

C) A somber narration of a difficult interaction

D) An invitation to reinterpret a series of memories

14

In the first paragraph (lines 1–16), the author presents a contrast in her description of

A) the scent of the honeysuckle and the feeling of the sun on her face.

B) emotions experienced in her recent past and those she would experience in the near future.

C) her mother's vague signs and the hurried preparations taking place in the house.

D) the anger she felt while she was ill and her passionate struggle to recover.

15

As used in line 15, the word "succeeded" most nearly means

A) accomplished.

B) split.

C) followed.

D) remedied.

16

The author's reference to being "at sea in a dense fog" (lines 17–18) emphasizes that she felt

A) afraid, because she felt like she was sinking in her dark, still life.

B) angry, because she could not control her life.

C) confused, because her new teacher was trying to teach her too much.

D) lost, because she had difficulty communicating with the world.

17

The author's reference to "finger play" in line 41 emphasizes her

A) childish need to learn by playing games with dolls and toys.

B) teacher's technique for teaching her grammar.

C) initial inability to understand that she was spelling words with her hands.

D) opinion that learning sign language was as easy as a child's game.

18

Which choice provides the best evidence for the answer to the previous question?

A) Lines 38–40 ("When . . . d-o-l-l")

B) Lines 46–48 ("I did . . . existed")

C) Lines 49–51 ("But my . . . name")

D) Lines 56–58 ("Earlier . . . w-a-t-e-r")

19

The author includes the memory of breaking the doll in order to

A) provide details useful in illustrating her emotional state.

B) offer an example of her teacher's strong reactions.

C) recount an incident of poor behavior for which she felt little remorse.

D) establish the combative nature of her relationship with her teacher.

20

It can be inferred from the passage that the author would most likely agree with which of the following statements?

A) Without language, humans are destined to feel anger and bitterness.

B) People often destroy treasured objects without fully realizing the consequences of their actions.

C) Learning can free people from the barriers they construct around themselves.

D) Children need positive role models to help shape their lives.

21

Which choice provides the best evidence for the answer to the previous question?

A) Lines 1–5 ("I guessed . . . steps")

B) Lines 66–69 ("I was . . . outburst")

C) Lines 78–80 ("As the . . . rapidly)

D) Lines 88–92 ("That . . . away")

Answers and Explanations for Questions 14, 16, 17

Check the answers for questions 14, 16, and 17 below. If you missed any of these questions, go back and read the window around the reference for the question. Then consider the answer choice you chose—was it one of the College Board's common trap answers?

Question 14

The question asks what the author *presents a contrast* between in the first paragraph. Read the first paragraph as the window. In lines 11–16 the author states, *I did not know what the future held of marvel or surprise for me. Anger and bitterness had preyed upon me continually for weeks and a deep languor had succeeded this passionate struggle.* The author contrasts the emotions *marvel* and *surprise* with *anger and bitterness*. Eliminate answers that don't match this prediction. Eliminate (A) because, although both *honeysuckle* and the *sun* are mentioned, the author does not *contrast* them with one another. Did you catch the Right Answer, Wrong Question trap answer? Choice (B) matches the prediction: the author experienced emotions of *anger and bitterness* in her recent past, and she is going to experience *marvel* and *surprise* in her near future. Keep (B). Choice (C) doesn't answer the right question, and it also mixes up words from the passage. The passage says, *I guessed vaguely from my mother's signs*; it doesn't describe the mother's signs as *vague*. Eliminate (C). Eliminate (D) because, although the author says that she experienced *anger* and went through a *passionate struggle*, she doesn't say that she was angry *while she was ill* or that her struggle was a *struggle to recover*. Additionally, *anger* and *passionate struggle* are not contrasted. The correct answer is (B).

Question 16

The question asks what the author is emphasizing about her feelings when she uses the phrase *"at sea in a dense fog."* Read a window around the given line reference. In lines 17–27, the author compares herself to a ship that *groped her way toward the shore.* She also says that she was *without compass or sounding-line, and had no way of knowing how near the harbour was.* This imagery suggests that the author felt lost. Eliminate answers that don't match this prediction. Although the author mentions being *tense and anxious*, she doesn't say that she was *afraid* or use an image of *sinking*, so eliminate (A). The author doesn't mention being *angry* in this paragraph, and that is not what the image of *being at sea in a dense fog* emphasizes. Eliminate (B). Eliminate (C) because the author is describing how she felt before her teacher arrived. Did you catch the trap answers? Some are Could Be True traps that describe emotions the author plausibly could be feeling, but that aren't directly supported by the text. Some are Right Answer, Wrong Question trap answers that include emotions that are mentioned in the text, but that aren't connected to the image the question asks about. Keep (D) because it matches the prediction. The correct answer is (D).

Question 17

The question asks what the author emphasizes with the reference to *finger play*. Read a window around the given line reference. Lines 46–49 state, *I did not know that I was spelling a word or even that words existed; I was simply making my fingers go in monkey-like imitation.* The author calls it "finger play" because at first, it was a game to her; she didn't understand that she was spelling words. Eliminate answers that don't match the prediction. Eliminate (A) because the author thought she was playing a game; she didn't *need to learn by playing games.* Did you recognize the Right Words, Wrong Meaning trap answer? Eliminate (B) because the teacher is not teaching *grammar.* Keep (C) because it matches the prediction. Eliminate (D) because she does not find the learning *easy.* The correct answer is (C).

Vocabulary-in-Context Questions

There is no need to memorize lists of obscure five-syllable vocabulary words, but the SAT will test your ability to recognize the context-dependent meaning of words and phrases. You will likely see one or two of these "Vocabulary-in-Context" questions per passage in the SAT Reading Test. In Vocabulary-in-Context questions, you'll see familiar words, but they'll be used in less familiar ways. The key to these questions is to make sure you're going back to the text and reading carefully! Don't make an assumption about the word's meaning based on outside knowledge. Instead, find clues in the text that allow you to replace the word with another word or phrase that has a similar meaning. Consider question 15.

15

As used in line 15, the word "succeeded" most nearly means

A) accomplished.

B) split.

C) followed.

D) remedied.

Vocabulary-in-Context Approach

1. Find the word in the passage and cross it out.
2. Read 1–2 sentences for context.
3. Jot down your own word or phrase.
4. Use Process of Elimination.

Find the word *succeeded* in line 15 and cross it out. For Vocabulary-in-Context questions, you typically don't need to read the full 10- to 12-line window that you use for other question types, but carefully read a sentence or two around the target word (or phrase). Then jot down your own word or phrase that captures the meaning of the target word as it is used in the passage. Lines 13–16 state, *Anger and bitterness had preyed upon me continually for weeks and a deep languor had succeeded this passionate struggle.* The word *succeeded* could be replaced with a phrase such as "come after." Eliminate answers that don't match the prediction. Choice (A) is a possible definition for *succeeded*, but *accomplished* doesn't match the word's meaning in the context of the passage, making (A) a Could Be True trap answer. Eliminate (A). Neither *split* nor *remedied* matches "come after," so eliminate (B) and (D). Choice (C) matches the prediction and is the correct answer.

Best Evidence Questions

When you answered question 17, you may have noticed that it is paired with question 18.

17

The author's reference to "finger play" in line 41 emphasizes her

A) childish need to learn by playing games with dolls and toys.

B) teacher's technique for teaching her grammar.

C) initial inability to understand that she was spelling words with her hands.

D) opinion that learning sign language was as easy as a child's game.

18

Which choice provides the best evidence for the answer to the previous question?

A) Lines 38–40 ("When . . . d-o-l-l")

B) Lines 46–48 ("I did . . . existed")

C) Lines 49–51 ("But my . . . name")

D) Lines 56–58 ("Earlier . . . w-a-t-e-r")

You will likely see one, two, or even three of these "Best Evidence" questions in each passage of the SAT Reading Test. When a Best Evidence question is paired with a specific question, like question 17, simply follow the Basic Approach. Step 4 is to Predict the Correct Answer by underlining evidence in the passage. In many cases, you can simply use the underlined text to answer the Best Evidence question. For example, the prediction for question 17 came from lines 46–49, *I did not know that I was spelling a word or even that words existed; I was simply making my fingers go in monkeylike imitation.* Now use Process of Elimination on the answer choices for question 18.

Many Best Evidence questions present a "buy one, get one free" situation—the prediction from the first question will only appear in one answer for the Best Evidence question, and you will have essentially answered two questions by working one. The lines that gave the prediction for question 17 appear in (18B), which is the correct answer.

Some Best Evidence questions are paired with general questions rather than specific ones, and some are not paired with other questions at all. We'll discuss strategy for those questions later in this chapter. For now, let's keep working the questions in order.

Purpose Questions

Many of the questions on the SAT ask *what* the author said or suggested, but some ask *why* the author said something. These "Purpose" questions might ask why the author used a particular word or included a particular detail, or they may ask about the main purpose of a paragraph or of the whole passage. Consider question 19.

19

The author includes the memory of breaking the doll in order to

The question asks *why* the author includes this particular memory. The question doesn't include a line reference, but remember that you can use the question sequence to help you find the window. You read the fourth paragraph while answering questions 17 and 18 and didn't see anything about breaking a doll. So, starting with the fifth paragraph, scan the passage looking for the lead word *doll* and in particular a reference to breaking the doll. The reference is in the fifth paragraph, which reads

> One day, while I was playing with my
> new doll, Miss Sullivan put my big rag
> doll into my lap also, spelled "d-o-l-l" and
> 55 tried to make me understand that "d-o-l-l"
> applied to both. Earlier in the day we had a
> tussle over the words "m-u-g" and "w-a-
> t-e-r." Miss Sullivan had tried to impress
> it upon me that "m-u-g" is mug and that
> 60 "w-a-t-e-r" is water, but I persisted in
> confounding the two. In despair she had
> dropped the subject for the time, only to
> renew it at the first opportunity. I became
> impatient at her repeated attempts and,
> 65 seizing the new doll, I dashed it upon the
> floor. I was keenly delighted when I felt
> the fragments of the broken doll at my
> feet. Neither sorrow nor regret followed
> my passionate outburst. I had not loved
> 70 the doll. In the still, dark world in which
> I lived there was no strong sentiment or
> tenderness.

Of course, the author does not directly state *why* she includes this memory, and you might think that you need to supply your own interpretation. In an English class, that's probably what your teacher would expect. However, for SAT Reading, even the answer to a Purpose question depends on the text. Be sure to read a wide enough window to determine what the author is up to, then eliminate answer choices that don't match the text. On Purpose questions, be especially wary of Could Be True trap answers that you can't prove based on the text, as well as Right Answer, Wrong Question traps that match *what* the author said, but that don't answer the *why* question. Consider the answer choices for question 19.

19

The author includes the memory of breaking the doll in order to

A) provide details useful in illustrating her emotional state.

B) offer an example of her teacher's strong reactions.

C) recount an incident of poor behavior for which she felt little remorse.

D) establish the combative nature of her relationship with her teacher.

What trap answers do you notice? Choice (B) is a Mostly Right, Slightly Wrong trap answer, since the author rather than the *teacher* is having a strong reaction. Choice (C) is a Right Answer, Wrong Question trap: it describes *what* the author does, but not *why* she does it. Choice (D) is a Could Be True trap answer: it could be a reason for including such a story, but it is not supported by the context of the passage as a whole, which presents the relationship with her teacher positively. Choice (A) matches the text: evidence for this answer includes the phrases *I became impatient, I was keenly delighted, Neither sorrow nor regret followed my passionate outburst,* and *there was no strong sentiment or tenderness.* The correct answer is (A).

The correct answers to some Purpose questions may not feel very satisfying since you are used to deeper critical thinking in your classes at school. That's why it's so important to tackle these questions through Process of Elimination and to match answer choices to predictions from the passage. Don't be too smart for the test.

General Best Evidence Questions

Earlier we looked at a Best Evidence question paired with a specific question. As long as you underlined your prediction while working the first question, those questions were a two-for-one deal. However, some Best Evidence questions will be paired with general questions that ask about the passage as whole, or questions that are so open-ended that it's difficult to make a prediction for the first question.

Take a look at questions 20 and 21.

20

It can be inferred from the passage that the author would most likely agree with which of the following statements?

A) Without language, humans are destined to feel anger and bitterness.

B) People often destroy treasured objects without fully realizing the consequences of their actions.

C) Learning can free people from the barriers they construct around themselves.

D) Children need positive role models to help shape their lives.

21

Which choice provides the best evidence for the answer to the previous question?

A) Lines 1–5 ("I guessed . . . steps")

B) Lines 66–69 ("I was . . . outburst")

C) Lines 78–80 ("As the . . . rapidly)

D) Lines 88–92 ("That . . . away")

If you try to answer question 20 first and then find the answer to question 21, you'll be taking part in one of the worst scavenger hunts ever. There are no line references or lead words to tell you where to go in the passage, and the best evidence lines are scattered from the beginning to the end of the passage. If these questions occurred within the set of specific questions, you could use the order of the questions to help you narrow down your search to one section of the passage. However, this pair appears at the end of the questions, which means they might be general questions that don't fit into the typical order that the specific questions follow. Furthermore, question 20 is so open-ended that you wouldn't even know what kind of information to look for. Trying to answer these questions the same way you answered questions 17 and 18 will eat up your valuable time. Luckily, we have another strategy for you to use: it's called Parallel Process of Elimination, or Parallel POE.

Parallel POE is a strategy you can use to answer paired sets when you can't easily answer the first question on its own. Think for a moment about how paired questions must operate. The correct answer to the first question must be supported by an answer to the evidence question, and the correct answer to the evidence question must support an answer to the first question. In other words, if there is an evidence answer choice that doesn't support an answer for the first question, it is wrong. Period. Likewise, if there is an answer choice for the first question that isn't supported by an evidence answer, it is wrong. Period.

Let's use this to our advantage! Start by reading each answer choice for the evidence question. If an evidence answer choice doesn't address the first question, or if it doesn't support any of the answer choices for the first question, eliminate it. If an evidence answer choice supports one of the answer choices for the first question, literally draw a line connecting the two choices. You should not expect to have four connections. If you are lucky, you will have only one connection: the correct answer pair. If you have more than one pair, compare the remaining choices and keep an eye out for trap answers. The important thing to remember is that any answer choice in the first question that isn't physically connected to an evidence answer—and any evidence answer that isn't connected to an answer in the first question—must be eliminated.

Let's take a look at how this first Parallel POE pass would work for questions 20 and 21. Start with the "best evidence" lines.

- The lines for (21A) say, *I guessed vaguely from my mother's signs and from the hurrying to and fro in the house that something unusual was about to happen, so I went to the door and waited on the steps.* Read through all four answer choices for question 20. Notice those lines don't support any of the choices for question 20, so you can eliminate (21A).
- The lines for (21B) say, *I was keenly delighted when I felt the fragments of the broken doll at my feet. Neither sorrow nor regret followed my passionate outburst.* Now read through the answer choices for question 20. These lines could support (20B), so physically draw a line connecting (21B) with (20B).
- The lines for (21C) say, *As the cool stream gushed over one hand she spelled into the other the word water, first slowly, then rapidly.* These lines don't support any of the choices for Q20, so eliminate (21C).
- The lines for (21D) say, *That living word awakened my soul, gave it light, hope, joy, set it free! There were barriers still, it is true, but barriers that could in time be swept away.* These lines support (20C), so draw a line connecting (21D) with (20C).

At this point, (20A) and (20D) don't have lines that support them. If there is no evidence given to support those choices, they cannot be right, so eliminate (20A) and (20D).

You have a lovely 50/50 split now. Compare the remaining answer choices, matching them back to question 20 and to the passage. Question 20 asks which statement the author would agree with. While she did destroy a possession without feeling remorse, there is no evidence that the author would agree people *often* destroy treasured objects. Eliminate (20B) and (21B). The correct answers are (20C) and (21D).

General Questions and the Golden Thread

Once you have read the windows, underlined predictions, and identified the correct answers for the specific questions, you will have a solid idea of what's happening in the text and how the general structure fits together. You will also have an understanding of what the test writers think is important. This will make the general questions more approachable and much more efficient to work than they would have been if you'd started with them.

Take a look at question 12, which we skipped at first. You still might not have read the entire passage—not every word from start to finish—but you'll see that it doesn't matter. You've read what you need.

12

The passage as a whole suggests that the author views language as

A) a necessary but frustrating part of life.

B) the key to her appreciation of the world around her.

C) a phenomenon that remains mysterious.

D) the only method she can use to express her feelings.

Without going back to the text, see what you can eliminate! Choice (A) is gone; although you could argue that the author sees language as necessary, her *frustration* happened before she began to learn language. Choice (B) looks pretty good, so we'll hang on to it. Choice (C) doesn't work, because language doesn't *remain mysterious* to the author; she learned to understand and use language. Choice (D) might initially look good, but think back to the passage. The author did a pretty good job expressing her frustration when she broke the doll, and that was before she had language. This is a good example of a Mostly Right, Slightly Wrong trap answer: the answer works, except for the word *only*. Eliminate (D). Choice (B) is the correct answer, and you can get there without having to read the whole passage.

Structure Questions

Question 13 asks about how the passage is structured. These "Structure" questions can be tough because their answers often include abstract language. (Some Purpose questions do too.) The key is to match the abstract language in the answer choices back to the specifics discussed in the passage. It may be easier to consider one piece of each choice at a time. As you do, eliminate answers that don't match the passage. Try question 13.

13

Which choice best describes the developmental pattern of the passage?

A) A personal account of a transformative experience

B) An objective evaluation of a new teaching method

C) A somber narration of a difficult interaction

D) An invitation to reinterpret a series of memories

Choice (A) describes the passage as a *personal account*. Does this match the passage? Sure—this is Helen Keller's account of something she experienced in her childhood. Choice (A) also says that the passage is an account of a *transformative experience*. Is there evidence in the passage that the experience changed the author's life? Yes—she is telling the story of how she came to understand language, and she says, *As we returned to the house every object which I touched seemed to quiver with life. That was because I saw everything with the strange, new sight that had come to me.* Keep (A). Eliminate (B) because the passage is a first-hand account of the author's personal memories, so it's not accurate to describe it as *objective*. Additionally, it's true that the passage describes a teaching method, but it doesn't *evaluate* the method or say that the method is *new*. Choice (C) describes the passage as *somber* and says that it is an account of a *difficult interaction*. However, the author expresses a range of emotions in the passage, and the passage culminates with an experience of joyful discovery. Eliminate (C). Although the passage is about *memories*, it doesn't mention any reinterpretation of those memories. Eliminate (D). The correct answer is (A).

ADDITIONAL QUESTION TYPES

Let's take a look at a few additional question types that appear on the SAT Reading Test.

Stand-Alone Best Evidence Questions

In addition to the paired Best Evidence questions discussed previously, you will probably see one or two "stand-alone" Best Evidence questions in the Reading Test. There is not an example of a stand-alone Best Evidence question in the passage above, but they look like this:

22

Which choice best supports the claim that the author and her family had a way of communicating with one another before her teacher arrived?

A) Lines 1–5 ("I guessed . . . steps")

B) Lines 30–31 ("I felt . . . mother")

C) Lines 82–86 ("Suddenly . . . me")

D) Lines 94–95 ("Everything . . . thought")

Try working question 22. Then check the explanation below.

The question asks for evidence that *best supports the claim that the author had a method of communicating with her family before her teacher arrived*. Look at the lines for each answer choice and eliminate those that do not support the claim in the question. In the lines for (A), the author mentions *my mother's signs* and indicates that those signs let her know that *something unusual was about to happen*, indicating that her mother was able to communicate some ideas to her. Keep (A). In the lines for (B), there is no mention of *a method of communicating*, so eliminate (B). In the lines for (C), the author says that she *felt a misty consciousness as of something forgotten—a thrill of returning thought*. While these lines suggest that the author may have been familiar with the word *"water"* at some time in her life before the teacher came, they don't mention *a method of communication with her family*, so eliminate (C). The lines for (D) describe something the author experienced after working with her teacher, so eliminate (D). The correct answer is (A).

Tone Questions

Questions about tone (also referred to as the author's "attitude") are not as common as the other question types we've discussed, but you may see one on the SAT Reading Test. There is not a "Tone" question in the passage above, but here is an example:

23

At the time she wrote the passage, the author's attitude toward her teacher was most likely one of

A) frustration.

B) uncertainty.

C) awe.

D) appreciation.

Try question 23, then check the explanation below.

The question asks for the *author's attitude toward her teacher* at *the time she wrote the passage*. Like Purpose and Structure questions, Tone questions are not answered directly in the passage, but the correct answer must be supported by evidence from the passage. Look for words and descriptions that reveal the author's feelings or point of view. As a first step, you might determine whether the author's tone is positive, negative, or neutral, and start your Process of Elimination accordingly.

The author expresses many feelings throughout the passage, but to answer this question you must find evidence of how she felt while she was writing the passage, rather than how she felt while she was experiencing the events she describes. In lines 32–35, the author describes an interaction with her teacher that reveals the ultimate nature of their relationship: *I was caught up and held close in the arms of her who had come to reveal all things to me, and, more than all things else, to love me.* In lines 88–90, the author describes the outcome of her teacher's efforts: *That living word awakened my soul, gave it light, hope, joy, set it free!* Both of these descriptions are positive. Eliminate answers that don't match this prediction. Neither *frustration* nor *uncertainty* is positive, so eliminate (A) and (B). Note that these are Right Answer, Wrong Question trap answers: they describe emotions the author experienced, but they don't describe the feelings she had about her teacher when writing the passage. Choice (C), *awe*, is a Could Be True trap answer—it's certainly possible that the author was in awe of what her teacher was able to do, but the text doesn't actually support this inference. Choice (D), *appreciation*, is supported by the author's description of what she gained as a result of her experiences with her teacher. The correct answer is (D).

Synthesis Questions

There are two types of questions that ask you to synthesize information from multiple sources: Quantitative questions and dual passage questions. Both of these question types are covered in Chapter 6.

Put your skills to work with the full passage drill on the next page.

BASIC APPROACH EXERCISE

Questions 1–11 are based on the following passage.

This passage is adapted from Henry James, *The Turn of the Screw*. Originally published in 1898. The narrator, a governess caring for two children at a remote estate, encounters an unfamiliar figure on the grounds.

There were hours, from day to day—or at least there were moments, snatched even from clear duties—when I had to
Line shut myself up to think. It was not so
5   much yet that I was more nervous than I could bear to be as that I was remarkably afraid of becoming so; for the truth I had now to turn over was, simply and clearly, the truth that I could arrive at no account
10 whatever of the visitor with whom I had been so inexplicably and yet, as it seemed to me, so intimately concerned. The shock I had suffered must have sharpened all my senses; I felt sure, at the end of three days
15 and as the result of mere closer attention, that I had not been practiced upon by the servants nor made the object of any "game." Of whatever it was that I knew, nothing was known around me. There
20 was but one sane inference: someone had taken a liberty rather gross. That was what, repeatedly, I dipped into my room and locked the door to say to myself. We had been, collectively, subject to an intrusion;
25 some unscrupulous traveler, curious in old houses, had made his way in unobserved, enjoyed the prospect from the best point of view, and then stolen out as he came. If he had given me such a bold hard stare,
30 that was but a part of his indiscretion. The good thing, after all, was that we should surely see no more of him.

There was a Sunday when it rained with such force and for so many hours,
35 I had arranged with Mrs. Grose that, should the evening show improvement, we would attend together the late service. The rain happily stopped, and I prepared for our walk. The day was gray enough,
40 but the afternoon light still lingered, and it enabled me, on crossing the threshold, not only to recognize, but to become aware of a person on the other side of the window and looking straight in. One step
45 into the room had sufficed; my vision was instantaneous; it was all there. The person looking straight in was the person who had already appeared to me. He appeared thus again with I won't say greater
50 distinctness, for that was impossible, but with a nearness that represented a forward stride in our intercourse and made me, as I met him, catch my breath and turn cold. He remained but a few seconds—long
55 enough to convince me he also saw and recognized.

I stood there, a sudden vibration of duty and courage. I bounded straight out of the door again, reached that of the
60 house, got, in an instant, upon the drive, and, passing along the terrace as fast as I could rush, turned a corner and came full in sight. But it was in sight of nothing now—my visitor had vanished. I stopped, I
65 almost dropped, with the real relief of this; but I took in the whole scene—I gave him time to reappear. I call it time, but how long was it? That kind of measure must have left me: they couldn't have lasted as
70 they actually appeared to me to last. The terrace and the whole place, the lawn and the garden beyond it, all I could see of the park, were empty with a great emptiness. There were shrubberies and big trees, but

75 I remember the clear assurance I felt that none of them concealed him. He was there or was not there: not there if I didn't see him. I got hold of this; then, instinctively, instead of returning as I had come, went to
80 the window. It was confusedly present to me that I ought to place myself where he had stood. I did so; I applied my face to the pane and looked, as he had looked, into the room.

1

In the passage, the visitor is presented primarily as

A) a familiar townsperson.

B) a shadowy figure.

C) a bold intruder.

D) a frightening criminal.

2

Which choice best summarizes the passage?

A) A character has an unsettling experience with an unknown person and attempts to explain it.

B) A character's unexpected arrival causes upheaval among the members of the household.

C) A character's descent into madness begins with a traumatizing experience in her home.

D) A character takes bold action to try to drive away an intruder.

3

It can most reasonably be inferred from the passage that the narrator's conclusion that her experience was not a "game" is

A) contrived, because she cannot remember all of the details of her experience.

B) inaccurate, because she and the visitor saw and recognized one another.

C) correct, because she is the only one who appears to be aware of the intrusion.

D) disappointing, because she hoped the incident was a practical joke.

4

Which choice provides the best evidence for the answer to the previous question?

A) Lines 7–12 ("for the . . . concerned")

B) Lines 18–19 ("Of whatever . . . me")

C) Lines 54–56 ("He remained . . . recognized")

D) Lines 74–76 ("There . . . him")

5

As used in line 16, the phrase "practiced upon" most nearly means

A) pursued.

B) surprised.

C) rehearsed.

D) fooled.

6

The narrator uses the phrase "my visitor" in line 64 in order to

A) imply that the visitor was her invited guest.

B) indicate that the visitor was invisible to others in the house.

C) emphasize her inability to find the visitor.

D) convey an impression of connection between her and the visitor.

7

Which choice best supports the conclusion that the narrator did not truly wish to find the intruder?

A) Lines 19–21 ("There . . . gross")

B) Lines 44–46 ("One step . . . there")

C) Lines 64–65 ("I stopped . . . this")

D) Lines 82–84 ("I applied . . . room")

8

With regard to the intruder, the narrator is best described as

A) tense but determined.

B) curious but hesitant.

C) shaken but vengeful.

D) nervous but hopeful.

9

The author most likely uses the phrase "empty with a great emptiness" to highlight the

A) narrator's loneliness at the isolated estate.

B) narrator's fear that the figure was of supernatural origin.

C) narrator's concern that the visitor has robbed the estate.

D) narrator's certainty that the figure was no longer present.

10

The author indicates that the narrator would most likely agree that the intruder

A) was pointedly seeking her out.

B) demonstrated cunning tactics in his intrusion.

C) desired a fine home for himself.

D) was unpleasant to encounter in person.

11

Which choice provides the best evidence for the answer to the previous question?

A) Lines 23–28 ("We had . . . came")

B) Lines 39–44 ("The day . . . in")

C) Lines 48–52 ("He appeared . . . intercourse")

D) Lines 76–78 ("He was . . . him")

Summary

Let's revisit our list of challenges from the beginning of this chapter. We said the following things make SAT Reading difficult:

o   There's not enough time to read the passage and work the questions.

o   The passages are long, so it's easy to lose your focus.

o   You end up reading a ton of stuff you don't need.

o   The questions are written in a confusing way.

o   It often seems like more than one answer could work.

The Basic Approach addresses these difficulties:

o   When we skip or skim the passage rather than reading it in its entirety, we save a tremendous amount of time.

o   When we are guided by the questions, we read only what we need to answer those questions.

o   When we rephrase the questions, we make them clearer and more answerable.

o   When we use the text to predict and defend the answer, we are much less likely to pick trap answers.

Chapter 5
Reading Exercises: Answers and Explanations

CHAPTER 3: READING INTRODUCTION EXERCISE ANSWERS

1. **C** The question asks about the whole passage, but it also quotes a specific line, so begin there. The narrator's "complex about music" involves "hopes" that "crashed too low" (lines 1–3), and this led her to obsess negatively about the concert she performed in. If you stop there, (A) might seem like the correct answer, but instead, the narrator relates that while her poor performance at Town Hall made her doubt her ambition to be a singer, she eventually resolved to do it anyway. You can now eliminate (D), which is contradicted by the passage, and see that (C) offers the best summary. Choice (A) is incorrect because the passage doesn't tell you whether she changed careers, although it implies she did not. Choice (B) Could Be True, but it does not explain the complex.

2. **B** The question asks what "fortunate swimmers" means in this context. Read around the window for line 9, and it should be clear that this is an extended metaphor— "plunged" into "the mainstream of American musical life"—and that "fortunate swimmers" are those who performed at Town Hall. She had wanted, in other words, to be famous. Choice (B), "desire to be a popular singer," is basically saying that she wanted to be famous.

3. **A** The question asks what the quoted phrase is trying to convince readers of. By reading around line 12, you can see that the narrator's memories of the performance at Town Hall are either vivid or pushed (thrust) aside. The ones she remembers are negative, which eliminates (D), and the mood of panic is closest to (A), which essentially means "upset." There's nothing in the passage to suggest that the author resents anybody, (B), or is unstable, (C).

4. **B** The question asks which two contradictory statements or facts constitute the "misrepresentation." Reading the reference in context, you find that the narrator believes she might have performed better if she "had not been told the auditorium was full," and that a "misrepresentation like that can throw you off balance." Tying together these two statements, you can conclude that the misrepresentation refers to the number of people actually in attendance versus those the narrator expected to see. Choice (B) best expresses this relationship. Choice (A) is incorrect because the author's actual skill as a singer is not mentioned here. Choice (C) is incorrect because the reaction of the audience is never mentioned. Choice (D) is incorrect because the narrator's desire to please everyone is not mentioned in this paragraph.

5. **D** The question asks what happens in the third paragraph. Reading from there, after the Town Hall performance, the author "stopped going regularly to Mr. Boghetti's studio," because the "fiasco had shaken" her. In other words, the paragraph describes what happened to the author as a result of her Town Hall performance. Choice (D) matches this. While the passage implies that she attended rehearsals with Mr. Boghetti, their importance, (A), is not mentioned in the passage. Choices (B) and (C) are also misleading—the mother is kind in another passage, but is not a stranger, and while the passage concludes with a decision to return to singing as a potential career, it doesn't happen in the specified third paragraph.

6. **A** The question asks what the narrator means by saying she gave "critics the opportunity." According to the sentence, the author realizes that the "criticism was right" and that her performance had enabled them to write negative reviews. This suggests that the author knows that she had a role in earning the unfavorable criticism. This is best paraphrased by (A). Choice (C) contradicts this point and can be eliminated, as can (B), as there's nothing about "journalism" in this passage. Choice (D) Could Be True, but the passage doesn't actually say that this is something she recognized, and so it should be eliminated as well.

CHAPTER 4: BASIC APPROACH TO READING ANSWERS

1. **C** The question asks how the *visitor is presented*. Because this is a general question, it should be done after the specific questions. In the first paragraph, the narrator describes the visitor. Lines 23–30 say, *We had been, collectively, subject to an intrusion; some unscrupulous traveler, curious in old houses, had made his way in unobserved, enjoyed the prospect from the best point of view, and then stolen out as he came. If he had given me such a bold hard stare, that was but a part of his indiscretion.* Eliminate answers that do not match this prediction. Eliminate (A) because the visitor is not a *familiar townsperson*, the passage states that he is a *traveler*, and there is no indication that the narrator is *familiar* with him. Eliminate (B) because the visitor is not a *shadowy figure*; the narrator sees him clearly through a window later on in the passage. Keep (C) because it matches the prediction. Choice (D) is a Could Be True trap answer: there is no indication in the passage that the visitor is a *criminal*. Eliminate (D). The correct answer is (C).

2. **A** The question asks for a summary of the passage. Because this is a general question, it should be done after the specific questions. In the passage, the narrator describes two encounters with an unknown visitor. Lines 14–28 state, *I felt sure, at the end of three days and as the result of mere closer attention, that I had not been practiced upon by the servants nor made the object of any "game." Of whatever it was that I knew, nothing was known around me. There was but one sane inference: someone had taken a liberty rather gross.... We had been, collectively, subject to an intrusion; some unscrupulous traveler, curious in old houses, had made his way in unobserved, enjoyed the prospect from the best point of view, and then stolen out as he came.* In these lines, the narrator attempts to explain the encounter, determining that the visitor was a stranger who had snuck into the house. Eliminate answers that do not match this prediction. Keep (A) because it matches the prediction. Eliminate (B) because the passage does not describe *upheaval* among other *members of the household.* The narrator says, *Of whatever it was that I knew, nothing was known around me,* indicating that no one else in the house knew about the intruder. Eliminate (C) because there is no evidence that the narrator is descending *into madness.* Eliminate (D) because there is no indication that the narrator tried to *drive away* the intruder. The correct answer is (A).

3. **C** The question asks what can be *inferred* about *the narrator's conclusion that her experience was not a "game."* This is the first question in a paired set, but it easy to find, so it can be done on its own. Use lead words and the order of the questions to find the window. Q5 asks about line 16, so scan the first paragraph, looking for the lead word *game.* Lines 14–18 say, *I felt sure, at the end of three days and as the result of mere closer attention, that I had not been practiced upon by the servants nor made the object of any "game."* The narrator goes on to say, *Of whatever it was that I knew, nothing was known around me.* Therefore, the narrator concludes that no one is playing a trick on her, because she is the only one who knew about the *visitor.* Eliminate answers that do not match this prediction. Eliminate (A) because there is no indication that the narrator *cannot remember all of the details of her experience.* Eliminate (B) because there is no evidence that she and the visitor *recognized one other.* Keep (C) because it matches the prediction. Choice (D) is a Right Words, Wrong Meaning trap answer: although the narrator does consider that her experience could have been a *practical joke,* there is no indication that she *hoped* that it was or that she feels disappointed. Eliminate (D). The correct answer is (C).

4. **B** The question is the best evidence question in a paired set. Because the previous question was easy to find, simply look at the lines used to answer Q3. Lines 14–19 were used in the prediction: *I felt sure, at the end of three days and as the result of mere closer attention, that I had not been practiced upon by the servants nor made the object of any "game." Of whatever it was that I knew, nothing was known around me.* Only (B) includes any of these lines. The correct answer is (B).

5. **D** The question asks what the phrase *practiced upon* most nearly means in line 16. Go back to the text, find the phrase *practiced upon*, and cross it out. Then read the window carefully, using context clues to determine another word that would fit in the text. The text says, *I felt sure, at the end of three days and as the result of mere closer attention, that I had not been practiced upon by the servants nor made the object of any "game."* Therefore, *practiced upon* could be replaced by a word such as "tricked" or "deceived." Eliminate answers that do not match this prediction. *Pursued* does not match "tricked," so eliminate (A). *Surprised* does not match "tricked;" although a trick could be surprising, the two words do not have the same meaning. Eliminate (B). *Rehearsed* does not match "tricked;" this is a Could Be True trap answer based on another meaning of *practiced* that is not supported by the text. Eliminate (C). *Fooled* matches "tricked," so keep (D). The correct answer is (D).

6. **D** The question asks why *the narrator uses the phrase "my visitor."* Use the given line reference to find the window. In lines 46–64, the visitor appears twice to the narrator, and in lines 18–19, she indicates that he does not appear to anyone else. In this second encounter, the narrator says that she and the visitor *saw and recognized* one another and emphasizes that there was *a forward stride* in their connection. The narrator's use of the phrase *my visitor* is in keeping with her emphasis of the connection between them. Eliminate answers that do not match this prediction. Eliminate (A) because there is no evidence in the passage that the narrator *invited* the visitor, and in the first paragraph the narrator described the visitor's actions as an *intrusion*. Choice (B) is a Right Words, Wrong Meaning trap answer: although the narrator is the only one who is aware of the visitor, that is no indication that the visitor is *invisible* to others. Eliminate (B). Choice (C) is a Right Answer, Wrong Question trap answer: although the passage does indicate that the narrator is unable *to find the visitor*, (C) doesn't address the narrator's reason for using the phrase *my visitor*. Keep (D) because it matches the prediction. The correct answer is (D).

7. **C** The question asks for evidence that supports the conclusion that *the narrator did not truly wish to find the intruder.* Look at the line references given in the answer choices, and eliminate the statements that don't support this claim. The lines for (A)

say, *There was but one sane inference: someone had taken a liberty rather gross.* There is no mention of the narrator looking for the intruder nor any indication that she does not wish to find him, so eliminate (A). The lines for (B) say, *One step into the room had sufficed; my vision was instantaneous; it was all there.* Again, there is no mention of the narrator looking for the intruder nor any indication that she does not wish to find him, so eliminate (B). The lines for (C) say, *I stopped, I almost dropped, with the real relief of this.* The previous sentence says that *my visitor had vanished,* so her *relief* shows that *the narrator did not truly wish to find the intruder.* Keep (C). The lines for (D) say, *I applied my face to the pane and looked, as he had looked, into the room.* There is no evidence that the narrator did *not truly wish to find the intruder,* so eliminate (D). The correct answer is (C).

8.   **A**   The question asks how *the narrator is best described with regard to the intruder.* Since there is no line reference, use the order of the questions to find the window. Q6 asks about line 64 and Q9 asks about line 73, so scan the passage between those lines, looking for descriptions of the narrator's attitude toward the intruder. Lines 64–70 say, *I stopped, I almost dropped, with the real relief of this; but I took in the whole scene—I gave him time to reappear. I call it time, but how long was it? That kind of measure must have left me: they couldn't have lasted as they actually appeared to me to last.* The narrator is relieved about not finding the intruder but also does not give up immediately. Eliminate answers that do not match this prediction. Keep (A) because *tense* matches how the narrator felt as she ran outside to find the intruder and *determined* matches her waiting for him to reappear. Eliminate (B) because only *curious* is supported; there is no support for *hesitant.* Eliminate (C) because only *shaken* is supported; there is no support for *vengeful.* Eliminate (D) because only *nervous* is supported. *Hopeful* is a Could Be True trap answer: although the narrator waits for the intruder to reemerge, there is no indication in the text that she wants him to come back. The correct answer is (A).

9.   **D**   The question asks what the author means to highlight with the phrase *empty with a great emptiness.* Use the given line reference to find the window. In the third paragraph, the narrator goes outside to try to find the person she saw through the window, but she is unsuccessful. Lines 63–64 say, *But it was in sight of nothing now—my visitor had vanished.* The narrator describes what she sees: *The terrace and the whole place, the lawn and the garden beyond it, all I could see of the park, were empty with a great emptiness.* Therefore, the phrase *empty with a great emptiness* indicates that the visitor is nowhere to be seen. Eliminate answers that do not match this prediction. Choice (A) is a Could Be True trap answer: although the narrator could

be lonely, the text does not support this interpretation. The *emptiness* refers to the disappearance of the visitor, not the narrator's feelings. Eliminate (A). Choice (B) is also a Could Be True trap answer: although it is possible that the figure disappeared because it was a ghost, the text does not provide evidence that the visitor was of *supernatural origin*. Eliminate (C) because there is no indication that the visitor *robbed the estate*. Although the word *stolen* is mentioned in line 28, the passage says that the intruder had *stolen out as he came*, so this is a Right Words, Wrong Meaning trap. Keep (D) because it matches the prediction. The correct answer is (D).

10. **B** The question asks what *the narrator would most likely agree* with about *the intruder*. Notice that this is the first question in a paired set, so it can be done in tandem with Q11. Look at the answer choices for Q11 first. The lines for (11A) describe the intruder as *some unscrupulous traveler* and say that he *had made his way in unobserved, enjoyed the prospect from the best point of view, and then stolen out as he came*. These lines support (10B). Draw a line connecting (10B) and (11A). The lines for (11B) describe a gray afternoon when the narrator was able *not only to recognize, but to become aware of a person on the other side of the window and looking straight in*. These lines do not support any of the answers for Q10, so eliminate (11B). The lines for (11C) say that the intruder *appeared thus again with I won't say greater distinctness, for that was impossible, but with a nearness that represented a forward stride in our intercourse*. Although these lines mention a *forward stride* in the interactions between the narrator and the intruder, they do not support any of the answers for Q10. Eliminate (11C). The lines for (11D) say that the intruder *was there or was not there: not there if I didn't see him*. These lines do not support any of the answers for Q10, so eliminate (11D). Without any support in the answers from Q11, (10A), (10C), and (10D) can be eliminated. The correct answers are (10B) and (11A).

11. **A** (See explanation above.)

Chapter 6
Synthesis and Reading Drill

We have one more question category to look at, and then it's time to put the Basic Approach, POE Criteria, and Parallel POE to the test! Over the next several pages you will find sample passages from Science, History/Social Studies, and World Literature. As you work through the passages, the main question you should have in mind is, "Where is the support in the text?" When you circle your answer, you should have concrete evidence either from the text or from earlier questions to back up that circle. After you finish each drill, check your answers in the next chapter.

SYNTHESIS QUESTIONS

While most of the questions in your Reading passages will be consistent with what we've seen up to this point, there will be two additional question types that will show up somewhere in the Science or History/Social Studies passages.

1. **Quantitative Information (charts, graphs, tables)**
   You may see some type of graphic, like a chart, table, or graph, that connects to the passage in some way. The graphic will be straightforward. Make sure you identify the variables and read the graphic carefully. When you get to the question, the key is making sure you can put your pencil on the data point that supports keeping or eliminating the answer.

2. **Dual Passages**
   One of your Science or History/Social Studies passages will be a dual passage set. There will be two shorter passages about one topic. You will have a few questions about the first passage, a few about the second passage, and the remaining questions will ask about both passages together.

QUANTITATIVE QUESTIONS

This drill contains questions that ask about graphs in the passage. Follow the Basic Approach through the rest of the questions. When you get to the graphs, make sure you can put your pencil on the data point you need to answer the question.

QUANTITATIVE QUESTIONS READING DRILL

Questions 12–21 are based on the following passage and supplementary material.

This passage is adapted from Gerardo Chowell, Cécile Viboud, Xiaohong Wang, Stefano M. Bertozzi, Mark A. Miller, *Adaptive Vaccination Strategies to Mitigate Pandemic Influenza: Mexico as a Case Study.* © 2009 by PLoS Currents.

Virological subtyping of a novel pandemic virus can provide an early clue to target vaccination efforts. While
Line the elderly are normally at most risk
5 for severe outcomes during seasonal influenza, warranting the targeting of vaccination for direct protection to that group, they may have residual protection during pandemics. By contrast, younger
10 groups generally respond better to vaccine and provide a greater reduction of transmission. Given residual protection in seniors in early pandemic waves, younger age groups become a clear priority group
15 for pandemic vaccine allocation. In the current 2009 pandemic, those who were born between 1919 and around 1957 would have been first exposed to H1N1 during their childhood and may enjoy
20 protection against S-OIV infection and death, as observed in the early wave of S-OIV in Mexico.

Several studies have assessed the effects of potential vaccination strategies against
25 pandemic influenza in terms of reducing morbidity and mortality based on priority age groups, transmissibility, timing of vaccination efforts, and number of years of life lost. A recent study has evaluated
30 the influenza vaccine allocation problem considering a vaccination coverage of 35% at the pandemic onset or near the pandemic peak when the population is stratified by age and low and high risks.
35 Results suggest that vaccines should be allocated to individuals with high-risk complications whenever the vaccine becomes available late in the pandemic (close to the peak) while targeting high
40 transmitter groups (children) is more effective when the vaccine is available close to the start of the pandemic. Most studies of influenza vaccination strategies to date have assumed a given epidemiological
45 profile based on past influenza epidemics and pandemics but have not necessarily considered novel profiles that could arise in future pandemics. Given high levels of uncertainty as to the epidemiology of the
50 next outbreak of S-OIV or other novel influenza virus, unfortunately, no single strategy can fit all scenarios. Our adaptive strategy is flexible enough to accommodate a range of possible scenarios illustrating
55 our experience with past pandemics, and potentially new ones.

We note that other intervention strategies have been proposed to mitigate the burden of pandemic influenza. Social
60 distancing and facemasks have been suggested as mitigation strategies, but their efficacy against pandemics remains debated. Strategies involving antiviral treatments are helpful to mitigate disease
65 burden, but resources are limited and effectiveness assumes speedy delivery and susceptibility of circulating viruses. Any of these interventions could be used in combination with the adaptive vaccine
70 allocation strategy proposed here.

Mexico began vaccinating against seasonal influenza in 2004, and annual campaigns target children 6 to 23 months old, adults over 65 years, and those with
75 chronic conditions. In the past, Mexico has relied on other countries for influenza

vaccine production, which in the setting of a pandemic is likely to be available in limited supplies. Although a preparedness

80 and response plan against pandemic influenza for Mexico had been drafted with the objective of optimizing resources and conducting a timely response, it lacks guidance on how to define priority groups

85 in the scenario of a limited vaccine supply. Our study shows that even limited vaccine supplies, if used optimally, can have an impact on mitigating disease burden in a middle-income country like Mexico.

90 There are many limitations to policy models with respect to choice of parameter estimates and the incorporation of bio-medical, environmental, operational, political, economic features. No one model

95 can claim to incorporate all assumptions and features given the limited data on the epidemiology of novel pandemic viruses and paucity of data on contact rates, especially in Mexico. This model

100 illustrates a prioritization scheme based on age groups but does not further discriminate other sub-groups such as those persons with other medical conditions, including pregnancy. Models

105 do not necessarily provide answers but help articulate the questions, assumptions and numerous uncertainties in rapidly evolving circumstances as a tool to formulate rational policy based on the

110 best available evidence. Pandemics evolve rapidly relative to capabilities to enact policies; therefore, pre-formulated adaptive strategies can readily take into account new data. Knowledge of the

115 specific sub-type circulating and real-time information on age-specific rates of severe outcomes are crucial to help policy makers infer who may be at most risk, and tailor intervention strategies accordingly. These

120 adaptive pandemic strategies could be readily adopted by other countries.

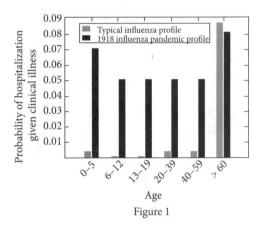

Figure 1

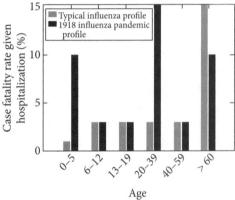

Figure 2

12

Based on the passage, the authors' statement "they may have residual protection during pandemics" (lines 8–9) implies that

A) younger people respond better to vaccines than older people do.

B) compared to younger people, elderly people aren't a priority during pandemics.

C) elderly people may be able to fight off pandemics better than younger people can.

D) younger people are less likely to get influenza.

13

The authors use the word "enjoy" in line 19 to indicate that children who are exposed to influenza

A) are unlikely to die from it as adults.

B) handle the effects of the illness well.

C) are happy to overcome it.

D) may have some immunity to it later in life.

14

A politician claims that Mexico is in dire need of more funds for creating its own vaccines, since, unless the majority of citizens are vaccinated, a pandemic could wipe out the population. Which of the following statements in the passage contradicts the politician's claim?

A) Lines 12–15 ("Given . . . allocation")

B) Lines 48–52 ("Given . . . scenarios")

C) Lines 86–89 ("Our study . . . Mexico")

D) Lines 94–99 ("No one . . . Mexico")

15

The authors' main purpose of including the information about how "Mexico has relied on other countries for influenza vaccine production" (lines 75–77) is to

A) provide a rationale for targeting vaccination efforts.

B) encourage Mexico to create more influenza vaccinations.

C) deter Mexico from seeking foreign vaccine producers.

D) discourage Mexico from venturing into a new industry.

16

As it used in line 102, the word "discriminate" most nearly means

A) differentiate.

B) rank.

C) condescend.

D) victimize.

17

The passage suggests that

A) a strategy that takes into account a variety of factors could lead to a better disease control policy.

B) young children should be given all doses of vaccine available at the beginning of a pandemic.

C) alternatives to vaccination have proven helpful in preventing the spread of pandemics.

D) viruses change too quickly for vaccine producers to adapt.

18

Which of the following provides the best evidence for the answer to the previous question?

A) Lines 9–12 ("By contrast . . . transmission")

B) Lines 59–63 ("Social . . . debated")

C) Lines 63–67 ("Strategies . . . viruses")

D) Lines 114–119 ("Knowledge . . . accordingly")

19

Based on the figures, which choice gives the correct percentage of the case fatality rate given hospitalization percentage for the 1918 influenza pandemic profile for ages 0–5?

A) 1%

B) 7%

C) 10%

D) 15%

20

Do the data in the tables support the authors' statement that elderly patients have some residual protection during pandemics?

A) Yes, the probability of hospitalization for age groups above 5 years and below 60 years is much higher for the 1918 pandemic than for the typical influenza profile.

B) Yes, the probability of hospitalization and the case fatality rate given hospitalization percentage for people older than 60 are higher for the typical influenza profile than for the 1918 pandemic.

C) No, the probability of hospitalization for age groups above 5 years and below 60 years is much higher for the 1918 pandemic than for the typical influenza profile.

D) No, the probability of hospitalization and the case fatality rate given hospitalization percentage for people older than 60 are lower for the typical influenza profile than for the 1918 pandemic.

21

According to the figures, which of the following pairs of percentages provides evidence in support of the answer to the previous question?

A) 15% and 10%

B) 15% and 5%

C) 15% and 2.5%

D) 10% and 7%

DUAL PASSAGES

Although the two passages will be about the same topic, there will also be differences that you'll need to pay attention to. Rather than attempting to read and understand both passages at the same time, just follow the Basic Approach and focus on one at a time.

The questions for Passage 1 will come before the questions for Passage 2, and the questions for each passage follow the order of the passage, just like single-passage questions. The questions about both passages will follow the questions for Passage 2.

Work the questions about Passage 1 first, then jot down the main idea of Passage 1. Then work the questions about Passage 2, and jot down the main idea of Passage 2. Next, jot down the relationship between the passages. For example, do the authors disagree with one another? Does one passage discuss a theory, while the other discusses an application of the theory? Does one passage present a historical perspective, while the other presents a more modern perspective on the same topic? Once you've considered the relationship between the passages, you're ready to tackle the questions that ask about both passages.

Always keep in mind that the same POE criteria apply, no matter how two-passage questions are presented.

- If a question asks what is supported by both passages, make sure that you find specific support in both passages, and be wary of all the usual trap answers.
- If a question is about an issue on which the authors of the two passages disagree or on how the passages relate to one another, make sure you find support in each passage for the author's particular opinion.
- If the question asks how one author would respond to the other passage, find out what was said in that other passage, and then find out exactly what the author you are asked about said on that exact topic.

The bottom line is that if you are organized and remember your basic reading comprehension strategy, you'll see that two-passage questions are no harder than single-passage questions! In the following drill, you'll have a chance to try a set of dual passages.

DUAL PASSAGE READING DRILL

Questions 22–31 are based on the following passages.

Passage 1 is adapted from Edwin E. Slosson, M.S., Ph.D., *Easy Lessons in Einstein: A discussion of the more intelligible features of the theory of relativity*. Published in 1920 by Harcourt, Brace and Howe. Passage 2 is adapted from D.J. McAdam, *Einstein's Relativity: A criticism*. Published in 1922 by Richard G. Badger.

Passage 1

All three of Newton's laws of motion are now questioned and the world is called upon to unlearn the lesson which
Line Euclid taught it that parallel lines never
5 meet. According to Einstein they may meet. According to Newton the action of gravitation is instantaneous throughout all space. According to Einstein no action can exceed the velocity of light. If the
10 theory of relativity is right there can be no such thing as absolute time or way of finding whether clocks in different places are synchronous. Our yardsticks may vary according to how we hold them and the
15 weight of a body may depend upon its velocity. The shortest distance between two points may not be a straight line. These are a few of the startling implications of Einstein's theory of relativity.
20 According to Einstein the size and shape of any body depends upon the rate and direction of its movement. For ordinary speeds the alteration is very slight, but it becomes considerable at rates
25 approaching the speed of light, 186,000 miles a second. If, for instance, you could shoot an arrow from a bow with a velocity of 160,000 miles a second, it would shrink to about half its length, as measured by
30 a man remaining still on earth. A man traveling along with the arrow could discover no change. No force could bring

the arrow or even the smallest particle of matter to a motion greater than the
35 speed of light, and the nearer it comes to this limit the greater the force required to move it faster. This means that the mass of a body, instead of being absolute and unalterable as we have supposed,
40 increases with the speed of its movement. Newton's laws of dynamics are therefore valid only for a matter in motion at such moderate speeds as we have to deal with in our experiments on earth and in our
45 observations of the heavenly bodies. When we come to consider velocities approximating that of light the ordinary laws of physics are subject to an increasing correction.

Passage 2

50 If it does those alarming things claimed for it, distort our bodies, make our clocks unreliable, shorten our yard-sticks, we ought to study it to see if we can invent some counter irritant.
55 Yet a glance through books that have been written from Slossen and Harlow at one end to Eddington, Cunningham and Einstein himself at the other, seems to discourage serious study. "In the history
60 of science, the year 1919 is not likely to be known as the year of the overthrow of the German Empire, but as the year of the overthrow of Newton's law of gravitation.
It is scarcely an exaggeration to say
65 that Einstein hitched the earth to space or the moon and jerked it up to hit Newton's apple. (Though he speaks of a stone falling.)
To any who may be disposed to

question his claim, he can say you are not
one of the eleven. He is reported to have
said that "not *twelve* men in the world
can read and understand fully his book."
This, probably, is a surer way to protect his
device than even an international patent.
Also it is a good way to thwart the critic.
The eleven men who break in will not give
it away, and those outside dare not criticize
what they cannot read. Besides, *eleven*
apostles is the standard, even another one
might be dangerous.

Maybe this astronomer would honestly
tell him that his yard-stick would contract
one-hundredth of the thickness of a cat's
hair, and if the cloth did not change and
the yard-stick did, when he had measured
two million yards of cloth he would gain
an inch.

It is a little provoking that not alone
sensational writers, whom we could
disregard, but men of learning and who
seem to speak with authority, speak of our
bodies, yard-sticks and clocks as if they
had found something seriously wrong
affecting them.

22

The author of Passage 1 takes a position
that he would most likely describe as

A) critical of the stated implications of
    Einstein's theory.

B) sensational and unworthy of serious
    study.

C) analogous description to provide a
    frame of reference.

D) dismissive of Newton's laws.

23

Which choice provides the best evidence
for the answer to the previous question?

A) Lines 1–5 ("All three . . . meet")

B) Lines 26–30 ("If . . . earth")

C) Lines 55–59 ("Yet a . . . study")

D) Lines 89–95 ("It is . . . them")

24

The primary purpose of the first
paragraph of Passage 1 (lines 1–19) is to

A) introduce the basic elements of
    Newton's laws of motion.

B) rebuff arguments against the new
    ideas mentioned in the paragraph.

C) contrast familiar assumptions with
    unexpected assertions.

D) qualify a claim by providing an
    appropriate context.

25

Which of the following hypothetical situations most nearly matches the illustration in the second paragraph (lines 20–49) of Passage 1?

A) An archer shoots an arrow at 200 miles per hour in a competition and the arrow appears much smaller to a watching crowd

B) A comet traveling at 170,000 miles a second appears the same size to both an observer on the comet and one on a nearby planet

C) A speck of dust travels at 190,000 miles a second, and appears as different sizes from different frames of reference

D) A grain of sand traveling at 175,000 miles a second appears as different sizes from different frames of reference

26

As used in line 54, "irritant" most nearly means

A) problem.

B) itch.

C) devastation.

D) salve.

27

The rhetorical effect of the sentence in lines 79–81 ("Besides, *eleven* . . . dangerous") is to

A) imply that if more than eleven people worked with Einstein, there would be an unacceptable margin of error in the calculations.

B) demonstrate the fervor with which Einstein promotes and protects his theories.

C) suggest, through a religious example, that those who attempt to refute Einstein's theories are betraying the progress of science.

D) emphasize through a reference the author's stance that trusting Einstein's theories requires faith.

28

Which choice provides the best evidence for the answer to the previous question?

A) Lines 69–71 ("To any . . . eleven")

B) Lines 74–75 ("This . . . patent")

C) Lines 77–79 ("The eleven . . . read")

D) Lines 89–95 ("It is . . . them")

29

The author of Passage 1 would most likely respond to the claim in lines 89–95 ("It is . . . them") of Passage 2 by

A) countering that relatable examples do more to educate than to harm.

B) agreeing that there is nothing wrong with our yard-sticks and clocks.

C) arguing that the discrepancies in yard-sticks and clocks change aspects of everyday life.

D) adding that more study should be done before accepting any new theories.

30

The opinions of the author of Passage 1 and the author of Passage 2 differ in that the author of Passage 2

A) disagrees with Einstein's theories and supports Newton's laws, while the author of Passage 1 discards Newton's laws for Einstein's theories.

B) disagrees with those who use mundane analogies to describe Einstein's theories, while the author of Passage 1 utilizes such methods.

C) acknowledges limits to his argument, while the author of Passage 1 does not.

D) believes that Einstein's theories have no application, while the author of Passage 1 believes those theories apply to sports and travel on earth.

31

Both authors would most likely agree that

A) Einstein's theories are unsound.

B) Einstein's theories are of significant value.

C) application of Einstein's theories is not always necessary.

D) exaggerations of Einstein's theories should be restricted.

ADDITIONAL DRILLS

Here are two more passages for you to try. Remember to focus on the text!

Additional Drill 1

Questions 1–9 are based on the following passage.

The following passage was adapted from Booker T. Washington, *Up From Slavery: An Autobiography*. Published in 1901.

I was born a slave on a plantation in Franklin County, Virginia. I am not quite sure of the exact place or exact date of my
Line birth, but at any rate I suspect I must have
5 been born somewhere and at some time. As nearly as I have been able to learn, I was born near a cross-roads post-office called Hale's Ford, and the year was 1858 or 1859. I do not know the month or the day. The
10 earliest impressions I can now recall are of the plantation and the slave quarters— the latter being the part of the plantation where the slaves had their cabins.

The first pair of shoes that I recall
15 wearing were wooden ones. They had rough leather on the top, but the bottoms, which were about an inch thick, were of wood. When I walked they made a fearful noise, and besides this they were
20 very inconvenient since there was no yielding to the natural pressure of the foot. In wearing them one presented an exceedingly awkward appearance. The most trying ordeal that I was forced to
25 endure as a slave boy, however, was the wearing of a flax shirt. In the portion of Virginia where I lived it was common to use flax as part of the clothing for the slaves. That part of the flax from which
30 our clothing was made was largely the refuse, which of course was the cheapest and roughest part. I can scarcely imagine any torture, except, perhaps, the pulling of a tooth, that is equal to that caused by

35 putting on a new flax shirt for the first time. It is almost equal to the feeling that one would experience if he had a dozen or more chestnut burrs, or a hundred small pin-points, in contact with his flesh.
40 Even to this day I can recall accurately the tortures that I underwent when putting on one of these garments. The fact that my flesh was soft and tender added to the pain. But I had no choice. I had to wear
45 the flax shirt or none; and had it been left to me to choose, I should have chosen to wear no covering. In connection with the flax shirt, my brother John, who is several years older than I am, performed one of
50 the most generous acts that I ever heard of one slave relative doing for another. On several occasions when I was being forced to wear a new flax shirt, he generously agreed to put it on in my stead and wear
55 it for several days, till it was "broken in." Until I had grown to be quite a youth this single garment was all that I wore.

I pity from the bottom of my heart any nation or body of people that is so
60 unfortunate as to get entangled in the net of slavery. I have long since ceased to cherish any spirit of bitterness against the Southern white people on account of the enslavement of my race. No one section
65 of our country was wholly responsible for its introduction, and, besides, it was recognized and protected for years by the General Government. Having once got its tentacles fastened on to the economic
70 and social life of the Republic, it was no easy matter for the country to relieve itself of the institution. When persons ask me in these days how, in the midst of what sometimes seem hopelessly discouraging

75 conditions, I can have such faith in the future of my race in this country, I remind them of the wilderness through which and out of which, a good Providence has already led us.

1

The author's attitude can be best described as

A) amused.

B) bitter.

C) determined.

D) tempered.

2

The primary purpose of the passage is to

A) detail the author's life and current situation.

B) illustrate an optimism gained through trials.

C) describe a particular suffering endured by the author.

D) seek sympathy for a group of people.

3

Which choice provides the best evidence for the answer to the previous question?

A) Lines 1–2 ("I was . . . Virginia")

B) Lines 23–26 ("The most . . . shirt")

C) Lines 58–61 ("I pity . . . slavery")

D) Lines 72–79 ("When persons . . . us")

4

In the context of the passage as a whole, the principal rhetorical effect of the first paragraph, lines 1–13, is to

A) demonstrate that the author has a sense of humor within a serious subject.

B) engage the reader with a universal uncertainty about the exact circumstances of a person's birth.

C) hint at the author's main point through an extended analogy that relates "birth" with a deeper concept.

D) provide context for the events recounted in the passage.

5

The author uses the word "accurately" (line 40) primarily in order to

A) emphasize the intensity of an experience.

B) provide evidence for the clarity of the author's memory.

C) give support for the following sentence.

D) show the author's gratitude towards his brother.

6

The sentence in lines 44–47 ("I had . . . covering") most directly suggests that

A) the author had been ordered by the plantation owners to wear a shirt.

B) no other forms of clothing were available.

C) some choices were not left to the author's discretion.

D) the author would have enjoyed not wearing clothing.

7

As used in line 62, "cherish" most nearly means to

A) prefer.

B) keep secret.

C) love.

D) hold resolutely.

8

Based on the passage, which of the following best describes the author's position regarding responsibility for the institution of slavery?

A) The slave owners bear full responsibility for their actions.

B) No one is responsible for the institution of slavery.

C) The responsibility rests most strongly on the government.

D) Responsibility is shared among many parties.

9

Which choice provides the best evidence for the answer to the previous question?

A) Lines 58–61 ("I pity . . . slavery")

B) Lines 61–64 ("I have . . . race")

C) Lines 64–68 ("No one . . . Government")

D) Lines 75–79 ("I can . . . us")

10

As used in line 77, "wilderness" most nearly means

A) an uncultivated terrain.

B) difficult circumstances.

C) a desert.

D) slavery.

Additional Drill 2

Questions 32–41 are based on the following passage.

This passage is adapted from H.G. Wells, *A Short History of the World*. Published in 1922. The excerpt begins with the aftermath of the French Revolution and describes the rise and fall of Napoleon Bonaparte.

For some time the French thrust towards Italy was hung up, and it was only in 1796 that a new general, Napoleon
Line Bonaparte, led the ragged and hungry
5 republican armies in triumph across Piedmont to Mantua and Verona. Says C. F. Atkinson, "What astonished the Allies most of all was the number and the velocity of the Republicans. These
10 improvised armies had in fact nothing to delay them. Tents were unprocurable for want of money, untransportable for want of the enormous number of wagons that would have been required, and also
15 unnecessary, for the discomfort that would have caused wholesale desertion in professional armies was cheerfully borne by the men of 1793–94. Supplies for armies of then unheard-of size could
20 not be carried in convoys, and the French soon became familiar with 'living on the country.' Thus 1793 saw the birth of the modern system of war—rapidity of movement, full development of national
25 strength, bivouacs, requisitions and force as against cautious manœuvring, small professional armies, tents and full rations, and chicane. The first represented the decision-compelling spirit, the second the
30 spirit of risking little to gain a little."
And while these ragged hosts of enthusiasts were chanting the Marseillaise and fighting for *la France,* manifestly never quite clear in their minds whether they
35 were looting or liberating the countries

into which they poured, the republican enthusiasm in Paris was spending itself in a far less glorious fashion.
Unhappily for France and the world a
40 man arose who embodied in its intensest form this national egotism of the French. He gave that country ten years of glory and the humiliation of a final defeat. This was that same Napoleon Bonaparte who had
45 led the armies of the Directory to victory in Italy.
Throughout the five years of the Directorate he had been scheming and working for self-advancement. Gradually
50 he clambered to supreme power. He was a man of severely limited understanding but of ruthless directness and great energy. He had begun life as an extremist of the school of Robespierre; he owed his first
55 promotion to that side; but he had no real grasp of the new forces that were working in Europe. His utmost political imagination carried him to a belated and tawdry attempt to restore the Western
60 Empire. He tried to destroy the remains of the old Holy Roman Empire, intending to replace it by a new one centring upon Paris. The Emperor in Vienna ceased to be the Holy Roman Emperor and became
65 simply Emperor of Austria. Napoleon divorced his French wife in order to marry an Austrian princess.
He became practically monarch of France as First Consul in 1799, and he
70 made himself Emperor of France in 1804 in direct imitation of Charlemagne. He was crowned by the Pope in Paris, taking the crown from the Pope and putting it upon his own head himself as
75 Charlemagne had directed. His son was

crowned King of Rome.

For some years Napoleon's reign was
a career of victory. He conquered most
of Italy and Spain, defeated Prussia and
80 Austria, and dominated all Europe west of
Russia. But he never won the command
of the sea from the British and his fleets
sustained a conclusive defeat inflicted by
the British Admiral Nelson at Trafalgar
85 (1805). Spain rose against him in 1808 and
a British army under Wellington thrust
the French armies slowly northward out
of the peninsula. In 1811 Napoleon came
into conflict with the Tsar Alexander I,
90 and in 1812 he invaded Russia with a great
conglomerate army of 600,000 men, that
was defeated and largely destroyed by the
Russians and the Russian winter. Germany
rose against him, Sweden turned against
95 him. The French armies were beaten back
and at Fontainebleau Napoleon abdicated
(1814). He was exiled to Elba, returned to
France for one last effort in 1815 and was
defeated by the allied British, Belgians and
100 Prussians at Waterloo. He died a British
prisoner at St. Helena in 1821.

The forces released by the French
revolution were wasted and finished. A
great Congress of the victorious allies met
105 at Vienna to restore as far as possible the
state of affairs that the great storm had
rent to pieces. For nearly forty years a sort
of peace, a peace of exhausted effort, was
maintained in Europe.

Map of Napoleon's French Empire and satellite states, in 1811

French Empire, including parts of Belgium and Italy
Satellite states of the French Empire
Non-French Empire

32

The author's rhetorical style can be
described as a

A) meticulous examination of minute
   particulars.

B) rapid overview interspersed with
   specific detail.

C) reverential regard for objective
   depictions of historical events.

D) callous nonchalance towards all
   depicted parties.

33

Which choice provides the best evidence for the answer to the previous question?

A) Lines 18–22 ("Supplies for . . . country")

B) Lines 43–46 ("This was . . . Italy")

C) Lines 97–100 ("He was . . . Waterloo")

D) Lines 103–107 ("A great . . . pieces")

34

The author's attitude towards the French armies is best characterized as

A) contemptuous.

B) ambivalent.

C) approving.

D) apathetic.

35

As used in line 13, "want" most nearly means

A) lack.

B) desire.

C) requirement.

D) gain.

36

The author supports his description of Napoleon as "a man of severely limited understanding" primarily by

A) providing an example in which Napoleon made a decision that alienated his French compatriots.

B) indirectly referencing a state of affairs that is implied to have had an impact on Napoleon's success.

C) refuting claims that Napoleon had no real grasp of matters beyond his own extremist background.

D) demonstrating Napoleon's lack of response to overtures from other heads of state which could have altered the course of events.

37

Which choice provides the best evidence for the answer to the previous question?

A) Lines 39–41 ("Unhappily for . . . French")

B) Lines 42–43 ("He gave . . . defeat")

C) Lines 55–57 ("but he . . . Europe")

D) Lines 65–67 ("Napoleon divorced . . . princess")

38

In the sixth paragraph, lines 77–101, the author primarily contrasts

A) Napoleon's defeat of Austria with his last effort to return to power.

B) types of victories won by Napoleon.

C) the responses of different nations.

D) multiple outcomes of an extended endeavor.

39

As used in line 103, "wasted" most nearly means

A) spoiled.

B) lost.

C) used up.

D) thrown away.

40

The passage suggests that Napoleon did not have significant success in which of the following regions?

A) Russia

B) Belgium

C) Prussia

D) Spain

41

Based on the map and the passage, it can be inferred that

A) Napoleon's armies were separated by hostile territory.

B) Napoleon had no interest in Britain or Portugal.

C) Napoleon never attacked Greece.

D) Napoleon held some influence in areas he did not directly rule.

Chapter 7
Reading Drill:
Answers and
Explanations

READING DRILL ANSWERS AND EXPLANATIONS

Quantitative Questions Drill

12. **C** The question specifically asks what the authors mean by "they will have residual protection during pandemics." The "they" is referring to the elderly, and the "protection" is immunity acquired during previous outbreaks. Eliminate (A) and (D) because they don't mention the elderly. Choice (B) is incorrect because while the authors do state that younger people should get vaccines before the elderly, the answer choice doesn't address the reason, which is that older people may have some immunity due to previous exposure.

13. **D** The question asks what the authors are trying to indicate by using the word "enjoy." Choices (B) and (C) assume that "enjoy" means to take pleasure in something. While the word does have a positive meaning in context, it simply means "to have." In this case, children who might have been exposed to influenza in the past may grow up to have some form of immunity to it that prevents it from becoming fatal. Choice (A) is too strong, since people can still die from it later in life, even if they were exposed as children, as is clear from the charts. Choice (D) is based on the statement in the first paragraph: "While the elderly are normally at most risk for severe outcomes during seasonal influenza, warranting the targeting of vaccination for direct protection to that group, they may have residual protection during pandemics."

14. **C** The question asks which statement contradicts the politician's statement. Choices (B) and (D) somewhat support the idea that there's no simple way to protect against a pandemic, so they do not contradict it. Choice (A) discusses which age group should be a priority for vaccination, but doesn't support the idea that Mexico needs vaccines for a majority of the population. Only (C) contradicts the politician by stating that it's possible to protect the population with a limited supply of vaccines.

15. **A** The question asks for the purpose of the statement "Mexico has relied on other countries for influenza vaccine production." Use the given line reference to find the window. Lines 75–77 indicate that "Mexico has relied on other countries for influenza vaccine production" and thus could face a vaccine shortage if the world suffers a pandemic. Lines 86–88 state that "even limited vaccine supplies, if used optimally," can help lessen disease. The previous paragraphs discuss effective ways

to target vaccines to certain parts of the population. Therefore, the authors mention Mexico's reliance on other countries' vaccines to show that using vaccines effectively is important. Eliminate answers that don't match this prediction. Keep (A) because it matches the prediction. Choice (B) is a Could Be True trap answer: it may seem logical that the authors would mention reliance on other countries to encourage Mexico to create more of its own vaccines. However, the authors do not actually mention creating more vaccines, so this answer is not supported by the passage. Eliminate (B). Choice (C) is also a Could Be True trap answer, since the authors do not actually state that Mexico should not seek vaccine producers in other countries. Eliminate (D) because the author does not discourage Mexico from producing vaccines. The correct answer is (A).

16. **A** Remember to read for the word in context, and not just to leap to a conclusion based on your prior knowledge. The passage says, "This model illustrates a prioritization scheme based on age groups but does not further discriminate other sub-groups such as those persons with other medical conditions including pregnancy." The use of the term "sub-groups" means breaking up the sample into smaller groups, which means to differentiate them. The correct answer is (A).

17. **A** This question asks what is suggested by the passage. The authors suggest that creating a flexible strategy that takes into account several factors such as age will help policy makers prepare for a pandemic. Choice (A) best reflects that. Choice (B) is too strong, since the passage doesn't say children should have all of the vaccine. The passage says that the other methods have "debatable efficacy," which means it's unclear how much they help. They definitely aren't "proven" to help, so (C) is incorrect. The passage does imply that viruses may not be susceptible to vaccines but it's unclear whether producers can't adapt or whether it's a matter of getting the vaccines delivered to people who need them, so (D) is incorrect. The correct answer is (A).

18. **D** This question asks for the evidence you used to answer the previous question, so if you can't find something to support your answer to question 17, take a moment to reassess. In this case, only (D) supports the idea that creating a flexible strategy that takes into account several factors such as age will help policy makers prepare for a pandemic. The correct answer is (D).

19. **C** The question asks for the correct percentage of the case fatality rate given hospitalization percentage for the 1918 influenza pandemic profile for ages 0–5. First, find the graph for fatality rate given hospitalization (figure 2), and then look

for the number that corresponds to the 1918 influenza pandemic profile (the darker of the bar graphs) and ages 0–5. The case fatality rate the question asks for is about 10%. The correct answer is (C).

20. **B** The question asks for evidence that elderly people have some sort of immunity or protection against pandemics. If this were true, it would mean that fewer get sick and die, so that's the information you are looking for in the figures. Choice (B) agrees with the information in the figures and supports the authors' contention that the elderly "may have residual protection during pandemics," since fewer elderly people get sick and die from a pandemic than from typical Influenza. The correct answer is (B).

21. **A** Remember to keep an eye out for questions that are related to one another. In this case, you should already have the answer from the previous question: figure 2 shows the percentages for people over 60 as 15% for the typical influenza outbreak and 10% for the 1918 pandemic, which suggests that elderly people have protection against pandemics. The correct answer is (A).

Dual Passage Drill

22. **C** This is a General Paired question, so see the explanation for Question 23.

23. **B** This is a General Paired question, so approach questions 22 and 23 together. Choice (A) for question 23 could match (D) for question 22. Choice (B) for question 23 could match (C) for question 22. Choice (C) for question 2 could match (B) for question 23. Choice (D) for question 23 could match (B) for question 22. Choice (A) for question 22 does not match any line reference for question 23, so it is not the best answer. Now, look closely at question 22, which asks how the author of Passage 1 would describe his own position. Because (B) for question 22 is supported only by references from Passage 2, it does not represent how the author of Passage 1 would "most likely describe his own position," so both 22 (B) and 23 (D) can be eliminated. Look more closely at Passage 1: "Newton's laws of dynamics are therefore valid only for...our experiments on earth and in our observations of the heavenly bodies." Because the author of Passage 1 states situations in which Newton's laws are valid, he is not "dismissive" of those laws, eliminating (D) for question 22 as well as (A) for question 23. The best answers are (C) for Question 22 and (B) for question 23.

24. **C** The question asks for the purpose of the first paragraph of Passage 1. Use the given line reference to find the window. The paragraph describes how Einstein's theories change our understanding of the way the world works, including Newton's laws of motion, the notion that parallel lines never meet, and the fact that yardsticks may vary according to how we hold them. The last sentence of the paragraph states, "These are a few of the startling implications of Einstein's theory of relativity." Therefore, the purpose of the paragraph is to present some surprising consequences of Einstein's theory. Eliminate answers that don't match this prediction. Eliminate (A) because the paragraph focuses on Einstein's theories, rather than Newton's laws. Eliminate (B) because the author of Passage 1 does not "rebuff" (which means "disagree with") Einstein's theories. Keep (C) because "unexpected assertions" matches the author's use of the phrase "startling implications," and the phrase "familiar assumptions" matches the examples of ideas we previously took for granted. Eliminate (D) because the author of Passage 1 does not "qualify" (which means "state the limits of") a claim. The correct answer is (C).

25. **D** The question asks what hypothetical situation most nearly matches the illustration in the second paragraph of Passage 1. Begin by summing up the illustration: an object at ordinary speed has a slight alteration, whereas one that approaches the speed of light undergoes a major alteration. Underline the illustration and its description in the first through fifth sentences of the second paragraph of Passage 1. Choice (A) is not the best answer because it describes an arrow shot only at a speed of 200 miles per hour, which does not approach the speed of light, and which would therefore not appear much smaller. Choice (B) is not the best answer because while the comet matches the considerable alteration of rates, it is contradictorily described as remaining the same size. Choice (C) is not the best answer because it describes an object going faster than the speed of light, which the passage asserts is impossible. Choice (D) is therefore the best answer, as it describes an object "approaching the speed of light" and "appearing as different sizes," which matches the information in Passage 1. The correct answer is (D).

26. **A** This question asks what the word "irritant" means. According to Passage 2, "if [relativity] does those alarming things claimed for it, distort our bodies, make our clocks unreliable, shorten our yard-sticks, we ought to study it to see if we can invent some counter irritant." The word "counter" indicates that the "irritant" refers to the "alarming things." Underline the first sentence of Passage 2. Choices (B) and (D) do not match the prediction. Choice (C) Could Be True, but "devastation" is more extreme than anything supported by Passage 2. The best answer is (A).

27. **D** The question asks for the rhetorical effect of the last sentence of the fourth paragraph of Passage 2. According to Passage 2, if you "question [Einstein's] claim, he can say you are not one of the eleven...men in the world [who] can read and understand fully his book.... The eleven men who" understand his book "will not give it away, and those outside dare not criticize what they cannot read." Rhetorically, "eleven apostles" is an allusion to the apostles in the Christian faith. Even without knowledge of that particular reference, the word "apostle" means "missionary," and the context suggests that Einstein's theories are difficult to criticize because few can understand those theories, and those who don't understand may feel that they have to agree. In other words, the author suggests that most people must accept Einstein's theories on faith. Choice (A) is not the best answer because it does not match the prediction. Choice (B) is a Right Answer, Wrong Question trap answer: earlier in the paragraph, the author suggests that Einstein is trying to "protect his device," but this is not the effect of the last sentence, so eliminate (B). The confusing language of (C) resolves to mean the opposite of what the author states, so it is not the best answer. Choose (D) because it matches the prediction: trusting Einstein's theories requires faith. The correct answer is (D).

28. **C** This is a Specific Paired question, so look at what was underlined as support for question 27. The sentence underlined for question 27 is the second-to-last sentence of the fourth paragraph of Passage 2, so (C) is the best answer.

29. **A** This question asks what the author of Passage 1 would most likely give as a response to the claim in the last paragraph of Passage 2. Begin by paraphrasing that claim: even men of learning and authority alter facts in order stick to their claims against relativity. Given that the author of the first passage uses the analogy of the arrow in order to describe an event which could not literally happen to an arrow, it can be shown that he disagrees with the author of Passage 2 and is willing to use a relatable example in order to educate. The best answer is therefore (A). Choices (B) and (D) do not match the prediction, and while (C) Could Be True, the author of Passage 1 suggests the opposite by stating that Newton's laws apply only to his Earth-bound experiments, which means it is not the best answer.

30. **B** This question asks what is different between the two authors' opinions. There are many potential differences, so evaluate the answer choices. According to Passage 1, "if...you could shoot an arrow from a bow with a velocity of 160,000 miles a second, it would shrink to about half its length." According to Passage 2, "it is a little provoking that...writers...speak of our bodies, yard-sticks and clocks as if they had found something seriously wrong affecting them." These references support (B),

which is the best answer. Choice (A) is Mostly Right/Slightly Wrong because the author of Passage 1 seems to support Einstein's theories but states that Newton's laws are valid for experiments on Earth. Eliminate (C) because neither author *acknowledges limits to his argument.* Eliminate (D) because the mention of shooting an arrow and a person traveling along with the arrow in Passage 2 are illustrations to help explain Einstein's theories; the author is not arguing that Einstein's theories *apply to sports or travel on earth.*

31. **C** This question asks what both authors would most likely agree about. According to Passage 1, "Newton's laws...are...valid...for...our experiments on earth and in our observations of the heavenly bodies, and when we come to consider velocities approximating that of light the ordinary laws...are subject to...correction." The author of Passage 2 writes that "men of learning...speak of our...yard-sticks...as if they had found something seriously wrong affecting them," which implies that the contraction of "one-hundredth of the thickness of a cat's hair" isn't alarming, and thus is not something that we necessarily ought to study. Both authors acknowledge that Einstein's theories do not significantly change some calculations, so (C) is the best answer. Choice (A) Could Be True for Passage 2, but is not the best answer because it does not match Passage 1. Choice (B) Could Be True for Passage 1, but is not the best answer because it does not have support from Passage 2. Choice (D) is supported by Passage 2, and Could Be True for Passage 1, but the author of Passage 1 uses an analogy of having a man travel along with an arrow moving with a velocity of 160,000 miles a second, which implies that the author of Passage 1 is willing to utilize hypothetical situations that are unlikely to be literally true in order to explain elements of Einstein's theories. This means that (D) can be eliminated, as the author of Passage 1 doesn't agree with it.

Additional Drill 1

1. **D** This question is asking for the author's attitude, or tone. While this can often be challenging to discern, this passage provides direct evidence: "when persons ask me how...I can have such faith...I remind them of the wilderness through which and out of which, a good Providence has already led us." This suggests that the author has a faith that is strengthened by living through hard circumstances. Choice (A) is not the best answer, because it does not match the prediction. Choice (B) is not the best answer because it does not match the prediction, and the author states "I have long since ceased...any spirit of bitterness." Choice (C) is not the best answer because it does not match the prediction. Moreover, the author uses artistic phrases,

such as "I suspect I must have been born somewhere and at some time," and the discussion about the author's first pair of shoes demonstrates that the author's attitude goes beyond simple determination. Choice (D) matches the prediction, and is the correct answer, because *tempered* means strengthened through hardship.

2. **B** This is a General Paired question, so see the explanation for Question 3.

3. **D** Choice (A) for question 3 could match (A) for question 2. Choice (B) for question 3 could match (C) for question 2. Choice (C) for question 3 could match (D) for question 2. Choice (D) for question 3 could match (B) for question 2. Because all the answer choices for question 3 could match a choice for question 2, nothing can be eliminated yet. Look more closely at what exactly the choices for question 3 support to eliminate weak matches. Choice (A) for question 2 contains the phrase *current situation*, which is not supported by the matching (A) for question 3, so both choices can be ruled out. Now, look closely at question 2, which asks for the *primary purpose of the passage*, and consider why the author wrote the passage. Choice (C) for question 2, and (B) for question 3 suggest that the author wrote the passage in order to *describe* [the] *particular suffering* of *wearing...a flax shirt*. Because the final paragraph of the passage broadens the scope of the passage to talk about *slavery* in general, and *the future of my race in this country*, the author did not write the passage in order to discuss *wearing...a flax shirt*, so (C) for question 2 and (B) for question 3 can be eliminated. Now, determine whether the author wrote the passage to *seek sympathy* or *illustrate an optimism gained through trials*. The best evidence to answer the question is (D) for question 3, which states that the author has *such faith in the future of* [his] *race in this country* due to *the wilderness through which and out of which* his race has been *led*. The hopeful tone with which the author ends the passage will help to eliminate (D) for question 2 and (C) for question 3, and supports (B) for question 2 and (D) for question 3.

4. **D** This question asks for the "rhetorical effect" of the first paragraph in the context of the passage. Because the question asks about the context of the passage as a whole, treat it as a general question and work it after the specific questions. In lines 1–13, the author details the uncertain circumstances of his birth as a slave on a plantation. In the rest of the passage, the author discusses some of his experiences and his thoughts on slavery. Therefore, the first paragraph provides an introduction for the rest of the passage. Eliminate answer choices that don't match this prediction. The author does not include any "humor" about his birth, so eliminate (A). He makes no mention of other people's births, so eliminate (B). The passage treats birth as a

literal (instead of figurative) concept, so eliminate (C). Keep (D) because it matches the prediction: an introduction provides context for what is to be discussed. The correct answer is (D).

5.　**A**　This question asks why the author uses a specific word. According to the passage, the author "can scarcely imagine any torture...that is equal to that caused by putting on a new flax shirt." The author continues to emphasize the painful nature of the experience with analogies about "chestnut burrs" and "a hundred small pin-points." Because memories are known to fade over time, the author uses the word "accurately" in order to continue emphasizing the painful nature of putting on a new flax shirt. This matches (A) and eliminates (B), which does not match the context. Choice (C) is not the best answer, because "the following sentence" describes another element that "added to the pain," which means that both sentences are support. Choice (D) Could Be True, in that John does the author the favor of breaking in a new shirt for him, but it doesn't have anything to do with the use of the word "accurately."

6.　**C**　This question asks what is most directly suggested by the sentence. Begin by underlining it, and then focus on which answer choices are supported by the text. Choice (A) is not the best answer, because although the passage states that the author was forced to wear a shirt on at least "several occasions," it is not directly stated in the text that the plantation owners forced this upon him. Choice (B) is not the best answer, because the author states that "it was common to use flax as part of the clothing," not that flax was the only available option, which means that it can be eliminated as Mostly Right, Slightly Wrong. Choice (D) is not the best answer, because the author "would have chosen to wear no covering" instead of the flax shirt, and while it Could Be True, it is not directly supported by the text. Choice (C) is the best answer, because the author wore the shirt, and states that "had it been left to me to choose," he would not have worn the shirt, which directly suggests that he was not given a choice.

7.　**D**　This question asks what "cherish" most nearly means in context. According to the passage, the author has "long ceased to cherish any spirit of bitterness" towards a group of people. Because the author follows that statement by adding that "no one section of our country was wholly responsible," the author means that he does not feel bitter, so he must have "long ceased to have any spirit of bitterness." Underline the second and third sentences of the last paragraph. Only (D) matches this prediction.

8. **D** This question asks for the author's position on slavery. According to the passage, "no one section of our country was wholly responsible for [slavery's] introduction," so the author feels that responsibility is shared, (D). This directly contradicts (A), so eliminate it. Choice (B) is Mostly Right, Slightly Wrong because "no one section... was wholly responsible" does not mean that "no one is responsible at all," so (B) is not the best answer. Choice (C) Could Be True, because the author states that slavery "was recognized and protected for years by the...Government," but the author does not directly state that the government has *most* of the responsibility, so this is not the best answer.

9. **C** This is a Specific Paired question, so look at what was used as support for question 8, which makes (C) the best answer.

10. **B** This question asks what the word "wilderness" most nearly means as it is used in line 77. Go back to the text, find the word "wilderness," and cross it out. Then read the window carefully, using context clues to determine another word or phrase that would fit in the text. The author says that when people ask "how, in the midst of what sometimes seem hopelessly discouraging conditions, I can have such faith in the future of my race in this country, I remind them of the wilderness through which and out of which, a good Providence has already led us." The word "wilderness" could be replaced by a phrase such as "difficult conditions." Eliminate answers that don't match this prediction. Choices (A) and (C) are literal interpretations of the word "wilderness," whereas the author uses the word figuratively. Eliminate (A) and (C). Keep (B) because it matches the prediction. Eliminate (D) because "past" does not match "difficult circumstances." The correct answer is (B).

Additional Drill 2

32. **B** The question asks for a description of the "author's rhetorical style." This is the first question in a paired set, so it can be done in tandem with question 33. Look at the answer choices for question 33. first. The lines for (33A) state, "Supplies for armies of then unheard-of size could not be carried in convoys, and the French soon became familiar with 'living on the country.'" Check to see whether these lines provide an example of any of the rhetorical styles mentioned in question 32's answer choices. There is no match, so eliminate (33A). The lines for (33B) state, "This was that same Napoleon Bonaparte who had led the armies of the Directory to victory in Italy." These lines don't exemplify any of the rhetorical styles mentioned in the answer choices for question 32, so eliminate (33B). The lines for (33C) state, "He

was exiled to Elba, returned to France for one last effort in 1815 and was defeated by the allied British, Belgians and Prussians at Waterloo." These lines match (32B). They provide a "rapid overview" ("He was exiled to Elba, returned to France for one last effort in 1815 and was defeated") along with specific detail (the location of the defeat and the list of armies that defeated him). Draw a line connecting (32B) with (33C). The lines for (32D) state, "A great Congress of the victorious allies met at Vienna to restore as far as possible the state of affairs that the great storm had rent to pieces." These lines don't provide an example of any of the rhetorical styles mentioned in question 32's answer choices, so eliminate (33D). Without any support in the answers for question 33, (32A), (32C), (32D) can be eliminated. The correct answers are (32B) and (33C).

33. **C** (See explanation above.)

34. **B** This question asks for the best characterization of "the author's attitude towards the French armies." This is a general question, so it should be done after the specific questions. Throughout the passage, the French armies are described in both positive and negative ways, ranging from "enthusiasts" who are "cheerfully" accepting of "discomfort" to "never quite clear in their minds whether they were looting or liberating the countries into which they poured." Eliminate (A) because "contemptuous" doesn't account for the author's mixed feelings. Keep (B) because "ambivalent" indicates that the author expresses contradictory characterizations of the armies. Eliminate (C) because "approving" doesn't account for the author's mixed feelings. Eliminate (D) because "apathetic" means "showing little interest," but the author expresses interest by describing the armies. The correct answer is (B).

35. **A** The question asks what the word "want" most nearly means as it is used in line 13. Go back to the text, find the word "want," and cross it out. Then read the window carefully, using context clues to determine another word or phrase that would fit in the text. The text says that "tents were unprocurable for want of money." Because "unprocurable" means "could not be obtained," "want" could be replaced by a phrase such as "not having." Keep (A) because "lack" matches "not having." Eliminate (B) because "desire" does not match "not having." Note that (B) is a Could Be True trap answer based on another meaning of "want" that is not supported by the text. Eliminate (C) because "requirement" does not match "not having." Eliminate (D) because "gain" does not match "not having." The correct answer is (A).

36. **B** This question asks what the author uses to support his description of Napoleon as "a man of severely limited understanding." Read the sentences immediately following that quote until you get to a list of Napoleon's actions, which is where the window cuts off. Underline the portion that states "he had no real grasp of the new forces that were working Europe," as this demonstrates that there were things he did not understand. This should lead to (B), as it implies that Napoleon failed due to his poor comprehension of the political state of affairs—"new forces that were working in Europe." Choice (A) Could Be True, because Napoleon "divorced his French wife," but that doesn't mean that the French felt alienated. Choice (C) is a Right Words, Wrong Meaning trap answer. "Refuting" means "denying," but the author says that Napoleon "had no real grasp of the new forces that were working in Europe," so he does not deny that Napoleon had no real grasp of matters. Eliminate (C). And (D) can be eliminated, for while it Could Be True that he received "overtures from other heads of state," there's no proof to support this.

37. **C** This is a Specific Paired question, so look at what was underlined as support for question 36. The sentence underlined for question 36 is the fourth sentence of the fourth paragraph, so (C) is the best answer.

38. **D** The question asks what ideas the author primarily contrasts in the sixth paragraph. Read the sixth paragraph as the window. In lines 77–81, the author provides examples of Napoleon's victories, but lines 81–101 describe a series of defeats that eventually led to Napoleon's death. Eliminate answers that don't match this prediction. Choice (A) is a Right Answer, Wrong Question trap answer: the author does mention Napoleon's victory over Austria and his final effort that ended in defeat, but these two specific examples are not what he "primarily contrasts." Eliminate (B) because the author contrasts Napoleon's victories with his defeats; he does not contrast different "types of victories." Eliminate (C) because the paragraph doesn't contrast different "responses" of nations; all of the nations responded by fighting, though some were successful while others weren't. Keep (D) because the victories and defeats were "outcomes" of Napoleon's "extended endeavor" to conquer other nations. The correct answer is (D).

39. **C** The question asks what "wasted" most nearly means in the context of the passage: "the forces released by the French Revolution were wasted and finished," and a group "met...to restore...the state of affairs" that had existed before the armies of the French Revolution had moved through Europe. Therefore, *wasted* and *finished* are used for the same meaning, and *wasted* means "finished," (C). Choice (A) doesn't fit the context, and (B) and (D) hint at a meaning that isn't present in the context.

40. **A** This question asks in what region "Napoleon did not have significant success." According to the passage, Napoleon's army "was defeated and largely destroyed by the Russians and Russian winter." Additionally, the passage states that Napoleon "dominated all Europe west of Russia." Underline that phrase, and note that (A) best matches it. Be careful of the trap answer at (B): while Belgium is later mentioned as part of the allied group that defeated Napoleon, "all Europe west of Russia" includes Belgium, as indicated by the map.

41. **D** This question asks what can be inferred based on the map and the passage. According to the passage, Napoleon "dominated all Europe west of Russia," but the map shows a large portion of "Europe west of Russia" that is neither part of the French Empire nor a satellite state. It can be inferred that Napoleon dominated areas that were not part of the French Empire or a satellite state, which matches (D). Choice (A) Could Be True, because the map shows a gap between the easternmost satellite state and the bulk of the territory controlled by Napoleon, but there's no support to show that this territory was hostile. Choice (B) contradicts the passage, for if Napoleon *never won the command of the sea from the British*, then he must have fought them at sea. Choice (C) Could Be True, in that Napoleon does not control Greece on the map, but there's no mention of it on the passage, which means that we cannot assume he didn't attack (and fail to capture) it.

Part III
Writing & Language

Chapter 8
Introduction to SAT Writing and Language Strategy

The Writing and Language section of the SAT takes 35 minutes and consists of 44 questions. In this chapter, we will talk about the unique format of some of these questions and a strategy that will help you to tackle any Writing and Language question you see.

INTRODUCTION

It might seem a little weird to test writing on a multiple-choice test. After all, wouldn't the best way to test how well you can write be to…make you actually write something? Well, the makers of the SAT tried that, but as of 2021, computers still can't accurately grade essays, and College Board thought it might be more sensible come up with a writing-*ish* test that can be scored by a Scantron machine. That's good news for you, though. Think of all the different skills you need in order to write something: good vocabulary, ability to explain something, creative thoughts, knowing when to start and stop a paragraph—not to mention proper spelling, grammar, and punctuation. How could one 44-question multiple-choice section test all of that? Luckily for you, it doesn't! The SAT Writing and Language Test covers a handful of punctuation and grammar rules, a tiny bit of vocabulary, and your ability to understand main ideas and how they flow within a passage. Throughout the Writing and Language section of this book, you'll get to know the specific topics that *are* tested on the SAT, and you can temporarily forget about the ones that aren't. Of course, we'll also take a closer look at some of the more challenging topics so that you can maximize your score. In this chapter, however, we're going to begin by focusing on strategy.

WHY DO I NEED A STRATEGY?

Believe it or not, students who are great writers and have a solid understanding of proper English can get into trouble on the Writing and Language section if they don't have a good strategy for how to approach this test. That's because they may view their job on this section as finding and correcting mistakes. That's not a completely wrong way of looking at the Writing and Language Test, but the tricky part about this SAT section is that you don't actually get to correct the errors yourself. Let's see an example:

The job of ice cream taster is not as easy as it **1** sounds, tasters may have to sample thirty flavors on an average day.

1

Reading this sentence, you might spot the error right away: a comma cannot be used between these two ideas, since they are both complete ideas, also known as independent clauses. We'll talk much more about this in the Punctuation chapter, but for now, just know that the comma doesn't work. Many high-scoring students might then have their own ideas about how the sentence should be corrected. For instance, you might decide that the sentence should use a period instead of a comma. Let's take a look at the answer choices now:

1

A) NO CHANGE
B) sounds. Tasters,
C) sounds: tasters
D) sounds because

Using the strategy of "correcting" the sentence, you might quickly circle (B) and move on. Let's take a closer look, though: (B) does change the comma to a period, but it adds a comma after *Tasters* that shouldn't be there. This is where you can go wrong if you try to fix the sentence yourself. Instead, you should use Process of Elimination with the answers that are actually there. Let's eliminate—so physically cross off—(A) and (B), since we know they are wrong, and compare (C) and (D). Choice (D) may be initially appealing; another way to correct the sentence would be to add the word *because*, but be careful. Choice (D) does not include the word *tasters*, so it reads ...*not as easy as it sounds because may have to...*, which of course isn't a complete sentence. Therefore, (C) has to be the answer. Most students probably wouldn't come up with the idea to put a colon in this sentence, but it is the only way to correct the sentence with the four given choices.

LET THE SAT HELP YOU

As you can see from the previous example, by looking at the answers, you can help yourself avoid making a mistake. The answer choices can help with much more, though: they can reveal errors you didn't notice when you read the sentence, and they can also show you what the question is testing. In school, you might be used to doing all of the work yourself. When it comes to the SAT, however, it's okay to be a little lazier. You don't have to come up with the answer yourself or even spot errors yourself. Don't do more work than you have to—use the answers as a guide! Let's look at another example.

Tasters are required to have a discerning palate, **2** but they have to be able to evaluate flavors objectively.

2

A) NO CHANGE

B) and

C) so

D) though

Here's How to Crack It

As you saw in the last question, most of the Writing and Language questions, like this one, won't actually ask a question. However, the SAT actually provides you with a good clue: the words or punctuation marks that are changing in the answer choices. Rather than just looking for any errors you can find in the sentence, instead use the answer choices to narrow down which rule or rules you need to consider. Most Writing and Language questions test just one or two rules, so this strategy makes the questions much easier.

What's changing in the answers in question 2? Only the transition words. This means you don't need to think about punctuation or tense or any of the other categories of rules that you might be familiar with. You can also compare the answers to identify any differences: you might notice that (A) and (D) contain opposite-direction transitions, while (B) and (C) go the same direction. Consider the two parts of the sentence. They both describe requirements of the job, so the ideas agree; eliminate (A) and (D). Compare (B) and (C). The transition *so* is used in a cause-and-effect relationship, which isn't the case here, so eliminate (C) and choose (B).

Let's try another one.

To prevent contamination of their palates, these "sensory analysts" have to avoid spicy foods and strong flavors for [3] at least a day prior to tasting.

[3]

A) NO CHANGE
B) at least a day or more
C) at least a day at the minimum
D) minimum one day or possibly more

Here's How to Crack It

As always, start with what's changing in the answers: the wording or number of words. The original might look okay, but don't automatically choose (A). It's important to consider the other choices, as errors are not always obvious. Choice (A) is the shortest answer, so consider whether the additional words in the other options offer any improvement. The phrase *at least* means that the given number is the minimum but leaves open the possibility of a higher number, so *or more* is already implied by *at least*. Eliminate (B). Likewise, *minimum* means the same thing as *at least*, so eliminate (C). Choice (D) doesn't include *at least*, but *minimum* and the possibility of *more* are redundant, so eliminate (D). Therefore, the shortest answer, (A), is correct.

Don't be afraid to pick NO CHANGE—it is correct about one-fourth of the time that it appears. However, you should never pick that option before considering the other answer choices. The writers of the SAT are very good at writing sentences that sound great but actually break rules. By examining the other answer choices, you'll save yourself the work of identifying errors and avoid making mistakes.

IT JUST DOESN'T SOUND RIGHT!

The title above is a direct quote from thousands of SAT students, when asked their reason for eliminating an answer choice on the Writing and Language. When reading the sentences and answer choices on this test, our instinct is to use our ears and choose answers based on how the phrasing sounds. However, we should recognize first that written English and spoken English are different. In spoken English, we don't use any punctuation, and we rarely speak in complete sentences, for example. However, the SAT tests your knowledge of written English. Relying on your ear, therefore, won't be a foolproof method. Let's see an example.

An ice cream manufacturer's creative team of food scientists focused on trends 4 churn out new flavors that tasters must test, even ones that seem a bit odd.

4

A) NO CHANGE

B) have churned

C) churns

D) churning

Here's How to Crack It

How does this sentence sound? For most people, it probably sounds okay. Nevertheless, let's remember to follow the basic approach. Identify the topic tested in the answer choices: verbs. Consider the difference between the original, *churn*, and (C), *churns*. One is singular, and one is plural (if you don't remember these rules, don't worry—they'll be covered later). Start by identifying the subject. The phrase *trends churn* or *scientists churn* might sound totally fine, but are the *trends* or the *scientists* the ones churning out new flavors? You might think the *scientists* are, but examine the structure of the sentence. The describing phrase *of food scientists* modifies *team*, and *focused on trends* modifies the *scientists*. Therefore, the subject of the sentence is *team*, since the phrases in between that word and the verb are just describing phrases. Since *team* is singular, a singular verb is needed. Eliminate (A) and (B) because they are both plural. Choice (C) is singular, so that works. Choice (D) makes the sentence incomplete, as an *-ing* verb cannot be the main verb in a sentence. Therefore, (C) is the answer.

Notice the importance of looking at the answers and considering the rules. The original sentence may have sounded perfectly fine, but it actually violated a grammar rule. POE saves the day!

RULES WERE MADE TO BE BROKEN

Of course, not every aspect of written English can be described using rules. Topics like the Oxford comma and the singular "they" have been debated by linguists for decades. This may make the Writing and Language section seem hazy, like your job is to intuit which answer *seems* correct. That couldn't be further from the truth. The fact is that the SAT Writing and Language only tests the English rules that everyone can agree on. You won't ever be tested on a rule that doesn't have a consensus among experts. As you go through this section, you'll learn which topics *are* tested on the SAT and the rules that come up regularly. Master these, and don't worry about the more ambiguous aspects of grammar and punctuation.

Of course, not all Writing and Language questions fall under universal rules (though the majority do). Let's see an example.

Not everyone can [5] hold eating ice cream for hours every day, starting at 9:00 in the morning or earlier.

5

A) NO CHANGE

B) poke

C) feel

D) handle

Here's How to Crack It

First, as always, check what's changing in the answer choices. In this case, it's the choice of word. Does any rule apply here? Not really. You simply need to know what each word means and how it should be used in context. The sentence implies that not everyone is able to eat ice cream all day. The words *hold*, *poke*, and *feel* are all words that relate to physical touch, which isn't the intended meaning in this sentence. Choice (D), *handle*, can be physical, but it can also mean "manage," which matches with the idea of being able to do something, so (D) is the answer. If you were not familiar with that definition of *handle*, you would just have to take your best guess.

Rest assured that you can expect to see only a few questions on the Writing and Language section that test your knowledge of how specific words and phrases work. Since there is virtually no limit to which ones could be tested, you can't adequately prepare for these questions (though the more books you read, the more you will become familiar with the different meanings of English words). Our best advice is to first master the rules that you will learn in this book. Just try your best on these questions and, if you have to, guess and move on.

Let's put those steps together into a simple basic approach.

> **Writing and Language Basic Approach**
>
> 1. Read to the end of the sentence with an underlined portion.
> 2. Look to the answers to see what's changing.
> 3. Use Process of Elimination.

GRAMMAR GLOSSARY

This is not an exhaustive list of grammar terms, but it's also more than we think you need. In fact, the only terms you really need to know are *subject, pronoun, verb, conjunction,* and *preposition.* Some other terms we included because we use them to explain how to spot and fix some of the more difficult questions on the SAT. We included still others just because you may be curious or think you have to know them. For example, you don't need to know what *predicate* or *subjunctive* means, but we included them to provide a comprehensive list of terms.

If you're not curious, you have our blessing to focus only on the big terms.

Active Voice: The construction used when the subject acts and the object receives. *The dog chases the car.* The dog is the subject, and the car is the object. See the contrast in *passive voice.*

Adjective: A descriptive word that always modifies a noun or a pronoun. *Pretty, vast, quick, yellow, bad*

Adverb: A descriptive word that always modifies a verb, adjective, or other adverb. *Hopefully, always, quickly, however*

Article: A short word that identifies a noun. *The, a, an*

Case: The function or behavior of a pronoun in a sentence. The three cases are *objective, possessive,* and *subjective* (or *nominative*). See *object pronouns, possessive pronouns,* and *subject pronouns.*

Clause: A group of words with a subject and a verb. See more under *dependent clause* and *independent clause.*

Comma Splice: Two complete ideas linked incorrectly by a comma. *The dog chased the car, I chased the dog.* One fix would be *The dog chased the car, **and** I chased the dog.*

Compound Noun: A noun made up of two elements that acts as a single noun. Depending on the item, the two elements that make up a compound noun might be linked with either a hyphen or space between them, or they can be merged as one word. *Swimming pool, check-out, whiteboard*

Conjunction: A word that joins words, phrases, or clauses together. See more under *coordinating conjunctions* and *subordinating conjunctions.*

Coordinating Conjunction: A word used to link elements of equal importance: adjectives, adverbs, nouns, phrases, or—with the help of a comma—even independent clauses. The acronym FANBOYS can help you remember the seven coordinating conjunctions: *for, and, nor, but, or, yet, so.*

Dependent Clause: An incomplete idea that contains a subject and a verb. The presence of a subordinating conjunction or a relative pronoun acting as a conjunction makes the clause dependent. A dependent clause is also known as a subordinate clause. *Because the dog chased the car, while the car was moving, when the dog chases brooms*

FANBOYS: The seven coordinating conjunctions. *For, and, nor, but, or, yet, so*

Future Perfect: A tense used to describe a future event that will be completed at a definite later time before a second event occurs. *I **will have cleaned** the whole house before the dog destroys the vacuum.* The helping verbs *will* and *to have* work with the past participle of the main verb to form the future perfect.

Future Perfect Progressive: A tense used to describe a future event that will be ongoing when a second event occurs. *By 5 pm, I **will have been cleaning** all day.* The helping verbs *will*, *to have*, and *to be* (its past participle *been*) work with the present participle to form the future perfect progressive.

Future Progressive: A tense used to describe an ongoing event in the future. *I **will be cleaning** all day tomorrow.* The helping verbs *will* and *to be* (the base form of *be*) work with the present participle to form the future progressive.

Gerund: The *-ing* form of the verb used as a noun. ***Drooling** is a sign of rabies.*

Idiom: An expression whose form and meaning can be determined by neither grammatical rules nor the usual definitions of its elements. The SAT usually tests idioms that involve a preposition. *Different from, in order to, focus on, argue over*

Independent Clause: A complete idea that contains a subject and a verb. *The dog chased the car. The car is moving. The dog chases brooms.*

Infinitive: The base form of the verb with *to* in front. *To bark. To run. To clean.* The presence of an infinitive does not meet the requirement of a verb needed to make a clause. An infinitive is like a car up on blocks, but a main verb in a clause is a car in drive. *The dog learned **to bark**. The dog wants **to run**. I need **to clean** the mess.*

Irregular Verb: A verb with a past participle that doesn't follow the usual pattern that regular verbs do of adding *-ed* at the end. See more under *past participle* and see *regular verb* for contrast. *The dog **ran** down the street. The dog has **run** away before. The dog ate the roast beef. The dog has **eaten** our dinner.*

Misplaced Modifier: Any kind of description that is in the wrong place in a sentence and at best creates confusion and at worst describes the wrong item. *I made a sweater for the dog **with pom-poms and sequins**.* The meaning would be clearer with *I made a sweater **with pom-poms and sequins** for the dog. **Running** down the street, **a car** almost hit me.* The meaning would be correct with either changing the item that the phrase describes or moving the phrase and changing it into a clause. ***Running** down the street, I was almost hit by a car.* Also correct would be *A car almost hit me when I was **running** down the street.*

Modifier: A word, phrase, or clause that describes something.

Noun: A person, place, thing, or idea. *Benjamin Franklin, Chicago, mother, dog, car, freedom*

Object: The receiver of the action, or the end of a prepositional phrase. *The dog chased **the car**. She gave **the dog** to me.*

Object Pronoun: A pronoun that replaces a noun as the object in a sentence. *Me, you, him, her, whom, us, them*

Passive Voice: The construction used when the subject receives the action and the object, if present, performs the action. *The car **is chased** by the dog.* The car is the subject, and the dog is the object. In passive voice, the helping verb *to be* works with the participle of the main verb, and the preposition *by* is used when the performer of the action is included as the object. See the contrast in *active voice.*

Past Participle: Past participles work with the helping verb *to have* to form the perfect tenses. *The dog **has chewed** the upholstery. The dog has **broken** the heirloom vase.* For regular verbs, the past participle is the *-ed* form of the verb and is indistinguishable in form from the simple past. *The dog **chewed** the upholstery.* For irregular verbs, the form of both the past participle and the simple past follows no predictable pattern, and they are usually different forms. *The dog **broke** my heirloom vase.* See more at *irregular verb.* Past participles can also function as adjectives. *The **chewed** upholstery can be replaced, but the **broken** heirloom vase can't.*

Past Perfect: A tense used to make clear the chronology of two events completed at a definite time in the past, one before the other. *I **had** just **calmed** the dog when the doorbell startled him.* The helping verb *to have* works with the past participle of the main verb to form the past perfect.

Past Perfect Progressive: A tense used to make clear the chronology of two events in the past, one of which is ongoing. *I **had been cleaning** for several hours and was ready to relax.* The helping verbs *to have* (in the past tense) and *to be* (its past participle *been*) work with the present participle of the main verb to form the past perfect progressive.

Past Progressive: A tense used to describe an ongoing action in the past tense. *The dog **was snoring.*** The helping verb *to be* works with the present participle of the main verb to form the past progressive.

Phrase: A group of words without a subject and a verb. *In most homes, snoring like a sailor*

Possessive Pronoun: A pronoun that indicates possession. *My, mine, your, yours, her, hers, his, its, whose, our, ours, their, theirs*

Predicate: The part of the sentence that provides information about the subject. The simple predicate is the verb. *The dog **is chewing** all of my shoes.* The complete predicate includes all the words that say something about the subject. In other words, everything but the subject. *The dog **is chewing all of my shoes.***

Preposition: A little word that describes relationships of time or place between words. *About, at, behind, between, by, in, of, off, on, to, with*

Prepositional Phrase: A group of words that begins with a preposition and ends with an object, almost always a noun or pronoun. *By the car, on the table, between you and me*

Present Participle: The *-ing* form of the verb, used with the helping verb *to be* to form the progressive tenses. *The dog **is drooling** on my leg.* Present participles can also function as adjectives. *I love a **drooling** dog.*

Present Perfect: A tense used to describe an event that began in the past and continues into the present, or to describe an event that was completed at some indefinite time before the present. *The dog **has lived** with me for 10 years. The dog **has attended** obedience school.* The helping verb *to have* works with the past participle of the main verb to form the present perfect.

Present Perfect Progressive: A tense used to describe an ongoing event that began in the past and continues into the present, or to describe an ongoing event that was completed at some indefinite, recent time before the present. *I **have been trying** to train the dog for 10 years. The dog **has been behaving**.* The helping verbs *to have* and *to be* (its past participle *been*) work with the present participle of the main verb to form the present perfect progressive.

Present Progressive: A tense used to describe an ongoing event. *The dog **is attending** obedience school.* The helping verb *to be* works with the present participle of the main verb to form the present progressive.

Pronoun: A word that takes the place of a noun in a sentence. *She, me, it, those, ours, who, that*

Regular Verb: A verb that uses *-ed* at the end to form its past participle. *The dog **listened** to my commands. I have **trained** the dog.* See more at *past participle* and see *irregular verb* for contrast.

Run-on Sentence: Two complete ideas linked incorrectly with no punctuation. *The dog chased the car I chased the dog.* One possible fix would be *The dog chased the car, **and** I chased the dog.*

Sentence Fragment: An incomplete idea left incorrectly on its own as a full sentence. *Because everyone recommends that dogs should be trained right away.* One possible fix would be *Because everyone recommends that dogs should be trained right away, I sent her to puppy class.*

Subject: The performer of the action in a sentence that is in active voice. *The **dog** chases the car. **She** gave the dog to me.* The receiver of the action in a sentence that's in passive voice. *The **car** was stolen. The **car** is chased by the dog.*

Subject pronoun: A pronoun that replaces a noun as the subject in a sentence. *I, you, she, he, who, we, they*

Subjunctive Mood: A type of sentence used to express wishes, recommendations, and counterfactuals. *I wish I **were** an Oscar Mayer Wiener. I recommend he **study** the basics. If I **were** a rich man, I would give all my money away.* In contrast, most sentences are in the indicative mood. *The dog **was** hungry. I **run** marathons.* The imperative mood is used for commands. ***Eat** your vegetables! **Sit**!*

Subordinating Conjunction: A word that precedes an independent clause and turns it into a dependent clause. For instance, *My dog likes to bark* is an independent clause, but *While my dog likes to bark* is a dependent clause because it's preceded by the subordinating conjunction *while. Since, because, while, though, although, when, as.*

Tense: The form of the verb that tells the time of an event (*past, present, future*). *I **chased** the dog. I **chase** the dog. I **will chase** the dog.* These examples can also be referred to as the simple past, simple present, and simple future. The perfect and progressive tenses provide more information about the duration and status of events within each of the three timeframes of past, present, and future.

Verb: A word that expresses an action, a feeling, or state of being. *Attend, be, calm, came, chase, chew, clean, drool, give, have, live, ring, run, snore, steal, train*

Verbal: A word derived from a verb that doesn't function as a verb in a sentence. Infinitives, participles, and gerunds are all verbals. *The dog was a challenge for me **to train**. The **training** class meets every Wednesday. **Training** a dog requires patience. A **trained** dog is a good dog.*

Summary

- The Writing and Language Test on the SAT is 35 minutes long and contains 44 questions.

- Many of the "questions" on the Writing and Language Test aren't exactly questions; instead, you'll be presented with a series of passages with underlined portions.

- **Check what's changing in the answer choices.** The answer choices not only tell you what a particular question is testing, but also reveal mistakes that you might not have otherwise seen.

- Use POE to get rid of the incorrect choices. If you can't eliminate three choices, pick the shortest one that is most consistent with the rest of the sentence.

Chapter 9
Punctuation

Writing and Language on the SAT will include
many questions on punctuation. When do you use
different punctuation marks? This chapter will review the different punctuation marks that are tested
on the SAT and how to use them.

WHERE DO WE BEGIN?

Many of us use punctuation without thinking about it a lot, and for our everyday lives, that works. But on the SAT, punctuation rules matter. This chapter will look at the rules for the different punctuation marks you will see on the test, including the less common ones. Once you learn the rules, you'll be able to easily answer punctuation questions.

The first step in correctly answering a punctuation question is to recognize that it is testing punctuation.

> Start by asking, "What's changing in the answer choices?"

If you see any punctuation marks (like commas, periods, or apostrophes), then it's a punctuation question. Once you know that the question is focusing on punctuation, it's time to ask the big question we will return to again and again:

> Does this punctuation need to be here?

There's More

When punctuation is changing in the answer choices, sometimes the question is testing only punctuation, but not always. Make sure to check for differences in both punctuation and words in the answer choices.

If you are choosing an answer choice that includes punctuation, there must be a reason for the punctuation. Every punctuation mark has a specific role to play within or between sentences. If there is no reason for it, leave it out. In the following pages, we'll review the seven situations in which punctuation is needed.

COMPLETE AND INCOMPLETE IDEAS

Before we get into the rules of punctuation marks, we need to take a slight detour to discuss complete and incomplete ideas.

> Complete Ideas can be sentences on their own.
>
> Incomplete Ideas are missing something and cannot be sentences on their own.

Let's take a look at some different phrases and decide whether they are complete or incomplete ideas. Here's a simple one to start with:

Sharks eat

Is this a complete idea? In other words, can this be a sentence on its own? Yes, this is a complete idea. It has a subject and verb and nothing is missing. Is it a good sentence? It's pretty short, and it doesn't provide a lot of information, but whether or not it's a good sentence doesn't matter on the SAT. All we want to know is whether it can be a sentence, and the answer is yes for this one. In short, a complete idea must have a subject and a verb.

Swims faster under certain conditions

Complete or incomplete? Well, we don't know who or what *swims*, so we're missing a subject. This idea is incomplete. Ideas are also incomplete if they are missing a verb:

The group of sharks

Missing a subject or verb is a clear indication that an idea is incomplete.

When sharks eat

Why is this an incomplete idea? We have a subject, *sharks*, and a verb, *eat*, so what's missing? The addition of words like *when*, *because*, and *although* makes ideas incomplete.

Clauses
In school, you may have learned the terms *independent clause* and *dependent clause*. A complete idea is the same as an independent clause, while incomplete ideas include dependent clauses and any other phrases that can't stand alone.

On the test, it's more likely that you will be working with longer phrases than the ones above, so let's take a look at a few more examples that are closer to what you'll see on the test.

Since the release of Jaws *in 1975, people have misunderstood sharks as fearsome beasts*

Is this a complete or incomplete idea? The word *Since* makes the first idea incomplete, but that incomplete idea is connected to a complete idea, which here makes the whole sentence complete. When you are deciding whether a phrase is complete or incomplete on the test, you have to read the entire phrase. If you read only part of it, you may incorrectly identify what type of idea you have.

The small number of shark attacks that have occurred

Complete or incomplete? Although it has a subject and verb, the word *that* introduces an incomplete idea, and the subject, the *small number of shark attacks*, is not followed by a verb to complete the idea. Incomplete ideas can interrupt complete ideas. Remember, incomplete ideas are missing something.

Now that we've looked at complete ideas and incomplete ideas, let's see the different ways we can link them.

STOP, GO, AND THE VERTICAL LINE TEST

FANBOYS = **F**or, **A**nd, **N**or, **B**ut, **O**r, **Y**et, **S**o

The SAT consistently tests the same punctuation marks, from the basic (like periods) to the more complex (like semicolons). In order to learn how to use the punctuation on the test, we've put together a chart that divides the punctuation into three different categories based on when they can be used.

STOP
- Period
- Semicolon
- Comma + FANBOYS
- Question mark
- Exclamation Mark

HALF-STOP
- Colon
- Long dash

GO
- Comma
- No punctuation

STOP punctuation can link ONLY complete ideas.

HALF-STOP punctuation must be *preceded* by a complete idea.

GO punctuation can link anything EXCEPT two complete ideas.

Let's start with the first group. When we use STOP punctuation, it will look like this:

Complete Idea STOP Complete Idea

As we saw before, a complete idea can look like this:

> *Sharks eat a variety of foods.*

Notice that we have STOP punctuation, a period, at the end of the complete idea. If we want to link this complete idea to another idea, it would look like this:

> *Sharks eat a variety of foods. They don't prey on humans.*

Since we have two complete ideas, we can use the other punctuation in the STOP category instead of the period. Our two complete ideas could look like this:

> *Sharks eat a variety of foods; they don't prey on humans.*

When it comes to punctuation on the test, periods and semicolons work the same way. We can also link the two complete ideas with a comma + FANBOYS like this:

> *Sharks eat a variety of foods, but they don't prey on humans.*

We could also use HALF-STOP punctuation in this situation, or in other cases when we are linking two ideas and the first one is complete. When we use HALF-STOP punctuation, it will look like this:

Complete Idea HALF-STOP Complete Idea

Complete Idea HALF-STOP Incomplete Idea

Note that in order to use HALF-STOP punctuation, the second part of the sentence must be related to the first. It could be an explanation, definition, or related list.

So we can also write our sentence like this:

> *Sharks eat a variety of foods: they don't prey on humans.*

Or

> *Sharks eat a variety of foods—they don't prey on humans.*

We can also use HALF-STOP punctuation to connect a complete idea to an incomplete idea, like this:

> Jaws *portrayed sharks in a negative light: deadly and prone to hunting humans.*

Or

> Jaws *portrayed sharks in a negative light—damaging scientists' efforts to protect them.*

HALF-STOP punctuation cannot be used after an incomplete idea, so these examples are not correct:

> *Many people were afraid to go swimming after—watching Jaws.*

> *My three favorite sharks are: whale sharks, hammerhead sharks, and tiger sharks.*

A list can follow a colon, but only when the first idea is complete. Since *My three favorite sharks are* is not a complete idea, this sentence is incorrect. Instead, it should have no punctuation at all, since it has two incomplete ideas.

When connecting two ideas that are not both complete, GO punctuation can be used. When we use GO punctuation, it will look like this:

Complete Idea GO Incomplete Idea

Incomplete Idea GO Complete Idea

Incomplete Idea GO Incomplete Idea

Comma or Nothing?

Generally, if you are connecting a complete idea and an incomplete idea and there is a shift in ideas, use a comma. If the two phrases are really part of the same idea, no comma. If you are connecting two incomplete ideas, no punctuation is used between them.

So we could write these ideas:

Many people were afraid to go swimming after watching Jaws.

Jaws *had real consequences, especially for shark conservation.*

These are the three types of punctuation (STOP, HALF-STOP, GO) you'll need to know in order to do well on the test. Although there is some overlap among the categories, the broad differences will serve you well. The SAT will not test you on the differences between types of punctuation in the same category; in other words, a period and a semi-colon are the same on the test. As long as you can identify which type of punctuation is needed, you'll be all set.

Let's take a look at some example questions. We'll also take a look at a particular strategy you can use for punctuation questions: the Vertical Line Test.

———————————————

Whale sharks are the biggest fish in the ocean, reaching up to 45 feet in length and weighing several **1** tons although they are sharks, their diet is more similar to that of whales.

1

A) NO CHANGE

B) tons, although they

C) tons; although they

D) tons. Although they,

Here's How to Crack It

First, we look to see what's changing in the answer choices. The words are the same in each answer choice; it's the punctuation that's changing. The types of punctuation in this question are STOP (the period and the semicolon) and GO (the comma).

When you see STOP punctuation changing in the answer choices, you can use a strategy called the Vertical Line Test (different from the one you may have learned in math!).

To use the Vertical Line Test, draw a vertical line where you see the STOP punctuation. In this case it's between the words *tons* and *although*. Then read the sentence from the beginning to the vertical line and determine if the idea is complete or incomplete: *Whale sharks are the biggest fish in the ocean, reaching up to 45 feet in length and weighing several tons.* This is a complete idea. Next, read from the vertical line to the end of the sentence: *although they are sharks, their diet is more similar to that of whales.* That idea is also complete.

What type of punctuation can link two complete ideas? STOP or HALF-STOP. We can eliminate (A) and (B) because no punctuation and a comma are both types of GO punctuation. Although (C) and (D) are both STOP punctuation, (D) adds a comma after the word *they.* There's no reason for a comma to be there, so we can eliminate (D). The correct answer is (C).

Let's try another.

Whale sharks are filter feeders that eat **2** plankton; small creatures like krill and copepods.

2

A) NO CHANGE
B) plankton. Small
C) plankton, they eat small
D) plankton: small

Here's How to Crack It
What's changing in the answer choices? Punctuation. Since we see STOP punctuation in the answer choices, we can use the Vertical Line Test. Draw a line between the words *plankton* and *small.*

The first idea, *Whale sharks are filter feeders that eat plankton,* is a complete idea. The second idea, *small creatures like krill and copepods,* is an incomplete idea. Since we have a complete idea and an incomplete idea, we cannot use STOP punctuation. Eliminate (A) and (B).

Choice (C) includes GO punctuation (a comma) and adds the words *they eat.* By adding a subject and verb, the second idea becomes a complete idea. Can we use GO punctuation between two complete ideas? No, so we must eliminate (C). The colon in (D) is HALF-STOP punctuation. HALF-STOP punctuation can be used after a complete idea, so (D) is the correct answer.

You may have wanted to put a comma after *plankton*, which is what makes (C) tricky. A comma could work, but not if the second phrase is complete, as (C) does. Although a colon might not have been the obvious choice, it does work based on the punctuation rules we went over. This problem is a good reminder to follow our basic approach and use POE rather than trying to fix the sentence yourself!

Let's look at another one.

From the Bay of Fundy, Canada, in the North to Victoria, Australia, in the **3** South—their habitat encompasses most of the ocean.

3
A) NO CHANGE
B) south. Their
C) south, their
D) south, their,

Here's How to Crack It

Punctuation is changing in the answer choices. Since there's STOP punctuation, let's use the Vertical Line Test. Draw the line between *South* and *their*. The first idea, *From the Bay of Fundy, Canada, in the North to Victoria, Australia, in the South,* is an incomplete idea. The second idea, *their habitat encompasses most of the ocean,* is a complete idea. Without two complete ideas, we can't use STOP punctuation, so eliminate (B). The first idea is not complete, so we can't use HALF-STOP punctuation; eliminate (A). Between the two remaining choices, there is no reason to put a comma after *their,* leaving (C) as the correct answer.

Let's see one more.

_____⌣_____

Not only are whale sharks swimming miles throughout the world's oceans, **4** but also diving to depths of up to a mile.

4
A) NO CHANGE
B) but also dive
C) but they also dive
D) they also dive

Here's How to Crack It

Punctuation is changing in the answer choices. Do you notice any STOP or HALF-STOP punctuation? It may not be as obvious as in the other questions, but there is STOP punctuation. A comma plus a FANBOYS words is another type of STOP punctuation. In this case, we have a comma plus the word *but*. When we have a comma + FANBOYS, we are going to draw the vertical line through the word *but* because the word *but* is being treated as part of the punctuation, not part of either idea. Now check the ideas. The first idea, *Not only are whale sharks swimming miles throughout the world's oceans*, is a complete idea. The second idea, *also diving to depths of up to a mile*, is an incomplete idea. STOP punctuation cannot be used between a complete idea and an incomplete idea, so eliminate (A). Although (B) changes *diving* to *dive*, the second idea is still incomplete, so eliminate (B). Choice (C) adds the subject *they* to the second idea. The second idea, *they also dive to depths of up to a mile*, is now complete, so STOP punctuation can be used. Choice (D) adds *they* but eliminates *but*. A comma, which is GO punctuation, cannot link two complete ideas. The correct answer is (C).

_____⌒_____

COMMAS

Commas can feel a bit trickier than other punctuation marks. They are sometimes treated like seasoning, sprinkled into sentences whenever you want to pause. This isn't helpful for doing well on the test, though. On the SAT, there are specific reasons to use commas.

> If you can't cite a reason to use a comma, don't use one.
>
> On the SAT, there are only 4 reasons to use a comma.
> - In STOP punctuation, with one of the FANBOYS words
> - In GO punctuation, sometimes, between a complete idea and an incomplete idea, in either direction
> - In a list of three or more things
> - Before and after unnecessary information

We've already seen the first two reasons in action, so let's take a look at the other two.

Scientists, ■5 conservationists: and wildlife enthusiasts are all interested in learning more about the lives of whale sharks.

5

A) NO CHANGE

B) conservationists, and

C) conservationists and,

D) conservationists; and

Here's How to Crack It

First, notice that punctuation is changing in the answer choices. We do see STOP and HALF-STOP punctuation. A quick application of the Vertical Line Test reveals that the first idea, *Scientists, conservationists*, is an incomplete idea, so we can eliminate (A) and (D).

Now we can focus on the comma. It's important to note that the SAT wants a comma after every item in the list, other than the final item. The comma before the *and* makes the meaning of sentences clearer. Take a look at this sentence:

I dedicate this book to my parents, my cat Fluffy and my dog Finn.

Without the comma, it sounds like the author potentially has a very interesting set of parents. To make the sentence clearer, add the comma:

I dedicate this book to my parents, my cat Fluffy, and my dog Finn.

Now with this knowledge, let's take a look back at the question. The sentence contains a list—*scientists, conservationists, wildlife enthusiasts*—so there should be a comma after *conservationists*. There is no reason to put a comma after the word *and*, so eliminate (C). The correct answer is (B).

———————————————⌒———————————————

Let's take a look at the fourth reason to use a comma.

———————————————⌒———————————————

Scientific research on whale sharks has increased in recent years, since aspects of their **6** lives, such as their migratory patterns and birthing process, have remained mysteries.

6

A) NO CHANGE

B) lives such as their migratory patterns and birthing process

C) lives, such as their migratory patterns and birthing process

D) lives such as, their migratory patterns and birthing process,

Here's How to Crack It

What's changing in the answer choices? Only commas. Therefore, we don't need to use the Vertical Line Test—that's only for when you see STOP or HALF-STOP punctuation. The commas are around the phrase *such as their migratory patterns and birthing process*. When commas are around a word, phrase, or clause, the question is testing necessary versus unnecessary information.

To check whether the information is unnecessary, read the original sentence without the phrase. *Scientific research on whale sharks has increased in recent years, since aspects of their lives have remained mysteries.*

Now we check to see if the new sentence is complete and has the same meaning. Yes on both counts, so the phrase is unnecessary and should be surrounded by commas (similar to how two parentheses work). The correct answer is (A).

It's worth noting that not all questions that test this rule require you to identify whether the phrase is necessary or unnecessary. Start by eliminating any answer that has only a comma before or after the phrase or has an unexplainable comma, like (C) and (D)

above. In many cases, that will eliminate three wrong answers, and you'll be left with the right one. You'll also see many of these questions where the non-underlined portion already either contains or doesn't contain a comma before or after the phrase, so you simply need to be consistent.

Let's do a little more practice with unnecessary information.

Necessary/Unnecessary Information Drill

Directions: Determine whether the italicized phrase is necessary or unnecessary. If it is unnecessary, add commas before and after. Answers can be found on page 142.

1. Sharks *that are carnivorous* have sharp teeth.

2. People are generally familiar with the hammerhead shark *which has an unusual head shape.*

3. The shark *that was portrayed in Jaws* was a great white shark.

4. Rachel Graham *who is a conservation scientist* studies whale sharks with the Wildlife Conservation Society.

5. Shark researcher *Eugenie Clark* has studied sharks since the 1980s.

Let's look at one more comma question.

A Couple of Dashes
A pair of dashes works the same way as a pair of commas; a pair of dashes can surround an unnecessary phrase. If you see a dash in the answer choices, make sure to check the rest of the sentence. If you see another dash, the question may be testing unnecessary information, rather than HALF-STOP rules.

That and Which
Phrases beginning with *that* will never be surrounded by commas (they're always necessary). Phrases beginning with *which* are usually unnecessary and thus typically use commas.

Scientists [7] expect, whale sharks will be similar, to other shark species, that eat similar foods.

7

7

A) NO CHANGE

B) expect, whale sharks will be similar, to other shark species

C) expect whale sharks will be similar to other shark species

D) expect, whale sharks will be similar, to other shark species,

Here's How to Crack It

Check to see what's changing in the answer choices. The location and number of commas are changing. Remember that there must be a reason to use a comma. If you can't find a reason, don't use one.

It looks like commas are surrounding the phrase *whale sharks will be similar*. To find out if the phrase is necessary information, reread the original sentence and then read the sentence without the phrase. The new sentence is *Scientists expect to other shark species that eat similar foods*. The new sentence has a new meaning and is no longer complete; the phrase is necessary. In addition, there is no reason to put a comma after *species*.

There are no reasons to use commas in this sentence. The correct answer is (C). The SAT likes to add extra, unnecessary punctuation to make answer choices incorrect. Remember, there must be a reason for every punctuation mark within and between sentences.

APOSTROPHES

Another punctuation mark that will appear on the test is the apostrophe. Apostrophes are difficult because they do not change how the words sound. Check it out: *their* and *they're* sound exactly the same. As with the other punctuation in this chapter, it's important to notice when apostrophes are changing in the answer choices.

You must have a reason to use an apostrophe, and there are only two reasons to do so.

> If you can't cite a reason to use an apostrophe, don't use one.
>
> On the SAT, there are only two reasons to use an apostrophe.
> - Possessive nouns (NOT pronouns)
> - Contractions

Let's take a look at an example.

Innovative technology has improved **8** scientist's method's of studying these elusive giants.

8
A) NO CHANGE
B) scientists' method's
C) scientists' methods
D) scientists methods

Here's How to Crack It
Look at what's changing in the answer choices. We see that the words are staying the same, but the apostrophes are changing. Remember, we need a reason to use an apostrophe, so let's check whether any of the apostrophes are necessary.

When apostrophes are used with nouns on the SAT, they indicate possession. Let's start with the word *method*. The word after *method* is *of*. Does *of* belong to *method*? No, so there is no need to use an apostrophe with the word *method*; eliminate (A) and (B).

Now let's check *scientists*. Do the *methods* belong to the *scientists*? Yes, so we do need an apostrophe; the correct answer is (C).

Let's try another.

---○---

9 It's possible to recognize whale sharks by they're unique patterns of spots.

9

A) NO CHANGE

B) It's possible to recognize whale sharks by their

C) Its' possible to recognize whale sharks by their

D) Its possible to recognize whale sharks by they're

Here's How to Crack It

What's changing in the answer choices? We notice that there are apostrophes in some of the answer choices on the words *it* and *they*.

When an apostrophe is used with a pronoun, it's a contraction. We want to say *It is possible*, so we need to use *it's*; eliminate (C) and (D). *Its* is used to show possession. *Its'* is not a word but will show up sometimes on the test. Let's take a look at the next apostrophe possibility. *Their* is a possessive pronoun, and *they're* is a contraction of *they are*. Is it correct to say *they are unique patterns of spots*? That changes the meaning of the sentence, which we don't want to do, so we can eliminate (A). Choice (B) correctly indicates that the *unique patterns* belong to the whale sharks.

---○---

Try the following exercise for more practice with apostrophes.

Apostrophes Drill

Circle the option that works. Keep in mind the important question: apostrophes or no apostrophes? Answers can be found on page 142.

1. *Rachel's/Rachels* friend said *she's/shes* excited to see whale sharks in *their/they're* natural habitat.

2. If *your/you're* interested, you can come with *us'/us*.

3. *Their/They're* buying tickets soon, so *well/we'll* need to decide soon.

4. *Whose/Who's* going to want *their/they're* own room?

5. *Its/It's* going to be fun to see whale *sharks/sharks'* swimming.

THE IMPORTANCE OF PUNCTUATION

Knowing how punctuation is used, especially with complete and incomplete ideas, can help you answer harder Writing and Language questions. As you work through Writing and Language questions, pay attention to the punctuation that is not in the underlined portion.

Let's take a look at an example.

People can upload photos of whale sharks to the Wildbook for Whale Sharks website, **10** it is a visual database that marine biologists can use in their study of whale sharks.

10

A) NO CHANGE

B) this is

C) that being

D) which is

Here's How to Crack It

In this example, we only see the words changing. There's no punctuation in the answer choices, so how can punctuation help us answer this question? Well, let's take a look at the punctuation in the sentence. Before the underlined portion, we see a comma, which is GO punctuation. Now let's check the phrase before the comma. The phrase, *People can upload photos of whale sharks to the Wildbook for Whale Sharks website*, is a complete idea.

We know that GO punctuation cannot be used between two complete ideas, so the phrase after the comma cannot be a complete idea. *It is a visual database that marine biologists can use in their study of whale sharks*, is a complete idea, so eliminate (A). Changing *it* to *this* doesn't change the idea into an incomplete one, so eliminate (B). Between (C) and (D), *which is* makes the second idea incomplete and uses a concise verb, so the correct answer is (C).

Watch for questions in which subjects and verbs change. Remember that adding or deleting a subject, verb, or conjunction can change whether an idea is complete or incomplete. While these questions don't test punctuation directly, your knowledge of what kinds of ideas can be connected by which types of punctuation will be key to correctly answering these trickier questions.

Let's try one more.

The efforts of volunteers and the application of artificial intelligence have greatly helped whale shark researchers: they can collect photos and identify individual whale sharks quickly, and **11** scientists, they are interested in answering the big questions about whale sharks, can focus more of their time on analyzing the results.

11

A) NO CHANGE
B) scientists being
C) scientists
D) scientists,

Here's How to Crack It

Look at what's changing in the answer choices. We see commas changing as well as words. Remember that we need a reason to use a comma. When we look later in the sentence, we see a comma after the word *sharks*. Remember that every comma needs a reason to be there. We can rule out three of the four comma rules: there's no FANBOYS words, the comma comes between the subject and verb, so it's not GO punctuation, and there isn't a list. Therefore, the comma must be there to indicate unnecessary information, so the phrase *interested in answering the big questions about whale sharks* must be an unnecessary phrase describing the scientists. We can eliminate (B) and (C) because they don't have a comma before the unnecessary phrase. Notice that we didn't need to decide whether the phrase was unnecessary, which can sometimes be hard to figure out, because the punctuation in the non-underlined portion told us it was unnecessary. When comparing (A) to (D), notice that (A) adds in the words *they are*, which changes the phrase into a complete idea. We cannot interrupt the complete idea *scientists can focus more of their time on analyzing the results* with another complete idea. Therefore, the correct answer is (D).

A NOTE ON GRANULARITY

Sorry for the weird word in the title of this section, but it's one that, we think, is worth knowing. We'd like to be able to give you a little extra "advanced" set of tips, but so far as punctuation is concerned, there's nothing more to say. That's because the SAT couldn't be quite so granular as to ask you to know the difference between a period and semicolon. They want to see that you have a basic knowledge of grammar, not that you understand that words like *however* are conjunctive adverbs, whereas words like *whereas* are subordinating conjunctions.

As a result, these rules about STOP, GO, HALF-STOP, commas, and apostrophes can be more useful to you than you may think. First of all, they can remind you that the SAT couldn't possibly make you choose between a semicolon and a period. If you get a list of answer choices that looks like the following, you can reason your way into the correct answer:

A) NO CHANGE
B) choose. The following
C) choose; the following
D) choose the following

In this instance, you know that the answer can't be (B) or (C) because both of those answers contain basically identical punctuation. Even if the idea of STOP and GO punctuation may seem a little simplistic, you can apply the concepts in more complex ways.

It can also help to remember that a lot of grammatical stuff is basically beyond consensus, and that stuff therefore can't be tested. For instance, let's say you're talking about a novel by Henry James. Would you call it *Henry James' novel* or *Henry James's novel*? The SAT wouldn't make you choose because there's not enough consensus around which one is right. Some style guides say add only the apostrophe after any noun that ends in *s*; some say *'s* after any singular noun.

The same goes for subordinating conjunctions—words like *because, although, if, since,* and *when*. When you use one to link two ideas, do you need a comma or not? For instance, which one of these is correct?

> *It's tough to say whether a comma is necessary because grammar experts don't agree.*

> *It's tough to say whether a comma is necessary, because grammar experts don't agree.*

So which one is it? Tough call, and even grammarians disagree with one another. A comma before a subordinating conjunction is a style choice, so the SAT couldn't make you pick between these answers:

A) necessary, because grammar

B) necessary because grammar

Those two answers are separated by nothing more than a stylistic choice, so how could you be expected to pick between them as if one were correct and the other incorrect?

In short, once you've mastered all the punctuation and techniques in this chapter, take the next step by looking to apply this knowledge on the meta-level. If you're stuck between two answers, at least give some consideration to the fact that if the answers are really that similar, there's probably something else wrong.

CONCLUSION

We've looked at the rules of punctuation that you need to know for the SAT. A lot of what we covered in this chapter was a refresher on rules that you already knew. Always check to see what is changing in the answer choices so you can figure out when a question is testing punctuation, and use Process of Elimination to get to the correct answer.

Remember the big question: does this punctuation need to be here?

> Know why you are using punctuation, whether that punctuation is STOP, HALF-STOP, GO, commas, or apostrophes. If you can't cite reasons to use these punctuation marks, don't use them!

On the next page, check your answers for the drills on pages 133 and 137 and then test out everything you've learned on punctuation!

CHAPTER DRILL ANSWERS

Necessary/Unnecessary Information Drill Answers

1. NECESSARY to the meaning of the sentence (no commas). If you remove the italicized part, the sentence is not adequately specific.

2. UNNECESSARY to the meaning of the sentence (commas). If you remove the italicized part, the sentence is still complete and does not change meaning.

3. NECESSARY to the meaning of the sentence (no commas). If you remove the italicized part, the sentence is not adequately specific.

4. UNNECESSARY to the meaning of the sentence (commas). If you remove the italicized part, the sentence is still complete and does not change meaning.

5. NECESSARY to the meaning of the sentence (no commas). If you remove the italicized part, the sentence does not work, as *shark researcher* cannot be the subject of a sentence without "a" or "the" before the phrase.

Apostrophes Drill Answers

1. Rachel's, she's, their
2. you're, us
3. They're, we'll
4. Who's, their
5. It's, sharks

PUNCTUATION DRILL
Time: 7 minutes

Questions 1–11 are based on the following passage.

Cold Process Soap-Making: A Traditional Process is Cool Again

Commercial soaps are traditionally made **1** with harsh, irritating chemicals and weaker fragrances, **2** both were initially rejected by consumers and artisans. However, as research presented the benefits of consistent hand-washing, these cheaper products gained popularity. Ingredient shortages during wartime—especially World War I and World War **3** II led to the development of synthetic detergents that were used instead of soap made with natural ingredients. Commercial soaps relied less on animal byproducts, hard to find during rationing, and incorporated vegetable-based fats. Today, some artisans have returned to the historic roots of the **4** craft; but hobbyists are making their own soap out of natural ingredients through the cold process method.

1
A) NO CHANGE
B) with harsh, irritating, chemicals,
C) with, harsh irritating chemicals,
D) with harsh irritating chemicals—

2
A) NO CHANGE
B) both of which
C) of whom both
D) both of them

3
A) NO CHANGE
B) II,
C) II;
D) II—

4
A) NO CHANGE
B) craft, therefore,
C) craft,
D) craft, and

Through the cold process **5** method;
(which utilizes an exothermic chemical
reaction called saponification), fatty acids
react with a base to produce glycerol. The
cold process method requires knowledge of
how to safely work with lye (a caustic metal
hydroxide that can burn skin), since the base
can have harmful **6** effects. As experts
suggest using gloves, goggles, and protective
clothing to ensure safety. To create soap using
this method, soap-makers heat oils to about
100 degrees Fahrenheit, then mix lye and
water into the oils until the mixture thickens.
Fragrant essential oils, dyes, scouring agents,
and emollients, such as sand, oatmeal, and
milk, are then added to the mixture. The
mixture is then poured into a mold to harden
for 24 hours and cure for four to six weeks.
Once cured, the mixture is cut into **7** bars
and packaged as soap.

5
A) NO CHANGE
B) method, which
C) method (which
D) method which

6
A) NO CHANGE
B) effects; as
C) effects:
D) effects,

7
A) NO CHANGE
B) bars and packaged (as soap).
C) bars—and packaged as soap.
D) bars, and packaged, as soap.

The cold process method has many benefits, but it also has a few challenges. There are issues that can arise throughout the process. When done correctly, the cold process method can produce creamier soaps with more intense fragrances, colors, and lathers, but when the solution is overmixed, the [8] "trace," or point when the lye and oils reach complete emulsification, is surpassed. This can cause the mixture to seize up and become too thick to work with or generate air bubbles. Improper temperatures or humidity levels can cause cracks to develop within the mold. Fragrance oils can cause separation of ingredients or grainy textures in the soap.

One successful soap-maker who has relied on traditional methods is Bindu Chopra. In 2015, she created a skin-care company that creates homemade soaps with the goal of providing affordable and natural products to customers. The [9] companys products utilize ingredients that remind Chopra of her childhood and emphasize the beauty of darker skin.

8

A) NO CHANGE

B) "trace" or point when the lye and oils reach complete emulsification,

C) "trace" or point, when the lye and oils reach, complete emulsification

D) "trace" or, point, when the lye and oils reach complete emulsification

9

A) NO CHANGE

B) companys' product's

C) company's products'

D) company's products

Using traditional methods is not always easy: Chopra's methods require more time and initial effort, and she sometimes faces **10** criticism from other companies and consumers who doubt that the natural ingredients are worth the extra cost. Despite this feedback, Chopra continues to develop her company and is not afraid to experiment with different combinations of ingredients in her **11** products; such as essential oils with strong fragrances, coffee beans, and walnut shells to exfoliate skin. According to Chopra, "Nothing beats homemade products."

10

A) NO CHANGE

B) criticism–

C) criticism;

D) criticism,

11

A) NO CHANGE

B) products. Such as

C) products, included with these were

D) products, such as

Summary

o   Remember STOP, HALF-STOP, and GO punctuation.

o   STOP punctuation can link only complete ideas.

o   HALF-STOP punctuation must be preceded by a complete idea.

o   GO punctuation can link anything except two complete ideas.

o   When you see STOP or HALF-STOP punctuation changing in the answer choices, use the Vertical Line Test.

o   On the SAT, there are only four reasons to use a comma:
   - STOP punctuation (with one of the FANBOYS words)
   - GO punctuation
   - after every item in a list
   - before and after unnecessary information

o   On the SAT, there are only two reasons to use an apostrophe:
   - possessive nouns (NOT pronouns)
   - contractions

o   Know why you are using punctuation, whether that punctuation is STOP, HALF-STOP, GO, commas, or apostrophes. If you can't cite reasons to use these punctuation marks, don't use them!

Chapter 10
Words

The Writing and Language Test will also focus on words—mainly nouns, pronouns, and verbs. While we will discuss a few of these grammatical concepts along the way, this chapter will boil these many concepts down to three main terms: Consistency, Precision, Concision. With fewer minutiae to remember, you will be able to work through Words questions with confidence and ease.

DO IT FOR THE GRAM…MAR?

In the last chapter, you learned how to approach questions that involve punctuation and complete sentences. Now we're going to go over what to do when words change—mainly transitions, verbs, and pronouns.

Although there are more rules you'll need to learn for grammar questions, our basic strategy is the same. As we saw in the previous two chapters, when faced with an SAT Writing and Language question with no actual question, we should always do the following:

> Check what's changing in the answer choices and use POE.

At the end of the Writing and Language Introduction, we gave you a grammar glossary to help with the mechanics of writing, since many high-scorers want to take a deeper dive into how sentences are constructed. If you really want to learn the meaning of *subjunctive mood* or *present perfect progressive tense*, we won't try to stop you, but you certainly don't need to know those terms for the SAT. In the interest of saving you a lot of time and effort, we'll focus here on the limited set of grammar topics that are actually tested on the SAT and work with just three basic rules.

> **CONSISTENCY:** Correct answers are consistent with the rest of the sentence and the passage.
>
> **PRECISION:** Correct answers are as precise as possible.
>
> **CONCISION:** Barring other errors, correct answers are as concise as possible.

Let's look at some examples of each.

CONSISTENCY

Central California visitors are sure to spot distinctive yellow signs and bumper stickers advertising the intriguingly named Santa Cruz Mystery Spot. The roadside attraction, which opened in 1941, offers an experience that seems to defy the laws of physics. **1** Despite this, it has attracted both devotees who attest to the locale's unusual properties and cynics who chalk its appeal up to clever trickery.

1

A) NO CHANGE

B) Accordingly,

C) Similarly,

D) Instead,

Here's How to Crack It

First, as always, check what's changing in the answers: transitions. Most transition questions relate the sentence in question to the one before, so always look to the previous sentence to consider how the ideas are related. These questions can be tricky—one reason is that if you read the two sentences as written, you can easily be fooled by the underlined portion. Transitions are like road signs that tell you which direction to go. We aren't used to reading sentences with incorrect transitions, so we can be tricked into thinking the underlined portion reflects the actual direction the two sentences go. To avoid making a mistake, start by covering the underlined portion with your finger and just reading the two sentences, without the underlined portion. Then, determine whether the ideas agree or disagree.

In this case, the sentence before the underlined portion describes the Mystery Spot. The sentence with the underlined portion explains a result of the Mystery Spot's offerings. Therefore, the ideas agree. Begin by eliminating any answers that are not same-direction transitions: (A) and (D), both of which are opposite-direction transitions. Next, consider the difference between (B) and (C). *Accordingly* is used before a conclusion, and it essentially means "going along with this." Since the second sentence here is a result of the first sentence, that could be a good match, so keep (B). *Similarly* is used for two separate items that have something in common. In this case, both sentences are about the Mystery Spot, so this transition wouldn't work. Eliminate (C). Choice (B) is the correct answer.

Let's see another transition question.

In the late 1930s, an inventor and mechanic named George Prather was looking for land on which to build a vacation home. **2** By the same token, he purchased the hillside property that would become the Mystery Spot.

2

A) NO CHANGE

B) In other words,

C) Nevertheless,

D) To that end,

Here's How to Crack It

Check what's changing in the answer choices. Again, transitions change, so cover up the original underlined portion and determine the relationship between the ideas. The previous sentence provides information about what Prather wanted. This sentence explains what he then did. These ideas agree, so eliminate any opposite-direction transitions: (C). Next, eliminate any answers that don't accurately represent the relationship between the sentences. *By the same token* means "in the same way." The second sentence does not describe something that happened in the same way as something else, so eliminate (A). *In other words* is used when a sentence restates the previous information but using other words. That isn't the case here, so eliminate (B). *To that end* means "with that goal in mind." Since the first sentence states Prather's goal and this sentence tells what he did in pursuit of that goal, this correctly captures the relationship between the sentences.

Let's note here that not all transition questions will be as tricky as these two. You'll see plenty of questions that have more common transitions such as *for example, in addition,* and *however* as their correct answers. We've chosen to give you examples of some of the more challenging transition questions. Be sure to learn the meanings of the trickier transitions we have covered here and when they should be used, as they may be tested in harder questions.

Let's review the basic approach for transition questions.

When transitions are changing in the answers:

1. Cover the original transition to avoid misunderstanding the relationship between the ideas.

2. If the question tests the relationship between two sentences, as most do, read the previous sentence and the sentence with the underlined portion.

3. Eliminate any answers that have wrong-direction transitions. Then, use POE to eliminate any remaining answers that are inconsistent with the relationship between the ideas.

Consistency isn't only tested on transition questions. Let's see another example.

Magnetic anomalies related to the slope of the hill **3** was said to occur on the property.

3

A) NO CHANGE
B) are
C) has been
D) is

Here's How to Crack It

Check the answer choices first. Verbs are changing. You might easily spot verb tense changing (*was* versus *is*, for example), but verb number also changes (*are* versus *is*, for example—both of which are present tense). Number refers to whether a verb is singular or plural. To determine the correct number, locate the subject of the verb—the one doing the action. The subject almost always comes before the verb in a sentence, but it may not come immediately before. In fact, the writers of the SAT love to fill the space in between the subject and verb with describing phrases in order to trick you. It may seem that the sentence is saying "the hill was" or "the slope of the hill was," but the actual subject is *magnetic anomalies*, which is plural. The phrase *related to the slope of the hill* is merely a describing phrase that provides information about the anomalies. Therefore, (A), (C), and

(D) all have to be eliminated, as they are all singular. The answer is (B), and you didn't have to make a decision about tense at all.

If you are not sure whether a verb is singular or plural, try putting the pronouns "they" and "it" before the verb. You would say "they are," so "are" is plural. You would say "it is," so "is" is singular. When number changes in the answer choices, always find the subject and eliminate answers that don't agree with it. Watch for prepositional phrases (those that begin with prepositions, such as *in, on, of, with,* and *by*) and other types of describing phrases that separate the subject and verb—the subject and verb will never be inside a prepositional phrase, so you can cross out those phrases to help find the subject.

Try the following drill for more practice with subject-verb agreement.

Subject-Verb Agreement Drill

Directions: Circle the subject and underline the verb in each sentence. Watch out for phrases in between the subject and verb. Answers can be found on page 166.

1. The tissues in the box are almost gone.

2. Tamara is studying for her test.

3. Running outside on cold days can make you get sick.

4. The release of the commission's findings was timed carefully.

5. The students in the class have chosen to stay after school.

6. After a loss, the players on the visiting team leave the field quickly.

7. The article in the newspaper was about the proposed soda tax.

8. Going on a trip with your school band is something not everyone has experienced.

9. The girl who ordered waffles, a biscuit, and scrambled eggs is sitting over there.

10. An art therapist does not need to have a PhD.

On question 3, you didn't have to determine the correct tense because only one answer was consistent in number with the subject. However, some Writing and Language questions will test tense, so let's see an example.

From its opening, the Mystery Spot **4** faces skepticism from those who suggest that its owner simply wanted to make money.

4

A) NO CHANGE
B) had faced
C) has faced
D) will face

Here's How to Crack It

What's changing in the answer choices? Verb tense. Remember, it all goes back to consistency: the tense of the underlined portion must be consistent with the rest of the sentence. Look for clues that would help to determine what tense is needed. This sentence is tricky because it has a present tense verb (*suggest*) and a past tense verb (*wanted*). Many sentences contain verbs in different tenses, so you can't always just find another verb in the sentence to identify the tense you need.

Here, the clue comes from the beginning of the sentence: *From its opening.* This refers to something that started in the past and continues, so eliminate answers inconsistent with this idea. Choice (A) is present tense, which does not convey the meaning of something that started in the past, so eliminate it. The verb *had faced* would be used to refer to an action from the past that stopped at some point. The sentence implies that the attraction still faces skepticism, so (B) can't work. Keep (C) because *has faced* is the correct tense for something that started in the past and continues. Eliminate (D) because *will face* is future tense. Therefore, (C) is the answer.

Note that the SAT tests a fairly limited range of tenses. Start with whether you want past, present, or future, and focus on Process of Elimination. Remember to identify when the question tests number as well because knowing whether you need a singular or plural verb can allow you to avoid having to make many decisions about tense.

Here is the basic approach for verbs.

When verbs are changing in the answers:

1. If number changes, find the subject and eliminate answers that are not consistent in number with the subject.

2. If tense changes, look for clues in the non-underlined portion that indicate what tense is needed.

Sometimes consistency is tested in questions that don't fall under other categories. Here's an example.

Prather and his descendants claim that the land now occupied by the Mystery Spot attraction causes compasses and other instruments to **5** function improperly.

5

A) NO CHANGE

B) be really odd.

C) act weird.

D) not work, in an unusual way.

Here's How to Crack It

First, identify what's changing in the answer choices. Here, it's the wording. You might notice also that some of the answers are more casual or wordy than others. Use Process of Elimination to eliminate answers that are not consistent with the rest of the text. Keep (A) as it probably seems okay for now. Compare (B) to (A). Choice (B) is less precise and uses *really* in a casual way, which isn't consistent with the more academic tone of the text. Eliminate (B). Choice (C) is also less precise than (A), using *act* instead of *function*, and *weird* is overly casual, so eliminate (C). Choice (D) is longer, but the additional words in comparison to (A) do not help to clarify the meaning; this answer is also awkwardly worded. Eliminate (D), so the answer is (A).

There isn't a specific part of speech or grammar rule that is being tested here: it's just consistency. However, these questions are very predictable. The Writing and Language passages are generally all written to have a moderately formal, academic tone. You aren't likely to see a passage that uses much slang or casual language, so you can generally eliminate answers that include those types of words. Sometimes, you will also see answers that go to the opposite extreme: overly formal language. Do not assume that the writers of the SAT prefer the fanciest language possible; given the choice between a simple answer with a clear meaning and a complicated answer with extremely formal constructions, go with the simple one. Just make sure that the words are precise enough to accurately convey the intended meaning.

Another way consistency comes up is on comparison questions. Take a look at question 6.

Many of the tricks showcased to visitors, however, are similar to **6** the Oregon Vortex, another "mystery spot" attraction that Prather had seen prior to purchasing the land.

6

A) NO CHANGE

B) those found at the Oregon Vortex,

C) a site called the Oregon Vortex,

D) Oregon Vortex visitors,

Here's How to Crack It

Start by identifying what's changing in the answer choices. The answers are very similar. Choices (A) and (C) have very similar meanings, while (B) adds the word *those* and (D) adds the word *visitors*. Start by identifying what *those* in (B) could refer to. The sentence draws a comparison (using the word *similar*) between the Santa Cruz Mystery Spot and the Oregon Vortex. However, the comparison is really between their *tricks*, as that is the subject of the sentence and what the text says *are similar to* something. Ask yourself what they are similar to: the "tricks" at the Oregon Vortex. Therefore, (A), (C), and (D) must be eliminated because they do not refer to the "tricks." In (B), *those* refers back to *tricks*, so this is consistent and makes the correct comparison.

Comparison errors can be very difficult for students to spot, so these are considered harder questions. For one, the original sentence may sound fine. We can understand what the author means to say, but that's not good enough—the sentence must be correctly written. Another challenge with these questions is that we often find ourselves leaning toward a shorter answer on the SAT, as concision is tested (as we will see soon). However, a shorter answer is not automatically correct. If it violates a grammar rule, it must be eliminated.

———————————————————

Let's take a look at some more examples of comparison errors, since this topic can be more challenging.

> *I think the Phillies' bullpen is better than the Braves.*

What's actually being compared here? We know what the writer means, probably, but what it says here is that one team's *bullpen* is better than another *team*. In order to fix the comparison, then, we'd have to make sure to compare like things, so a clearer version of this sentence would be

> *I think the Phillies' bullpen is better than that of the Braves.*

Or

> *I think the Phillies' bullpen is better than the Braves' bullpen.*

Try these next few and see if you can rewrite each sentence to make it more logical.

> James Joyce's novels are more concerned with the geography of Ireland than Samuel Beckett.

> The tacos at Juan's are better than Jorge's.

> Poems by amateur writers can sometimes be as good as professionals.

In the first instance, you want to compare the *novels* of Joyce with the *novels* of Beckett: right now the *novels* of Joyce are being compared with *Beckett* himself. Rewrite the sentence to say *James Joyce's novels are more concerned with the geography of Ireland than* **are those of** *Samuel Beckett.*

The second sentence should compare tacos to tacos, not tacos to Jorge's. Fix the sentence this way: *The tacos at Juan's are better than* **those at** *Jorge's.*

The third sentence should compare poems to poems, not poems to professionals. Fix the sentence this way: *Poems by amateur writers can sometimes be as good as* **those written by** *professionals.*

All of these fixes make good logical sense when they are pointed out, but faulty comparisons can be tough to spot because we misuse them so frequently in our day-to-day speech. First and foremost, when you see nouns changing in the answer choices, make sure that those nouns are consistent. If the bad comparison doesn't jump out at you, look out for words like *more*, *better*, or *as*. Make sure your sentences are as internally consistent and precise as possible.

Let's see one more way consistency is tested on the SAT Writing and Language Test.

The fact that Prather had already seen a successful Mystery Spot in another state, skeptics argue, validates **7** their view that the site's supposed supernatural properties were invented for monetary gain.

7

A) NO CHANGE

B) its

C) they're

D) it's

Here's How to Crack It

Check what's changing in the answer choices: pronouns. Whenever pronouns are changing in the answer choices, always identify the noun or pronoun the underlined portion refers back to. Whose *view* is being discussed? The *skeptics'*. This word is plural, so eliminate answers that are singular: (B) and (D). Next, consider the apostrophes. *They're* means "they are," which isn't correct here. Eliminate (C). The answer is (A), which contains the correct plural possessive pronoun.

Some pronoun questions are fairly easy, while others are challenging. Watch out for tricky nouns like *team*, *family*, and *company*. Even though these all consist of multiple people, the words themselves are singular and would need to be referred to using the singular pronoun *it* rather than the plural pronoun *they*.

Pronouns are not only tested in terms of consistency; they will show up on precision questions as well. Let's move on to our second key term for the Writing and Language grammar questions.

PRECISION

Consistency is probably the most important thing on the SAT, but precision is a close second. Once you've made sure that the underlined portion is consistent with the rest of the sentence, then make sure that the underlined portion is as precise as possible. Perfect grammar is one thing, but it won't matter much if no one knows what the writer is talking about!

Let's hear that one more time.

> Once you are sure that a word or phrase is consistent with the non-underlined portion of the sentence, make that word or phrase as precise as you can.

Upon arrival at the Santa Cruz Mystery Spot, visitors may peruse a gift shop, and then a tour guide leads them up a steep hill to a slanted shack; **8** they claim that the cabin is tilted due to the mysterious gravitational effects on the hill.

8

A) NO CHANGE
B) it claims
C) those claim
D) the guide claims

Here's How to Crack It

As always, first identify what is changing in the answer choices. In this case, the pronouns change. The original sentence may sound fine, but remember to follow the strategy to avoid making a mistake. Like before, identify the noun the pronoun refers back to. The only plural noun in the first part of the sentence is *visitors*, but the sentence is not suggesting that the visitors are the ones claiming the *mysterious gravitational effects*. The underlined portion should refer back to someone working at the Mystery Spot. Eliminate (A) as well as (B), because *it* cannot refer to a person. *Those* is a plural noun, like *they*, so (C) must also be eliminated. Choice (D) corrects the error by changing the pronoun to an actual noun, which makes the meaning precise and clear. Once again, we can see that a longer answer may be correct if it is more *consistent* or *precise* than the short option, and we can see that it is not enough for the meaning to be able to be inferred; we probably understood what the sentence meant, but the sentence must be written in a precise way to be correct.

Here are our tips for pronoun questions.

When pronouns are changing in the answers:

1. Identify who or what the pronoun refers back to, and make it consistent with that noun or pronoun.

2. When given the option, on the SAT, strongly consider choosing an actual noun over a pronoun to make the sentence as precise as possible.

Try the following drill for more practice with pronouns.

Pronoun Drill

Directions: Identify and fix the pronoun error in each sentence. Answers can be found on page 166.

1. Certain dialects have obvious sources, but that doesn't make it any easier to understand.

2. Each of us speaks with an accent because of where they are from.

3. Whether word choice or pronunciation, it's usually easy to hear in someone's accent.

4. Everyone uses some kind of dialect words in their everyday speech.

5. Movies, TV, the Internet: it may be destroying differentiated dialects in the modern world.

Another, more common type of precision question you can expect to see is a vocabulary question, similar to question 5 from page 156. As we mentioned in the Writing and Language Introduction, besides just reading more books, you can't really prepare for these questions, as there is no limit to the possible words that can be tested. Just be sure to read the non-underlined portion of the sentence carefully and note any slight differences in how the words in the answers should be used. If all else fails, take your best guess and move on, as you're better off devoting your time to other questions.

Let's take a look at a final way precision is tested on the SAT.

Leading visitors into the shack in which both the floor and walls are tilted, **9** a table allows the tour guide to seem to defy gravity.

9

A) NO CHANGE

B) the tour guide's angle on a table seems to defy gravity.

C) the tour guide stands on a table at an angle that seems to defy gravity.

D) the rules of gravity seem to be defied by the tour guide, who stands on a table.

Here's How to Crack It

Start by determining what is changing in the answer choices. The answer choices seem to all say something similar, but the order of the words changes. You might also say that the subject changes, as each wording starts with a different idea. If you see the order of words or the subject changing, look to see whether the sentence contains a modifier, which is a describing phrase. These often appear at the beginning of a sentence and are followed by a comma—we have exactly that here with *Leading visitors into the shack in which both the floor and walls are tilted*. Consider whom or what this is supposed to describe and use Process of Elimination. The *table*, the *tour guide's angle*, and the *rules of gravity* are not *Leading visitors*, so (A), (B), and (D) must all be wrong. Choice (C) begins with *the tour guide*, and that is who is *Leading visitors*, so it is the correct answer.

As you can see, these questions can actually be very quick once you notice the modifier rule being tested. However, this can be tricky to spot, especially because some wrong answers may sound fine. Like with comparison errors, we understand what the author is trying to say, so the error isn't always obvious. Watch out for tricky answers like (B) above; it may seem like this answer correctly starts with *the tour guide*, but it's actually the *angle* of the tour guide, which does not work. Note that modifiers, while they often appear like this one, can occur anywhere in a sentence—we've seen the SAT test this topic with a parenthetical phrase, which, like other modifiers, must come directly after the person or thing it's describing.

Try the following drill for more practice with modifiers.

Modifiers Drill

Directions: Identify and fix the modifier error in each sentence. Note that there are multiple possible ways to fix these errors; the answers on page 166 contain example solutions.

1. With all its in and outs, many people find language a tough thing to study.

2. Dialects are really fascinating to anyone who wants to study them of a particular language.

3. Once opened up, you can find endless mysteries in the study of language.

4. I first learned about the Appalachian dialect from a professor in college at age 19.

5. Frankly pretty boring, Donald didn't pay much attention in his linguistics class.

CONCISION

You might have noticed that on several of the previous questions we did not pick the shortest answer. That's because consistency and precision are more important than concision. However, when you have two answers left and both convey the same meaning without containing any errors, choose the shorter and simpler one. Furthermore, eliminate any answers that contain repetitive information.

Let's see an example.

One of the most popular events at the Mystery Spot is when the tour guide places a ball on a slope and the ball **10** looks as if it is rolling in the wrong direction.

10

A) NO CHANGE

B) seems to the viewers to be moving in a direction that goes up the hill instead of down.

C) looks and appears to move incorrectly.

D) appears to roll uphill.

Here's How to Crack It

Start with what's changing in the answer choices. In this case, the answers seem to provide similar information, but the number of words changes, as some answers use more words than others. This is a good clue that the question could be testing concision. When you see that, start with the shortest option, in this case (D). Read the sentence with the wording from (D) and consider whether there are any errors. This seems okay, so check the other options against (D) to see whether they correct an error or clarify the meaning further. Choice (A) is overly wordy, as it uses more words to provide the same meaning as (D). The same is true for (B). Choice (C) isn't as long as (A) and (B), but it is redundant in saying both *looks* and *appears*, so eliminate (A), (B), and (C). The answer must be (D).

To summarize, always consider all four options carefully, as that will help you identify errors your ear might not have caught. If the shortest option has no errors and the longer options are not more consistent or precise, then choose the short answer.

Let's see one more example.

Whether a genuine gravitational anomaly **11** like no other place or nothing more than an optical illusion, the Santa Cruz Mystery Spot will likely continue to spark interest.

11

A) NO CHANGE

B) different from other places

C) not like other spots

D) DELETE the underlined portion.

Here's How to Crack It

First identify what's changing in the answers. In this case, (A), (B), and (C) all state something similar, and then there is the option to delete. When given this option, always try it, and see whether the sentence still works. In this case, deleting the phrase is fine. That's because of the word *anomaly*, which means something out of the norm. Therefore, (A), (B), and (C) are all redundant with *anomaly*, and no phrase here is needed, so the answer is (D). Luckily, even if you didn't know the meaning of *anomaly*, by paying attention to similarities and differences in the answers, you might realize that there really isn't a difference among the three phrasing options, so (D) would be a safe bet in that case.

When given the option to DELETE, try it. This option isn't always correct—remember, shorter isn't always better. However, there must be a reason not to DELETE.

As we have seen in this chapter, when the SAT is testing *words* (which it is any time the words are changing in the answer choices), make sure that those words are

- **Consistent.** Transitions, verbs, pronouns, and writing style should agree within sentences and passages.

- **Precise.** The writing should communicate specific ideas and events.

- **Concise.** When everything else is correct, the shortest answer is the best.

CHAPTER DRILL ANSWERS

Subject-Verb Agreement Drill Answers
1. Tissues; are
2. Tamara; is studying
3. Running; can make
4. Release; was timed
5. Students; have chosen
6. Players; leave
7. Article; was
8. Going; is
9. Girl; is sitting
10. Art therapist; does (not) need

Pronouns Drill Answers
1. *it* is the problem. *Certain dialects have obvious sources, but that doesn't make them any easier to understand.*
2. *they* is the problem. *Each of us speaks with an accent because of where he or she is from.*
3. *it* is the problem. Take it out and rearrange the sentence accordingly. *Word-choice and pronunciation are usually easy to hear in someone's accent.*
4. *their* is the problem. *Everyone uses some kind of dialect words in his or her everyday speech.*
5. *it* is the problem. *Movies, TV, the Internet: all three may be destroying differentiated dialects in the modern world.*

Modifiers Drill Answers
1. *Many people find language a tough thing to study because of all its ins and outs.*
2. *Dialects of a particular language are really fascinating to anyone who wants to study them.*
3. *Once opened up, the mysteries of a language can be endless.*
4. *I first learned about the Appalachian dialect from a college professor when I was 19 years old.*
5. *Donald didn't pay much attention in his linguistics class, which he found frankly pretty boring.*

WORDS DRILL
Time: 8 minutes

Questions 34–44 are based on the following passage.

Uncovering Dinosaurs in Scotland

In 2015, as they hiked along the coast of Scotland's Isle of Skye, Steve Brusatte and his team were on the lookout for signs of dinosaurs. Brusatte, a paleontologist, studies the history of life through fossils. Paleontologists had not considered Scotland a fossil-rich site (compared to areas like Mongolia and China), but the unearthing of a dinosaur bone changed all that: the discovery by Dr. Neil Clarke and Dougie Ross wasn't made until 1995, so much of **34** there has gone unexplored. The discovery was exciting since the fossils in Scotland were older than **35** the first human civilizations, giving paleontologists another glimpse into life before humans. Discoveries of small bits of dinosaur teeth and bones, along with footprints, prompted an optimistic Brusatte to move to Scotland to explore the area in search of more evidence of ancient life. "Right now is the best time in the history of dinosaur research," he said.

34

A) NO CHANGE
B) the region
C) that
D) it

35

A) NO CHANGE
B) the age of the
C) those of the
D) that of the

Brusatte and another researcher, Tom Challands, stumbled upon a barely [36] understandable site full of dinosaur tracks. Many of the features of the footprints, such as location and size, were similar to [37] tidal creatures. The location of the track site on the island's coast made fieldwork challenging, as the team had to contend with the elements. [38] However, they couldn't use drones to capture overhead images because of the cold winds, and they also had to be constantly mindful of the tides as the rising water routinely flooded the track site.

36

A) NO CHANGE
B) plain
C) obvious
D) perceptible

37

A) NO CHANGE
B) those of tide pools.
C) the formation of tide pools.
D) tide pools.

38

A) NO CHANGE
B) Therefore,
C) In other words,
D) Regardless,

Enduring the cold and wet of the island led to several significant discoveries. In 2015, the team **39** found a site full of tracks from sauropods (a group of dinosaurs **40** known as its large size). During field work in 2017, one of Brusatte's students found a dinosaur bone on Eigg, another Scottish island, marking the first dinosaur discovery in Scotland that wasn't on the Isle of Skye. Evidence of the stegosaurus was found in 2020; the team discovered that **41** those had walked among the other dinosaurs on the Isle of Skye.

39

A) NO CHANGE

B) stumbled upon a site full of sauropod tracks

C) came upon sauropod tracks filling a site

D) became aware of a site filled with sauropod tracks

40

A) NO CHANGE

B) knows that

C) knows

D) known for

41

A) NO CHANGE

B) we

C) it

D) they

These discoveries provide a wealth of new information about dinosaurs of the Middle Jurassic period that both **42** have encouraged further studies and have given some answers about how and where these animals lived. The Middle Jurassic species have not been studied as well as other dinosaurs have since their fossils are not found as often, so the research in Scotland greatly increases the knowledge about **43** it. Initially scientists thought sauropods spent most of their time in water until the discovery of their footprints on land disproved that theory. The footprints on the coast of the Isle of Skye suggest that they both walked on land and spent time in water.

Through these findings, **44** we paint a clearer picture of the lives of dinosaurs in the Middle Jurassic period. "Each new dinosaur fossil we find, whether it's a footprint on the Isle of Skye or a fossil bird in China, is a clue that helps fill in the picture of dinosaur evolution," Brusatte said.

42
A) NO CHANGE
B) encourages further studies and gives
C) encourages further studies and give
D) encourage further studies and give

43
A) NO CHANGE
B) them.
C) one.
D) him or her.

44
A) NO CHANGE
B) ancient sauropods
C) modern paleontologists
D) they

Summary

- When faced with an SAT Writing and Language question, always check what's changing in the answer choices and use POE.

- When you see verbs changing in the answer choices, make sure those verbs are consistent with their subjects as well as with other verbs in the sentence and surrounding sentences.

- When the nouns are changing in the answer choices, make sure those nouns are consistent with the other nouns in the sentence and the paragraph.

- Once you are sure that a word or phrase is consistent with the non-underlined portion of the sentence, make that word or phrase as precise as you can.

- Concision is key when you want to communicate meaning. As long as the grammar and punctuation are good to go, the best answer will almost always be the shortest.

Chapter 11
Questions

In the previous chapters, we've seen "questions" that don't have questions at all. In this chapter, we will deal with those questions that actually do contain questions and some of the strategies that can help to simplify them.

ANSWERING QUESTIONS ABOUT QUESTIONS

In the previous two chapters, we saw most of the concepts that the SAT will test. In this chapter, we're not going to learn a lot of new stuff in the way of grammar. Instead, we'll look at some of the questions the SAT asks.

As we've seen, a lot of the questions don't have questions at all. They're just lists of answer choices, and we start the process of answering them by asking a question of our own: "What's changing in the answer choices?"

Because you need to move quickly through this test, you may fall into the habit of not checking for questions. Even when you do read the questions, you may read them hastily or vaguely. Well, we are here to tell you that neither of these approaches will work.

> The most important thing about Writing and Language questions is that you *notice* those questions and then *answer* those questions.

This may seem like just about the most obvious advice you've ever been given, but you'd be surprised how much less precise your brain is when you're working quickly.

Here's an example. Do these next 10 questions as quickly as you can.

1. $2 + 1 =$
2. $1 + 2 =$
3. $3 + 1 =$
4. $3 + 2 \neq$
5. $1 + 2 =$
6. $2 - 1 <$
7. $2 \pm 2 =$
8. $3 + 1 =$
9. $3 + 2 =$
10. $3 + 3 \neq$

Now check your answers.

1. 3
2. 3
3. 4
4. Anything but 5
5. 3
6. Any number greater than 1 (but not 1!)
7. 0 or 4
8. 4
9. 5
10. Anything but 6

Now, it's very possible that you got at least one of those questions wrong. What happened? It's not that the questions are hard. In fact, the questions are about as easy as can be. So why did you get some of them wrong? You were probably moving too quickly to notice that the signs changed a few times.

This is a lot like the Writing and Language section. You might miss some of the easiest points on the whole test by not reading carefully enough.

As we will see throughout this chapter, most of the questions will test concepts with which we are already familiar.

INTROS, CONCLUSIONS, AND TRANSITIONS

In the lesson on Words, we went over how transitions connect two ideas. You'll see some Writing and Language questions that ask a question related to how ideas are connected.

Here's an example.

1 Most people with a full-time or part-time job get paid every two weeks. What most people don't realize is just how persistent that pay gap has been. The size of the pay gap may have narrowed, but we still have a long way to go. In some jobs, women earn only $0.83 for every dollar a man with the same title earns, and the statistics are even worse when only women of color are included.

1

Which choice is the best introduction to the paragraph?

A) NO CHANGE

B) The definition of "gap" is a hole or separation between two things.

C) It's common knowledge that older people are usually paid more than younger people are.

D) Most people are familiar with the idea of a gender pay gap.

Here's How to Crack It

First and foremost, it's important to notice the question. It's asking for an *introduction* to the paragraph. Should you just look at the four options and choose the one you like best? No! You can't know how to introduce the paragraph until you have read the paragraph. Ignore the underlined portion, as it may not be correct, and look to see what is discussed in the rest of the paragraph. The second sentence mentions *that pay gap*, so because of the word *that,* it must refer to a *pay gap* mentioned in the previous sentence. The paragraph goes on to clarify that it is a gap between *women* and *men*. Check the answers to see whether they relate to a *pay gap* between men and women. Eliminate (A) because it mentions pay but not a *gap*. Choice (B) defines *gap*, but it doesn't relate to pay, so it's wrong. Choice (C) describes a pay difference, but the paragraph is about gender, not age. Choice (D) mentions the *gender pay gap* and ties in to the second sentence by explaining what *Most people* know, where the second sentence contrasts that with what they *don't realize*. Therefore, (D) is the answer.

As you can see, it's extremely important to understand what the question is asking. For the Writing and Language questions that ask a question, typically all of the answers will have correct grammar and punctuation. You don't need to worry about those rules or about whether the sentence is concise. Your goal here is to choose the answer that is consistent with what the question is asking.

Note that you may need to read more for these questions, since they are more related to the content of the passage. Make it a habit to read the rest of the paragraph before answering these questions. Reading in between the sentences that have underlined portions and paying attention to the meaning of the text, not just the mechanics, will also help you to get more of these questions right.

Let's try another.

[2] Within the same jobs, African American women are paid on average less than people of other identities are. Some people assume the difference in pay is related to the types of careers that are more popular with particular genders or the reduced hours and time off many mothers take. However, the overall gap still exists between people of different genders even in the same position and with the same level of experience and education. The challenges women face in ascending to higher-paying leadership positions further contribute to the overall pay discrepancy.

2

Which choice provides the best transition from the previous paragraph to this one?

A) NO CHANGE

B) While statistics show a clear gender pay gap, they can't provide a simple and straightforward reason for this disparity.

C) The pay gap is calculated in two ways, one that controls for what jobs people have and one that takes all pay into consideration.

D) Inequality can be difficult to understand because people tend to think of personal prejudices more so than institutional issues.

Here's How to Crack It

First, be sure to read the question. It's asking for a *transition from the previous paragraph*. Like with question 1, we must read this paragraph before answering the question so that we can identify its main idea. We also need to know the main idea of the previous paragraph. The previous paragraph introduced the pay gap and ended with a statistic. Ignoring the underlined portion, this paragraph begins by speculating about what the pay gap is *related to* and goes on to aspects that *contribute to the overall pay discrepancy*. Therefore, it's focusing on why the pay gap exists.

A transition question requires you to pick an answer that moves smoothly from the previous topic to this topic. Use POE. Choice (A) relates closely to the final sentence of the previous paragraph, but it is not consistent with the topic from this paragraph, so it can't be correct. Choice (B) mentions *statistics* and the *reason* for the pay gap, so it ties in well with the end of the last paragraph and the focus of this one. Keep (B). Choice (C) discusses how the pay gap is *calculated*, but it doesn't relate to the reasons behind it, so eliminate (C). Choice (D) also does not have to do with the topic of this paragraph. Thus, the answer must be (B).

———————————————————

In general, when the question asks for an introduction, choose an answer that relates to the topic of the paragraph and sounds like it's introducing an idea (not one that sounds like it's starting in the middle of a topic). When the question asks for a transition, choose an answer that relates to both the topic of the previous paragraph and the topic of current paragraph. When the question asks for a conclusion, choose an answer that relates to the topic of the paragraph and sounds like it's wrapping up the ideas (not one that goes off in a different direction or introduces a new detail).

Let's look at another one that deals with some of the topics we've seen earlier.

The problem has certainly gained a good deal of traction in public debates. The fact that it has gained such traction makes us wonder why there isn't more significant action to combat the gender pay gap. **3**

3

Which of the following gives the best way to combine these two sentences?

A) The problem has certainly gained a good deal of traction in public debates; the fact that it has gained such traction makes us wonder why there isn't more significant action to combat the gender pay gap.

B) The problem has certainly gained a good deal of traction in public debates, which raises the question of why more isn't being done to combat the gap.

C) The problem has certainly gained a good deal of traction in public debates: this fact of more public attention raises a serious question of why more isn't being done to close that gap.

D) Having gained a good deal of traction in public debates, we may wonder why there isn't more significant action to combat the gender pay gap and the problem of it.

Here's How to Crack It

The question asks us to combine the two sentences. For these questions, start with the shortest option. In this case, that's (B). Choice (B) seems okay, so just check the remaining options to see whether they are any better. Choice (A) is repetitive, as it states the idea of gaining traction twice. Choice (C) repeats the idea of gaining traction and more public attention. Choice (D) creates a modifier error by implying that we have gained traction, when the problem is what has gained traction. Thus, the answer must be (B).

For these questions, the shortest option is usually correct. Don't automatically pick it, but start with that answer, and if it doesn't seem to have an error, just make sure the other options aren't better. The writers of the SAT do not like to repeat the same words or ideas twice, so eliminate any answer that does so.

Questions like #3 are why…

> The most important thing about Writing and Language questions is that you *notice* those questions and then *answer* those questions.

PRECISION QUESTIONS

Not all questions will be applications of punctuation and parts of speech. Some questions will ask you to do more specific things. Remember the three terms we kept repeating in the Words chapter: Consistency, Precision, and Concision. We'll start with the Precision-related questions. Even in those in which Precision is not asked about directly, or is mixed with Consistency or Concision, remember:

> Answer the question in the most precise way possible. Read literally!

Let's try one.

The question of unequal pay for women draws on many other broader social issues. **4**

4

The writer is considering deleting the phrase *of unequal pay for women* from the preceding sentence. Should this phrase be kept or deleted?

A) Kept, because removing it would remove a crucial piece of information from this part of the sentence.

B) Kept, because it reminds the reader of social injustice in the modern world.

C) Deleted, because it wrongly implies that there is a disparity between what women and men are paid.

D) Deleted, because it gives information that has no bearing on this particular text.

Here's How to Crack It

This question asks whether we should keep or delete the phrase *of unequal pay for women*. Without that phrase, the sentence reads, *The question draws on many other broader social issues*. Because nothing in this sentence or any of the previous ones specifies what this *question* might be, we should keep the phrase. We want to be as precise as possible!

And, as (A) says, we want to keep the phrase because it is crucial to clarifying precisely what *the question* is. Choice (B) is a little too grandiose a reason to keep the phrase, especially when the whole passage is about the particular injustice of the gender pay gap. Choice (A) is therefore the best answer.

Let's try another.

_____

The gender disparities persist in other areas than pay. It is a kind of open secret, for instance, that women have had the right to vote in the United States for less than a century. **5** There is a long history of misogyny written into the very cultural and social fabric of the United States.

5

At this point, the writer is considering adding the following true statement:

> The year that women's suffrage became legal in the United States was also the year that the American Football League was formed under the leadership of Jim Thorpe.

Should the writer make this addition here?

A) Yes, because it gives a broader context to the achievement of women's suffrage.

B) Yes, because it helps to ease some of the political rhetoric in the rest of the passage.

C) No, because it does not contribute in a significant way to the discussion of the gender pay gap.

D) No, because the question of gender pay is irrelevant when all football players are men.

Here's How to Crack It

The proposed sentence does contain an interesting bit of information, but that piece of information has no clear place either in these few sentences or in the passage as a whole. Therefore, it should not be added, thus eliminating (A) and (B).

Then, because it does not play a significant role in the passage, the sentence should not be added for the reason stated in (C). While (D) may be true in a way, it does not reflect anything clearly relating to the role the sentence might play in the passage as a whole. Read literally, and answer as literally and precisely as you can.

CONSISTENCY QUESTIONS

Just as questions should be answered as *precisely* as possible, they should also be answered with information that is *consistent* with what's in the passage.

When answering consistency questions, keep this general rule in mind:

> Writing and Language passages should be judged on what they *do* say, not on what they *could* say. When dealing with Style, Tone, and Focus, be sure to work with the words and phrases the passage has already used.

Let's look at two questions that deal with the idea of consistency.

[1] One need look no further than to the idea of the "traditional" family. [2] The shift, however, has yet to produce a substantive increase in how women, who are now nearly as likely to work as men, are paid. [3] In this idea, the father of the family earns the family wage 6 and gives the children their last names. [4] With such an idea bolstering what many consider to be the goal inherent in the "American dream," it is no wonder that women in the workplace should have a somewhat degraded position. [5] Shifting social and economic roles, however, have begun to change how people think about gender roles within the family. 7

6

Which of the following choices would best complete the distinction described in this sentence and the paragraph as a whole?

A) NO CHANGE

B) while the mother tends to the children and the home.

C) though his interest in "masculine" things like sports may vary.

D) but will only be able to achieve a wage commensurate with his skills and education.

7

The best placement for sentence 2 would be

A) where it is now.

B) before sentence 1.

C) after sentence 4.

D) after sentence 5.

Here's How to Crack Them

Let's look at question 6 first. In this case, the question tells us exactly what to look for: something that would *complete the distinction* in the sentence, a distinction made between what is expected of a man and a woman in a "traditional" family. Choices (A), (C), and (D) may be true in some definitions of what that a "traditional" family is, but none of those answers fulfills the basic demands of the question. Only (B) does so by describing what is expected of a *mother* in contrast to what is expected of a *father*, as described earlier in the sentence.

Now, as for question 7, we need to find some very literal way to make sentence 2 consistent with the rest of the paragraph. Look for words and phrases that will link sentence 2 to other sentences. Remember, it's not what the passage *could* say, it's what the passage *does* say. Sentence 2, we should note, starts with *the shift*, thus clearly referring to a shift that has been mentioned before it. As such, sentence 2 belongs definitively after sentence 5, which discusses *shifting social and economic roles*.

As we have seen, these questions are not difficult, but they do require very specific actions. Make sure you read the questions carefully and that you answer those questions as precisely and consistently as you can.

The same goes for Charts and Graphs on the Writing and Language section. Don't let the strangeness of the charts throw you off! Just read the graphs with as much precision as you can and choose the most precise answers possible.

⸺⚬⸺

Let's have a look at one.

⸺⚬⸺

Even as women's roles in high-level positions, such as Congress, have increased almost four-fold since 1981, **8** the pay that women receive relative to men has increased by less than 20%.

8

Which of the following choices gives information consistent with the graph?

A) NO CHANGE

B) women's wages have increased by over 80%.

C) the wages of women in Congress have decreased.

D) the efforts of women in Congress to raise wages have failed.

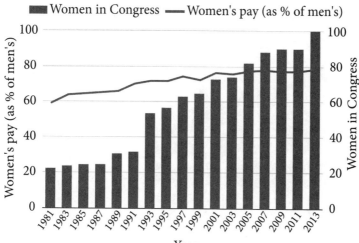

Women in Congress and Women's Pay

■ Women in Congress ── Women's pay (as % of men's)

Here's How to Crack It

This question is asking for what agrees with the graph. From what we have seen, these questions are usually pretty straightforward. You don't have to do anything overly complex with the graphs.

It looks like "Women in Congress" goes up significantly, whereas "Women's Pay" remains relatively consistent. The only choice that reflects that trend is (A). Choice (B) misreads the graph, and (C) and (D) can't be supported one way or the other. Choice (A) is therefore the best answer.

In general, graphs on the SAT Reading and Writing and Language sections are very straightforward, and the fundamental question they ask is, "Can you read a graph?" These are easy points as long as you read the graphs carefully and use POE.

CONCLUSION

As we have seen in this chapter, the SAT can ask a lot of different kinds of questions, but it's not going to throw anything really crazy at you. The biggest things to remember, aside from the punctuation rules, are *CONSISTENCY* and *PRECISION*. If you pick answers that are precise and consistent with other information in the passage, you should be good to go. Just be sure to answer the question!

QUESTIONS DRILL

Time: 10 minutes

Questions 1–11 are based on the following passage and supplementary material.

Zombies in the Movies

1 With the rise of movie streaming, the number of movies that are never shown in theaters increases every year. Horror, Western, and Sci-Fi movies are made every year, but the number of movies produced in each genre fluctuates annually. For example, as the number of Westerns has stayed at or below about 25 per year since the 1960s, the number of Zombie and Vampire films has **2** risen, with Zombie films increasing nearly six-fold.

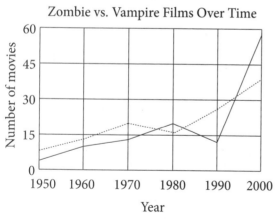

Zombie vs. Vampire Films Over Time

— Zombie Films (Maximum in a single year)

····· Vampire Films (Maximum in a single year)

1

Which of the following choices would best introduce the main point of the essay?

A) NO CHANGE

B) While many movie genres are staples in Hollywood, the popularity of these genres has changed over time.

C) Everyone knows that the highest form of Hollywood film is the drama.

D) There's a lot that you may not know about how films are made in Hollywood.

2

Which of the following gives information consistent with the graph?

A) NO CHANGE

B) risen, with Vampire films increasing nearly six-fold.

C) declined, with Zombie film production decreasing by a sixth.

D) declined, with Vampire film production decreasing by a sixth.

While the saying goes that there's "no accounting for the public's taste," **3** lots of people like lots of different things. Why should the number of Westerns have remained relatively low while the number of Zombie films has skyrocketed? Maybe we should ask the question another way: what do people today get from Zombie films that they don't from Westerns?

Westerns dominated the 1920s. Zombie films have dominated the 1990s and 2000s. **4** Beginning with these facts alone, we can start to see why these films might have been popular in different eras. The 1920s,

3

Which of the following choices would offer the most effective transition between the previous paragraph and the current one?

A) NO CHANGE

B) these trends nonetheless invite us to try.

C) a lot of people don't even care about Zombie movies.

D) science has not yet shown that zombies exist.

4

The writer is considering deleting the underlined sentence. Should the sentence be kept or deleted?

A) Kept, because it provides a logical transition between ideas in the paragraph.

B) Kept, because it explains why Westerns are now less popular than Zombie films are.

C) Deleted, because it is not directly related to the paragraph's focus on Zombie films.

D) Deleted, because it undermines the passage's claim about the declining popularity of Westerns.

for instance, was an American moment of crusade. **5** These were crusades altogether distinct from those conducted by the Catholic Church starting in 1095. Only a tough sheriff, the kind one might get in an old-west town, could find the perfect balance between **6** legit action and foul play. Thus, if the world could not be contained by law and order, at least here was an imaginary space that could be in the West.

5

Which choice best supports the idea in the previous sentence?

A) NO CHANGE

B) The United States is still interested in crusades today, so it's hard to see why they don't make as many Westerns anymore.

C) Led by Woodrow Wilson's plan for a U.S.-led League of Nations, the world, reeling from World War I, wanted justice among the outlaws.

D) The stock market wouldn't crash for another nine years, at which point people would really freak out.

6

Which choice best maintains the style and tone of the passage?

A) NO CHANGE

B) integrity and harshness.

C) being lit and cruelty.

D) justice and brutality.

[1] The 1990s and 2000s, dominated as they are by Zombie films, show that contemporary conflicts are not so far away. [2] Instead, we are interested in and suspicious of the people around us. [3] Although we now have the world at the click of a button, Zombie films show that we are not all that interested in that world. [4] Whether coworkers or fellow students, the people around us, especially when viewed as a mass, can seem almost "dead." [5] And the reasons for this are fairly obvious: our private or online personalities have become so robust that **7** we end up spending a lot of time designing avatars that match our personalities. **8**

7

Which choice would most effectively conclude the sentence and the paragraph?

A) NO CHANGE

B) sometimes it's hard to have face-to-face conversations with people.

C) many people now struggle with addictions to their Internet devices.

D) the "real world" outside cannot help but seem dull by comparison.

8

To make this paragraph most logical, sentence 2 should be placed

A) where it is now.

B) before sentence 1.

C) before sentence 4.

D) before sentence 5.

9 It may seem that genre conventions never change. Because they never change, it probably seems like a Western today follows the same set of rules as a Western from 100 years ago. What the rise in Zombie films shows, however, is that the genres themselves change, and they provide different things to different eras. **10** This is not to say that one genre is better than the other—that it's better,

9

Which choice most effectively combines the underlined sentences?

A) It may seem that genre conventions never change; because they never change, it probably seems like a Western today follows the same rules as a Western from 100 years ago.

B) It may seem that genre conventions never change; because of it, it could be argued that a Western today follows the same set of rules as a Western from 100 years ago.

C) It may seem that genre conventions never change: a Western today follows the same set of rules as a Western from 100 years ago.

D) Because Westerns today follow the same set of rules as they did 100 years ago, it seems to most outside observers that genre conventions never change.

10

At this point, the author is considering adding the following true statement:

For what it's worth, my personal favorite is Jacques Tourneur's *I Married a Zombie*, which is based loosely on *Jane Eyre*.

Should the writer make this addition here?

A) Yes, because the essay as a whole is filled with these kinds of examples and personal preferences.

B) Yes, because the author's quirky choice shows that he has an off-beat perspective.

C) No, because the author's strange choice disqualifies the author from discussing popular taste.

D) No, because the essay as a whole is not primarily focused on the author's personal preferences.

for instance, to watch a tough cowboy fight off a gang of cattle rustlers—but it is to say that these genres hold a lot more than their **11** bloodthirsty entertainment value.

11

Which choice most effectively suggests that Westerns offer more than what they seem superficially to represent?

A) NO CHANGE

B) mere

C) wholesome

D) engaging

Summary

- The most important thing about Writing and Language questions is that you notice those questions and then answer those questions. Don't miss out on some of the easiest points on the whole test by not reading carefully enough.

- When answering consistency questions, keep this general rule in mind: Writing and Language passages should be judged on what they do say, not on what they could say. When dealing with Style, Tone, and Focus, make sure to work with the words and phrases the passage has already used. As in the Words chapter, answer questions in the most precise way possible.

- There will be charts or graphs on the Writing and Language Test, but don't let that throw you off. Just read the graphs with the same focus that you'd use for a passage and choose the most precise answers possible.

Chapter 12
Writing & Language Exercises: Answers & Explanations

CHAPTER 9: PUNCTUATION DRILL ANSWERS

1. **A**   Punctuation is changing in the answer choices, so this question is testing STOP, HALF-STOP, and GO punctuation. Use the Vertical Line Test and identify the ideas as complete or incomplete. Draw the vertical line between the words *chemicals* and *and*. The first part of the sentence, *Commercial soaps are traditionally made with harsh, irritating chemicals*, is a complete idea. The second part, *and weaker fragrances,* is an incomplete idea. To connect a complete idea to an incomplete idea, HALF-STOP or GO punctuation is needed. Keep (A) because no punctuation is GO punctuation. Eliminate (B) and (C) because there is no reason to use a comma after *chemicals.* Eliminate (D) because there is no reason to separate the information with a dash, as *and weaker fragrances* is a continuation of the same idea from the first part of the sentence. The correct answer is (A).

2. **B**   Types of pronouns are changing in the answer choices, so this question is testing sentence structure. The pronoun refers back to *chemicals* and *fragrances*, so start by eliminating (C) because *whom* only refers to people. In choosing among the remaining options, consider the structure of the sentence, as *both of which* creates an incomplete idea, but *both of them* begins a complete idea. Use the Vertical Line Test to evaluate the parts of the sentence. Draw the line between *fragrances* and *both*. The first part of the sentence, *Commercial soaps are traditionally made with harsh, irritating chemicals and weaker fragrances* is a complete idea, and it's followed by a comma with no FANBOYS word. Therefore, the second part of the sentence must be incomplete, as two complete ideas cannot be connected with only a comma. Eliminate (A) and (D) because both make the second part of the sentence complete. Keep (B) because *both of which* makes the second part of the sentence incomplete. The correct answer is (B).

3. **D**   Punctuation is changing in the answer choices, so this question is testing how to set off unnecessary information. The phrase *especially World War I and World War II* is unnecessary information, so it should have commas, dashes, or parentheses both before and after it. There is a dash earlier in the sentence after *shortages during wartime*, so the answer must also include a dash. Eliminate (A), (B), and (C) because they don't include a dash. The correct answer is (D).

4. **D**   Punctuation is changing in the answer choices, so this question is testing STOP, HALF-STOP, and GO punctuation. Use the Vertical Line Test and identify the

ideas as complete or incomplete. The original sentences contains the FANBOYS word *but*, which connects the ideas but isn't part of them, so draw the vertical line through the word *but*. The first part of the sentence, *Today, some artisans have returned to the historic roots of the craft*, is a complete idea. The second part, *hobbyists are making their own soap out of natural ingredients through the cold process method*, is also a complete idea. To connect two complete ideas, STOP punctuation is needed. Either a semicolon or a comma plus FANBOYS is STOP punctuation, but a semicolon plus FANBOYS can't be used. Eliminate (A). A comma without the FANBOYS word is GO punctuation, so eliminate (B) and (C). Keep (D) because a comma plus a FANBOYS word is STOP punctuation. The correct answer is (D).

5. **C** Punctuation is changing in the answer choices, so this question is testing how to set off unnecessary information. The phrase *which utilizes an exothermic chemical reaction called saponification* is unnecessary information, so it should have commas, dashes, or parentheses both before and after it. There is a parenthesis later in the sentence after this phrase, so the answer must also include a parenthesis. Eliminate (B) and (D) because they don't include a parenthesis. Choice (A) has a parenthesis, but it uses a semicolon before that. The first part of the sentence, *Through the cold process method*, is an incomplete idea, so a semicolon doesn't work, as it can only link two complete ideas. Eliminate (A). The correct answer is (C).

6. **C** Punctuation is changing in the answer choices, so this question is testing STOP, HALF-STOP, and GO punctuation. Use the Vertical Line Test and identify the ideas as complete or incomplete. Draw the vertical line between the words *effects* and *As*. The first part of the sentence, *The cold process method requires knowledge of how to safely work with lye...since the base can have harmful effects*, is a complete idea. The second part, *As experts suggest using gloves, goggles, and protective clothing to ensure safety*, is an incomplete idea. To connect a complete idea to an incomplete idea, GO or HALF-STOP punctuation is needed. Eliminate (A) and (B) because they use STOP punctuation. Note that the remaining answers remove the word *as*, so reconsider the Vertical Line Test. Without the word *as*, the second part of the sentence becomes complete. In that case, a colon works, so keep (C). To connect two complete ideas, GO punctuation cannot be used, so eliminate (D). The correct answer is (C).

7. **A** Commas, parentheses, and dashes are changing in the answer choices, so this question is testing necessary versus unnecessary information. Keep (A) as it doesn't have any immediate error. For (B), parentheses should be used when the information is loosely related to the sentence's point but not necessary for the sentence's meaning. In this case, the phrase is not absolutely essential, but there is no reason to break the idea apart through the use of parentheses, so eliminate (B). Remember that there must be a good reason to use punctuation marks. Choice (C) adds a dash before the phrase *and packaged as soap*, but again, there is no real reason to take a pause in the sentence, as this part of the sentence is still part of the same idea as the first part of the sentence. Eliminate (C). Choice (D) makes an error by putting a comma before *and*, which can only be used when the sentence contains two complete ideas. Eliminate (D). The correct answer is (A).

8. **A** Punctuation is changing in the answer choices, so this question is testing how to set off unnecessary information. The phrase *or point when the lye and oils reach complete emulsification* is a definition of the word *"trace,"* so it should have commas both before and after it, as it is not essential to the meaning of the sentence. Eliminate (B), (C), and (D) because they all are missing a comma before the phrase. The correct answer is (A).

9. **D** Apostrophes are changing in the answer choices, so the question is testing apostrophe usage. When used with a noun, on the SAT, an apostrophe indicates possession. In this sentence, the *products* belong to *the company*, so an apostrophe is needed, and because *company* is singular, the apostrophe should be placed before the *s*. Eliminate (A) because it does not contain the apostrophe. The *products* do not own anything, so there should not be an apostrophe on that word. Eliminate (B) and (C). Keep (D) because it correctly places the apostrophe before the *s*. The correct answer is (D).

10. **A** Punctuation is changing in the answer choices, so this question is testing STOP, HALF-STOP, and GO punctuation. Use the Vertical Line Test and identify the ideas as complete or incomplete. Draw the vertical line between the words *criticism* and *from*. The first part of the sentence, *she sometimes faces criticism*, is a complete idea. The second part, *from other companies and consumers who doubt that the natural ingredients are worth the extra cost*, is an incomplete idea. To connect a complete idea to an incomplete idea, GO or HALF-STOP punctuation is needed. Keep (A) because no punctuation is GO punctuation. Keep (B) because a dash is

HALF-STOP punctuation. A semicolon is STOP punctuation, so eliminate (C). Keep (D) because a comma is GO punctuation. Next, consider that a comma or a dash can separate unnecessary information, which (B) and (D) both do. The source of the criticism is part of the point the author is trying to make, not unnecessary information, so there is no good reason to put a comma or a dash before that phrase. Eliminate (B) and (D). The correct answer is (A).

11. **D** Punctuation is changing in the answer choices, so this question is testing STOP, HALF-STOP, and GO punctuation. Use the Vertical Line Test and identify the ideas as complete or incomplete. Draw the vertical line between the words *products* and *such*. The first part of the sentence, *Despite this feedback, Chopra continues to develop her company and is not afraid to experiment with different combinations of ingredients in her products*, is a complete idea. The second part, *such as essential oils with strong fragrances, coffee beans, and walnut shells to exfoliate skin*, is an incomplete idea. To connect a complete idea to an incomplete idea, GO or HALF-STOP punctuation is needed. Both periods and semicolons are STOP punctuation, so eliminate (A) and (B). Keep (D) because it uses GO punctuation with the same wording. Consider (C): it adds some additional words. The phrase *included with these were essential oils with strong fragrances, coffee beans, and walnut shells to exfoliate skin* is a complete idea. Since (C) makes the second part complete, it does not work because it links two complete ideas with a comma. Eliminate (C). The correct answer is (D).

CHAPTER 10: WORDS DRILL ANSWERS

34. **B** Words are changing in the answer choices, so this question is testing precision. A pronoun can only be used if it is clear what the pronoun refers to. The word *there* seems to refer to *Scotland*, but the phrase "so much of there" is not a correct way to word this idea; eliminate (A). The words *the region* are precise, so keep (B). The pronoun *that* could refer to *the unearthing of a dinosaur bone* or *the discovery*, so the pronoun is not precise; eliminate (C). The pronoun *it* could refer to the *dinosaur bone* or the *fossil-rich site*; eliminate (D). *The region* is the most precise choice. The correct answer is (B).

35. **A** Vocabulary is changing in the answer choices, so this question is testing precision of word choice. Look for an answer choice with the correct comparison. The sentence says that *the fossils in Scotland were older than,* so the correct word should refer to something from the past. The sentence later says the fossils give *paleontologists another glimpse into life before humans.* Look for an answer that compares the fossils to something related to humans. Choice (A) compares the fossils to *the first human civilizations,* so keep (A). Choice (B) is not concise, and the meaning is clear without the phrase *the age of,* so eliminate it. Eliminate (C) because the phrase *those of* refers to what would be *fossils* of the first human civilizations, but the sentence already provides a clear meaning without this phrase, as it compares the age of the fossils to the age of the first human civilizations. Eliminate (D) because *that* does not clearly refer to some aspect of the human civilizations. The correct answer is (A).

36. **D** Vocabulary is changing in the answer choices, so this question is testing precision of word choice. Look for a word with a definition that is consistent with the other ideas in the sentence. The sentence says that a researcher *stumbled upon* the site and uses the adverb *barely* to describe something about it, so the correct word should mean "noticeable." Choice (A) has some support, but *understandable* relates more to knowledge than to being able to notice the site, so eliminate it. Choices (B) and (C) are similar in meaning, and neither works with the word *barely* that comes before, so eliminate (B) and (C). *Perceptible* means "noticeable," so keep (D). Choice (D) makes the meaning of the sentence most precise. The correct answer is (D).

37. **B** Vocabulary is changing in the answer choices, so this question is testing precision of word choice. Look for an answer choice with the correct comparison. The sentence compares *the features of the footprints* to something to do with *tide pools* or *tidal creatures,* so the correct word should refer to other features. Look for an answer that refers to features. Choice (A) compares the features to *tidal creatures,* which is not consistent, so eliminate (A). Choice (B) compares the features to *those of tide pools,* which could refer to *features.* Keep (B). Choices (C) and (D) compare the features to tide pools themselves, not the *features* of the tide pools, so they create a comparison error. Eliminate (C) and (D). The correct answer is (B).

38. **C** Transitions are changing in the answer choices, so this question is testing consistency of ideas. A transition must be consistent with the relationship between the ideas it connects. The sentence before the transition states that *The location of the*

track site on the island's coast made fieldwork challenging, as the team had to contend with the elements, and the sentence that starts with the transition states that *they couldn't use drones to capture overhead images because of the cold winds, and they also had to be constantly mindful of the tides as the rising water routinely flooded the track site.* The second sentence restates the previous idea in a more specific way, so eliminate (A) and (D), which both contain opposite-direction transitions. *Therefore* indicates a "cause-and-effect" relationship, and there is no relationship of this type referenced, so eliminate (B). *In other words* is a same-direction transition that is used for a restatement, so keep (C). The correct answer is (C).

39. **A** Words that come before a parenthetical phrase are changing in the answer choices, so this question is testing consistency with a modifier. The modifying phrase in the parentheses says *a group of dinosaurs known for its large size* and is describing something from earlier in the sentence. The underlined phrase must end with the term for this group of dinosaurs. Keep (A) because it ends with *sauropods.* Eliminate (B) and (D) because they both end with *sauropod tracks,* and the tracks are not *a group of dinosaurs.* Eliminate (C) because it ends with *site,* which is not *a group of dinosaurs.* The correct answer is (A).

40. **D** Verbs are changing in the answer choices, so this question is testing consistency of verbs. A verb must be consistent with its subject and with the other verbs in the sentence. The other verbs in the paragraph are *led* and *found,* which are in the past tense. To be consistent, the underlined verb must also be in the past tense. Eliminate (B) and (C) because they are not in past tense. The correct idiom is *known for.* The correct answer is (D).

41. **C** Pronouns are changing in the answer choices, so this question is testing consistency of pronouns. A pronoun must be consistent in number with the noun it refers to. The underlined pronoun refers to the noun *the stegosaurus,* which is singular. To be consistent, the underlined pronoun must also be singular. Eliminate (A), (B), and (D) because they contain the plural pronouns *those, we,* and *they.* Keep (C) because it contains the singular pronoun *it.* The correct answer is (C).

42. **B** Verbs are changing in the answer choices, so this question is testing consistency of verbs. A verb must be consistent with its subject and with the other verbs in the sentence. Start by identifying the subject, the person or thing encouraging something. The subject of the verb is *a wealth of new information,* which is singular.

To be consistent, the underlined verb must also be singular. Eliminate (A) because *have encouraged* is plural. Keep (B) because *encourages* and *gives* are singular. Eliminate (C) and (D) because they both contain the plural verb *give*. The correct answer is (B).

43. **B** Pronouns are changing in the answer choices, so this question is testing consistency of pronouns. A pronoun must be consistent in number with the noun it refers to. The underlined pronoun refers to the noun *Middle Jurassic species*. The word *species* could be either singular or plural, but look for other clues in the sentence. The sentence states that the *species have not been studied as well*, so because *have* is plural, *species* must be plural. Furthermore, the non-underlined part of the sentence refers to the species using the phrase *their fossils*. Therefore, to be consistent, the underlined pronoun must also be plural. Eliminate (A) and (C) because both contain singular pronouns. Keep (B) because *them* is plural and is consistent with *their fossils*. The pronouns *him and her* are singular, so eliminate (D). The correct answer is (B).

44. **C** Pronouns and nouns are changing in the answer choices, so this question is testing precision of word choice. Look for a word with a definition that is consistent with the other ideas in the sentence. The sentence says that *these findings* help someone or something *paint a clearer picture of the lives of dinosaurs*, so the correct word should refer to who is painting the picture. Eliminate (A) and (D) because *we* and *they* are not precise. Eliminate (B) because *ancient sauropods* are not clarifying the information. Keep (C) because *modern paleontologists* are clarifying the information. Choice (C) makes the meaning of the sentence most precise. The correct answer is (C).

CHAPTER 11: QUESTIONS DRILL ANSWERS

1. **B** Note the question! The question asks which choice *would best introduce the main point of the essay*, so it's testing consistency of ideas. Save this question for later, after reading the whole passage. Determine the subject of the passage and find the answer that is consistent with that idea. The paragraph says *Horror, Western, and Sci-Fi movies are made every year, but the number of movies produced in each genre fluctuates annually*. The rest of the passage continues this discussion of movie

genres. Eliminate (A) because *movie streaming* or *theaters* are not consistent with the main idea. Keep (B) because it focuses on *movie genres*, which is consistent with the main idea. Eliminate (C) because *drama* is not one of the genres mentioned. Eliminate (D) because *how films are made in Hollywood* is not consistent with *movie genres*. The correct answer is (B).

2. **A** Note the question! The question asks which choice *gives information consistent with the graph*, so it's testing consistency. Read the labels on the graph carefully, and look for an answer that is consistent with the information given in the graph. Choices (C) and (D) are not consistent with the figure since the number of *Zombie* and *Vampire* films has risen, so eliminate (C) and (D), respectively. Choice (B) is not consistent with the figure since the number of Vampire films has increased from around 15 to 40, which is not a six-fold increase, so eliminate (B). The graph does show that the number of Zombie films has increased six-fold since it goes from about 10 in the 1960s to nearly 60. The correct answer is (A).

3. **B** Note the question! The question asks which choice *would offer the most effective transition between the previous paragraph and the current one*, so it's testing consistency of ideas. Determine the subjects of the previous and current paragraphs and find the answer that is consistent with those ideas. The previous paragraph states that *the number of movies produced in each genre fluctuates annually* and *the number of Westerns* has not increased, while *the number of Zombie and Vampire movies has risen*. The current paragraph asks questions about that trend, like *Why should the number of Westerns have remained relatively low while the number of Zombie films has skyrocketed?* A consistent transition will link the trend and the discussion of the trend. Choice (A) is not consistent with either paragraph, so eliminate (A). Choice (B) mentions *trends,* and the phrase *invite us to try account for people's taste,* which is consistent with the questions in the paragraph, so keep (B). Choice (C) mentions *Zombie movies* but says that *people don't care*, which is not consistent with the information in the previous paragraph, so eliminate (C). Choice (D) mentions *zombies*, but not *Zombie movies*, so eliminate (D). The correct answer is (B).

4. **A** Note the question! The question asks whether a sentence should be deleted, so it's testing consistency. If the content of the underlined sentence is consistent with the ideas surrounding it, then it should be kept. The previous sentences state that *Westerns dominated the 1920s. Zombie films have dominated the 1990s and 2000s.*

The following sentence states that *The 1920s, for instance, was an American moment of crusade.* The sentence in question is consistent with the discussion of film genres and when they were popular, so the sentence should be kept; eliminate (C) and (D). Keep (A) because the sentence does provide *a logical transition.* Eliminate (B) because the sentence does not explain *why Westerns are now less popular than Zombie films are.* The correct answer is (A).

5. **C**   Note the question! The question asks which choice *best supports the idea in the previous sentence*, so it's testing consistency. Eliminate answers that are inconsistent with the previous sentence. The previous sentence states that *the 1920s, for instance, was an American moment of crusade.* Look for an answer choice that is consistent with and supports the idea of the 1920s being an American moment of crusade. Eliminate (A) because *the Catholic Church* and *1095* do not support America in the 1920s. Eliminate (B) because the *United States today* does not support the 1920s. Keep (C) because *the world, reeling from World War I, wanted justice among the outlaws* supports the 1920s being a moment of crusade. Eliminate (D) because it discusses what happened after the 1920s. The correct answer is (C).

6. **D**   Note the question! The question asks which choice *best maintains the style and tone of the passage*, so it's testing consistency. Eliminate answers that are inconsistent with the style and tone of the passage. The passage is written in a formal tone, so eliminate any answers that use slang or informal language. Eliminate (A) and (C) because *legit* and *being lit* are slang terms. Between (B) and (D), *brutality* is more consistent with the tone than *harshness*. The correct answer is (D).

7. **D**   Note the question! The question asks which choice would *most effectively conclude the sentence and the paragraph*, so it's testing consistency of ideas. Determine the subject of the sentence and the paragraph and find the answer that is consistent with that idea. The paragraph says *Zombie films show that we are not all that interested in that world* and that *the people around us, especially when viewed as a mass, can seem almost "dead."* The last sentence of the paragraph starts by saying *our private or online personalities have become so robust.* Eliminate (A) because *designing avatars* is not a contrast to *online personalities.* Eliminate (B) because *face-to-face conversations* being hard is not consistent with the main idea of the paragraph. Eliminate (C) because *addictions to…Internet devices* is not consistent

with the main idea of the paragraph. Keep (D) because *the real world* seeming *dull* is a contrast to *robust online personalities* and is consistent with *people around us* seeming *almost "dead."* The correct answer is (D).

8. **C**   Note the question! The question asks where sentence 2 should be placed, so it's testing consistency of ideas. The sentence must be consistent with the ideas that come both before and after it. Sentence 2 says that *Instead, we are interested in and suspicious of the people around us.* Therefore, that sentence must come after some mention of being *interested.* Sentence 3 says *we are not all that interested in that world.* Therefore, sentence 2 should follow sentence 3 and come before sentence 4. The correct answer is (C).

9. **C**   Note the question! The question asks how to effectively combine the underlined sentences, so it's testing precision and concision. Look for a sentence that is concise and maintains the meaning of the sentence. Eliminate (A) because it repeats the word *change*, which is not concise. Eliminate (B) because it repeats the word *it*, which is not concise. Keep (C) because it is concise, and the meaning is precise. Eliminate (D) because it is not as concise as (C). The correct answer is (C).

10. **D**   Note the question! The question asks whether a sentence should be added, so it's testing consistency. If the content of the new sentence is consistent with the ideas surrounding it, then it should be added. The paragraph discusses movie genres changing. The new sentence discusses the author's favorite Zombie film, so it is not consistent with the ideas in the text; the sentence should not be added. Eliminate (A) and (B). Eliminate (C) because there is no indication that the author's favorite movie is a *strange choice*, and the reason provided does not relate to the content of the passage. Keep (D) because it correctly states that *the essay as a whole is not primarily focused on the author's personal preferences.* The correct answer is (D).

11. **B**   Note the question! The question asks which choice *most effectively suggests that Westerns offer more than what they seem superficially to represent*, so it's testing consistency. Eliminate answers that are inconsistent with the purpose stated in the question. The sentence says *it is to say that these genres hold a lot more than their… entertainment value.* Look for an answer choice that is consistent with the idea that the films offer more than what they seem to represent. Eliminate (A), (C), and (D) because *bloodthirsty, wholesome,* and *engaging* do not suggest that there is more to the Western films than entertainment. Keep (B) because *mere* suggests the films are more than just entertainment. The correct answer is (B).

Chapter 13
Writing &
Language Drill

WRITING AND LANGUAGE DRILL

Questions 1–11 are based on the following passage.

A Little Pygmy Up

"When I last saw you, you were this tall," say aunts and grandmothers everywhere, as kids grow taller and taller. If you've ever thought that kids seem to be getting taller every generation, you may be right. Data from 1820 forward show that men from a large swath of **1** countries, with no exceptions, have grown in height, some by as much as 25 centimeters. The human species has, on the whole, grown taller since the earliest days of the species, whether from natural selection, improved health, or increased access to good food.

Median Male Height (cm) in Various Countries, 1820–2013

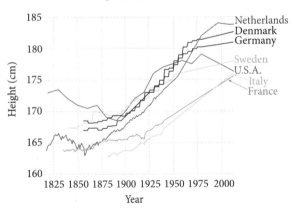

Source/Olson, Randy (2014): Historical median heights for various countries, 1818-2013. figshare. http://dx.doi.org/10.6084/m9.figshare.1066523

1

Which choice offers an accurate interpretation of information in the graph?

A) NO CHANGE

B) countries, particularly Italy and France, have grown in median height, while many others have shrunk by as much as 20 centimeters.

C) countries have all seen a growth in median height of over 15 centimeters.

D) countries, with the exception of the U.S.A., have grown in median height, some by as many as 20 centimeters.

In the discussion of human height, the pygmy populations of the equatorial rainforest regions of Africa have always been considered a curious outlier. In one pygmy population in Cameroon, the average male **2** gets up to only 150 cm, well below the averages for the European and American nations shown in the graph. A recent study from University of Pennsylvania professor Sarah Tishkoff, a leading **3** scholar, on African genetics, may have revealed the reason and raised some interesting questions besides.

2

A) NO CHANGE
B) scales the mountain to
C) climbs up to
D) reaches a height of

3

A) NO CHANGE
B) scholar, on African genetics
C) scholar; on African genetics
D) scholar on African genetics,

[1] The study documents the early-life factors that limit the height of the pygmy populations. [2] In children from the pygmy group Baka, infants are the same size as infants from other populations. **4** [3] A variety of environmental and genetic factors in each produced the slow growth, with a particular genetic variation in CISH. [4] This gene is linked to **5** resistances, to some equatorial diseases but may also account for the height particularities of these groups. **6**

4

At this point, the writer is considering adding the following information and adjusting the punctuation accordingly:

> but they grow at a slower rate than other infants, particularly during the first two years of life.

Should the writer make this addition here?

A) Yes, because it explains the pygmy data that is shown on the graph.

B) Yes, because it explains the distinction indicated in the first sentence of the paragraph.

C) No, because it suggests that pygmy mothers are not as caring as European mothers.

D) No, because it contradicts data in the previous paragraph that suggests human populations always grow taller.

5

A) NO CHANGE

B) resistances to

C) resistances to,

D) resistances: to

6

Where is the most logical place in this paragraph to add the following sentence?

> In a group like the Sua, however, the slowed growth is mainly prenatal—it occurs before the children are born.

A) After sentence 1

B) After sentence 2

C) After sentence 3

D) After sentence 4

The truly fascinating questions [7] that have emerged from this study and have related to intra-species evolution. It is well known in the scientific community that humans and baboons evolved from a common ancestor, but [8] it's less known that evolutionary factors may be at play within the relatively "young" human species as well. The study presents findings that [9] suggest that the Baka broke off from the Efé and Sua approximately 20,000 years ago, showing very significant evolutionary adaptation in the recent past. Africa is a particularly notable place because it has more genetic [10] distinction than any other continent. It is home to the pygmies, yes; [11] in this sense, it is also home to the Maasai and the Dinka, who are tall by any standard, and to the mixed populations that have resulted from many years of border crossing and European colonization.

Now we just need to figure out whether this information tells us that it's a small world after all, or if we're all one of a kind.

7

A) NO CHANGE

B) that have emerged from this study, in which they relate

C) to emerge from this study relate

D) to emerge from this study, they relate

8

A) NO CHANGE

B) its

C) they're

D) their

9

A) NO CHANGE

B) findings that suggest that it

C) findings that suggest that they

D) findings that are suggestive of its

10

A) NO CHANGE

B) relation

C) boundedness

D) diversity

11

A) NO CHANGE

B) nonetheless,

C) thus,

D) heretofore,

Questions 12–22 are based on the following passage.

B & O Cool Story

Because the people who would eventually found the United States were European, it should **12** be no surprise that the earliest population growth in the country took place on the Atlantic Coast. Some of the major population centers in the early **13** republic make obvious sense; Philadelphia and Boston, famed as the cities of Independence, and New York, renowned as the city of business and just about everything else. What may surprise us, however, is that in 1860, on the eve of the Civil War, the third-largest city in the United States was not Boston, Chicago, Los Angeles,

12

The writer wants to maintain an informative tone in the passage and avoid the appearance of mockery. Which choice best accomplishes this goal?

A) NO CHANGE

B) not blow your minds

C) not send us for a loop

D) be no big whoop

13

A) NO CHANGE

B) republic make obvious sense:

C) republic make obvious sense

D) republic—make obvious sense,

Atlanta, or Houston. The third-largest city in the United States at that time was Baltimore, **14** Maryland, though Baltimore today ranks 26th. In fact, even by 1880, Baltimore had slipped considerably, from third to sixth. In the meantime, three other cities—Boston, St. Louis, and Chicago—had assumed the third, fourth, and fifth spots, respectively. **15**

Populations of Major Cities in the United States, 1860–1900			
City	1860	1880	1900
New York	1,174,800	1,912,000	3,437,000
Philadelphia	565,500	847,000	1,294,000
Boston	177,800	363,000	561,000
Baltimore	212,400	332,000	509,000
Cincinnati	161,000	255,000	326,000
St. Louis	160,800	350,000	575,000
Chicago	109,300	503,000	1,698,000

Source/Bureau of the Census and Schatz, Phil: U.S. History. http://philschatz.com/us-history-book/contents/m50109.html

14

A) NO CHANGE
B) Baltimore, Maryland, which
C) Baltimore, Maryland. Baltimore
D) Baltimore, Maryland, and this city of Baltimore

15

The writer wants the information in the passage to reflect the information in the chart as accurately as possible. Given that goal and assuming that no other part of the sentence would not change, in what sequence should the three cities be named?

A) NO CHANGE
B) St. Louis, Chicago, Boston
C) Chicago, Boston, St. Louis
D) Chicago, St. Louis, Boston

[1] In some ways, Baltimore's relatively small population size today seems unremarkable. [2] For most people alive today, Baltimore **16** has been the home of a storied baseball team, and the fact that Chicago and St. Louis grew as much as they did in the late 1800s can be explained by a more general population shift to the West. [3] The more interesting question should point us in another direction: why did Baltimore have such a relatively large population in the second half of the nineteenth century? [4] Baltimore has always been ideally positioned for a robust shipping industry and **17** holy capable of handling lots of freight. [5] Located as it is near the Atlantic Ocean and directly on the Chesapeake Bay, Baltimore was a perfect channel for goods coming from Europe and moving to the interior of the country. **18**

16

Which choice most effectively completes the idea presented in this sentence and is consistent with the rest of the passage?

A) NO CHANGE

B) is a mere forty-five miles north of Washington, D.C.,

C) was reintroduced to the American public through a series of media portrayals,

D) has "always" been a relatively small city,

17

A) NO CHANGE

B) holy capable for

C) holey capable for

D) wholly capable of

18

To improve the organization and clarity of this paragraph, the writer wants to add the following sentence.

The answer is relatively simple and comes down to something fundamental: shipping.

The sentence would most logically be placed after

A) sentence 1.

B) sentence 2.

C) sentence 3.

D) sentence 4.

19 Fore it to come to the for in population, however, Baltimore also had to do something pioneering, and that something came with the growth of railroads. By the 1820s, Baltimore's prominence as a port was starting to decline after the opening and success of the Erie Canal, which enabled cargo **20** to travel by water from New York City to the Great Lakes, thus enabling easier delivery to the Midwest. In response, Baltimore officials pushed the development of a new and unknown technology, railroading, as a way to move goods through Baltimore to cities in the West, whether those cities had waterways or not.

The result of citizens' petitions and politicians' grand plans **21** have been the Baltimore and Ohio, or B&O, Railroad, which began operations in the late 1820s. While the B&O did have its share of struggles, it was nonetheless be one of the most powerful rail lines in the country for much of the nineteenth century. And it helped Baltimore to maintain its prominence at a time when the size of a city was largely a function of **22** how connected that city was to other places.

19
A) NO CHANGE
B) For it to come to the four
C) For it to come to the for
D) For it to come to the fore

20
A) NO CHANGE
B) traveling by
C) to travel in
D) traveling through

21
A) NO CHANGE
B) were
C) was
D) is

22
Which choice most effectively concludes the sentence and paragraph?
A) NO CHANGE
B) how many railroad lines and canals it had.
C) the number of people who thought of it as a large city.
D) a strong connection to both diversity and European roots.

Chapter 14
Writing &
Language Drill:
Answers and
Explanations

A LITTLE PYGMY UP: ANSWERS AND EXPLANATIONS

1. **D**   Use POE and the graph provided. Choice (A) can be disproven by the graph since no country has seen a growth of 25 cm in median male height. Choice (B) is not supported by the graph. Other countries (like the Netherlands) have experienced more growth in male height than Italy and France have. Furthermore, *many others* have not *shrunk* by as much as 20 cm. Choice (C) should be eliminated because not all countries saw a growth in median height of *over 15 cm* (in particular, the United States actually decreased) Therefore, by POE, the correct answer is (D), which is supported by the graph.

2. **D**   This sentence is about average male height, not the act of actually climbing up a mountain or another object. Eliminate (B) and (C). Choice (A) is not as precise as (D). Therefore, (D) is the best option since it best expresses the intended meaning of the sentence.

3. **D**   Notice the punctuation is changing in the answer choices. Since (C) contains a semicolon, check to see if both parts of the sentence are complete ideas. In this case, the first part (*A recent…scholar*) is incomplete, so a semicolon would be incorrect. Eliminate (C). The remaining answer choices vary the number and placement of the comma(s). The phrase *a leading scholar on African genetics* should be surrounded by commas since this information is unnecessary, which makes (D) the correct answer.

4. **B**   The suggested addition is necessary since it would add relevant details to the sentence. Eliminate (C) and (D). The graph does not contain data on the pygmy populations, so (A) is incorrect. The first sentence of this paragraph mentions that the study indicates that *early-life factors…limit the height of pygmy populations*. Thus, the additional information helps to explain the claim made in the beginning of this paragraph. Choice (B) provides the best reason for the writer to make this addition.

5. **B**   Notice the punctuation is changing in the answer choices. Since (D) contains a colon, check to see if the first part of the sentence is a complete idea. Technically, it is, but this represents an exception to the rule—you need to make sure that the rest of the sentence still makes sense. In this case, because the split occurs across an idiomatic phrase (*resistances to*), punctuation should be avoided in order to ensure that the flow of the sentence is not interrupted. This eliminates (A), (C), and (D) and makes (B) the correct answer.

6. **B** Notice the question. It is asking you to determine the most logical place for the sentence *In a group like the Sua, however, the slowed growth is mainly prenatal—it occurs before the children are born.* The *however* signals that this sentence provides a contrast to a previous sentence regarding the concept of *slowed growth.* Sentence 2 sets up this contrast by stating that the infants from the pygmy group Baka are the same size as normal infants. The new sentence, therefore, follows logically after sentence 2, so (B) is the correct answer.

7. **C** As written, this sentence is not a complete thought. There is no main verb in this sentence. Choices (B) and (D) do not fix this error. This makes (C) the only option. If you have trouble seeing the original error, try eliminating the filler-phrase *that have emerged from this study* to more easily identify the subject (*questions*) in order to see that a main verb (*relate*) is needed.

8. **A** Notice that the pronouns are changing in the answer choices. Since a possessive pronoun is not needed, (B) and (D) are incorrect. To see if the pronoun and verb should be singular or plural, look at the non-underlined portion. The sentence begins with *It is common knowledge….* In order to make the second part of the sentence consistent with the first, the correct answer is (A)—no change is necessary.

9. **A** Notice that the pronouns are changing in the answer choices. Since a possessive pronoun is not needed, (D) is incorrect. Of the remaining answer choices, only (A) provides clarity to the sentence. The *it* used in (B) could refer back to *the study* while the word *they* in (C) could refer back to *findings.* Neither of those is what broke off from the Efé and Sua. Thus, the correct answer is (A).

10. **D** Since all the answer choices mean essentially the same thing, choose the one that expresses the intended meaning of the sentence. In this case, the writer is conveying the idea that Africa has more genetic differences than any other continent. The only choice that would work in this context is (D). The remaining options do not mean "differences" in this context and, therefore, are not as precise as *diversity.*

11. **B** Notice that the transition word is changing in each answer choice. Since (A) and (C) have the same meaning, both can be eliminated since there can't be two right answers. Choice (D) means "before now," which is not appropriate in context. The writer is trying to set up a contrast—that the continent of Africa is home not only to the pygmies but also to many other populations as well. The only option that provides a contrast is (B).

B&O COOL STORY: ANSWERS AND EXPLANATIONS

12. **A** The question signals that you are looking for the answer choice that has a *sense of general interest* and will *avoid the appearance of mockery.* Choice (A) conveys that the location of population growth should be unsurprising given the context. It is informative and neutral in tone, so keep it. Choice (B) could seem to be mocking the reader, as it suggests the reader might be surprised but shouldn't be. Eliminate it. Choices (C) and (D) are both pretty informal; their casual tone is inconsistent with the neutral, informative tone of the passage. Eliminate them and choose (A).

13. **B** Choice (A) contains STOP punctuation, so check to see whether there are complete ideas on both sides of the semicolon. What follows the semicolon is not a complete idea, so eliminate (A). Choice (B) features a colon, which can be used to connect a complete idea to an incomplete idea that provides an example or illustration of the complete idea it follows. Keep (B). Choice (C) removes the colon, when some punctuation is needed to connect the ideas. Choice (D) adds an unnecessary dash. Eliminate (C) and (D) and choose (B).

14. **B** Choices (A), (C), and (D) all feature repetition of the word *Baltimore*, while (B) does not. Since that suggests that the question is testing concision, check to see whether (B) works. It effectively and correctly links the two ideas, so (B), the most concise answer, is correct.

15. **C** The writer wants this sentence to reflect the information in the chart as accurately as possible. The order in which the cities are listed in (A) is the order in which they appear in the "City" column. This is a trap answer though, because the *respectively* in the sentence tells us the cities should be listed from largest to smallest. If you scan down the column headed "1880," you can see that Chicago had a bigger population in that year than St. Louis or Boston. Eliminate (A) and (B) as they do not list Chicago first. Check to see that Boston had a larger population than St. Louis. It did, so eliminate (D). The correct answer is (C).

16. **D** The sentence that begins the second paragraph states that *Baltimore's relatively small population size today seems unremarkable.* Choices (A), (B), and (C) all provide information about Baltimore that may be familiar to people, but none of them address the size of Baltimore's population. Choice (D) does address population size, which connects both to the paragraph as a whole and to the information

about the growth in Chicago and St. Louis that is discussed in the rest of the sentence. Choose (D).

17. **D** The answer choices feature variations of the word *holy*. Look at the rest of the sentence to see what sense of the word you need. This paragraph is explaining how well-suited Baltimore is for shipping, so this sentence requires a word that means something like *very* or *entirely*. Choices (A) and (B) use *holy*, which means *sacred* and does not make sense in this context. Eliminate (A) and (B). Choice (C) uses *holey*, which means *having a lot of holes*; eliminate (C). Choice (D) uses *wholly*, which means *entirely*. The correct answer is (D).

18. **C** The sentence to be inserted begins with *The answer is*, which suggests that the sentence should be inserted after a question has been posed. Sentence 3 provides the *more interesting question* that the rest of the paragraph works to answer. Eliminate (A) and (B) since it doesn't make sense to answer a question that hasn't been asked yet. Inserting the new sentence between sentence 3 and the rest of the paragraph provides a concise answer that links the question that is posed and the details that explain the answer. Eliminate (D) and choose (C).

19. **D** The first and last words are changing in these answer choices. Eliminate (A), since it begins with *fore* and the phrase needs to begin with the preposition *for*. The paragraph is talking about what was required for Baltimore to get a big boost in population, so the expression must mean something like *become prominent* or *really stand out*. The word *fore* means *toward the front*, so the expression *come to the fore* means *come to the front*. Neither *four* nor *for* makes sense in the expression. Eliminate (B) and (C) and choose (D).

20. **A** Look at the differences in the answer choices and consider whether you need *to travel* or *traveling* to follow *which enabled cargo*. *To travel* completes the phrase correctly, so eliminate (B) and (D). Compare (A) and (C) and see which preposition completes the idea better. Choice (A) has the sense of traveling by means of water, while (C) has the sense of moving through the water. Choice (A) fits the context of the paragraph better, since the point is that linked bodies of water allowed cargo to be moved easily. Eliminate (C) and choose (A).

21.   **C**   Verbs are changing in the answer choices. Look to see whether you need a singular or plural verb. The subject of the sentence is *result*, which is singular. Eliminate (A) and (B). The B&O began running in the 1820s, so the past tense makes sense. Eliminate (D) and choose (C).

22.   **A**   Choices (C) and (D) feature ideas that are touched on in the passage, but neither highlights the main idea of the passage overall or fits well with the focus on railroads in the last two paragraphs. Eliminate them. Choice (B) mentions rail lines explicitly, but look carefully at (A). Its reference to *how connected a city was to other places* encompasses the means of connection (the rail lines and shipping) while emphasizing why those means were important (because they connected the city to other places). Eliminate (B) and choose (A).

Part IV
Math

Chapter 15
Introduction to
SAT Math

INTRODUCTION

If you're aiming for the highest score on the SAT, you probably already have a broad range of math skills. In fact, you probably already know the math required to answer almost every question on the typical SAT Math section. So why aren't you already scoring an 800?

You may be surprised to learn that what's holding you back is *not* content knowledge. Students who score in the high 600s have roughly the same amount of mathematical knowledge as those who score an 800. Knowing more math is not the key—you've likely already learned almost every concept that's on the Math Test.

The problem is that on the SAT, the questions are not so much difficult as they are hard to do under timed conditions. They can also contain tricky trap answers. The SAT is not a fair test; in fact, the test writers are out to get you! They restrict your time, then they expect you to do all sorts of time-consuming algebraic manipulation. They make you feel rushed and then give you answers you may get if you calculated something incorrectly or misread the question. They even take away your calculator on one section! To improve your score, you'll need to do the following four things:

- Learn when to use your calculator and how to get along without it.
- Learn to avoid traps and eliminate careless errors.
- Become familiar with the types of questions that appear on the SAT.
- Learn our strategies for recognizing and defeating these questions.

In this chapter, we'll focus on the first two of these points; in later chapters, we'll cover the other two.

AVOIDING TRAPS AND CARELESS ERRORS

If you want to score a 750 or higher on the Math section, you can't afford to make *any* careless errors. The first thing to do is slow down! This might seem counterintuitive. In order to score an 800, you must answer every single Math question correctly. But it doesn't matter if you get all the hardest questions right if you throw it all away on a few silly mistakes on the easier questions. Set a goal *right now* to avoid careless mistakes from here on.

To avoid careless mistakes, burn the following acronym into your brain: RTFQ. This stands for Read The Final Question. Consider the following question:

12

At what point (x, y) does the graph of $2y - x = 6$ intersect the x-axis in the xy-plane?

A) $(0, 3)$

B) $(0, 6)$

C) $(-6, 0)$

D) $(3, 0)$

This is a fairly typical SAT Math question. The majority of high scorers will expect to get it right. However, did you catch the trap? Read the question one more time. Which intercept are you looking for? Your math classes in high school have likely conditioned you to put this equation into the format $y = mx + b$, where b represents the y-intercept. If you did not read the question carefully and simply converted the equation to this format, you could easily fall for (A). However, the question is asking for the coordinates when $y = 0$. RTFQ! Slow down. Take a few extra seconds between reading this question and starting to solve it. Make sure you know exactly what you are looking for.

A closely related skill is Process of Elimination (POE). Focus on the word "process." This implies an action on your part. POE is not something that occurs in your head. You have a pencil; make sure that you use it to cross off wrong answers. Let's consider the above problem one more time. Assume that you read the question carefully and you caught that it was about the x-intercept. Use POE to cross off any answer choices that represent y-intercepts:

> **RTFQ and Word Problems**
> RTFQ is even more important on word problems, which may contain a lot of unnecessary information. By starting with the final question, you will know exactly what you are looking for. See the Word Problems chapter for more on this idea.

12

At what point (x, y) does the graph of $2y - x = 6$ intersect the
x-axis in the xy-plane?

A) (0, 3)

B) (0, 6)

C) (−6, 0)

D) (3, 0)

Notice how this simple technique allows you to avoid falling for the obvious traps. However, there are some less obvious traps as well. Choice (D) has the right y-coordinate, but this point is not even on this line. Does $2(0) - 3 = 6$? No, it doesn't, but $2(3) - 0 = 6$. Choice (D) is one you might get if you mixed up the x- and y-coordinates. Get rid of this trap as well, and you're left with only one answer.

12

At what point (x, y) does the graph of $2y - x = 6$ intersect the
x-axis in the xy-plane?

A) (0, 3)

B) (0, 6)

C) (−6, 0)

D) (3, 0)

The moral of the story is that the SAT is full of traps. Making sure to RTFQ and using your pencil to cross of bad answer choices can improve your score right now, just by helping you avoid careless mistakes.

Try the following questions, chock-full of typical, nasty SAT traps. To get the most out of the drill, don't just do the questions; instead, see if you can spot the traps in the questions and answers. When you're done, check out each explanation of how to crack it. Let's dive in.

13

The population of a certain town increased by 20% in one year. The following year, the town's population decreased by 20%. What was the net effect on the town's population over two years?

A) It increased by 4%.

B) It was unchanged.

C) It decreased by 4%.

D) It decreased by 10%.

Here's How to Crack It

The main trap answer in this question is (B). Many students will be tempted to think that the 20% increase is cancelled out by the 20% decrease. This just goes to show that on the SAT, if you arrive at an answer by simply thinking for a few seconds, that answer is probably wrong. To see why, use some real numbers. Let's say the population was originally 100. A year later, it will be 20% higher, or 120. The population then decreases by 20%, so take 20% of 120 and subtract by the total: 120 − (0.20)(120) = 96. The population decreased by 4%, so the correct answer is (C).

27

An exponential function is graphed in the xy-plane. If the graph of the function has a y-intercept of 15 and the function is always increasing, which of the following could be the equation of the function?

A) $-15(0.80)^x$

B) $-15(1.20)^x$

C) $15(0.80)^x$

D) $15(1.20)^x$

Here's How to Crack It

Without a good understanding of exponential functions, it is easy to look at the answers and assume that answers with positive 15 are the ones that are increasing. While that is not necessarily true, it's a good bet that the answer in (A) is not increasing, since it has a negative coefficient and a smaller value in the parentheses. After eliminating (A), use your knowledge of intercepts to determine which equation has a *y*-intercept of 15. This happens when *x* = 0, as an exponent of 0 makes any base equal 1. You can try it on your calculator for this question if you forget that. Choice (B) has a *y*-intercept of −15, so eliminate that too. If *x* was 1 instead of 0, (C) would decrease and (D) would increase, so the correct answer is (D). We'll cover a bit more on exponential growth in the Word Problems chapter.

16

Don's Travel Expenses

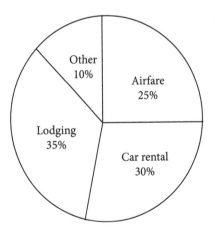

The pie chart above shows how Don spent $360 on a recent business trip. The amount Don spent on car rental was only a portion of the total cost of the car rental, because he shared the cost of the car equally with three other people. What was the total cost of the car rental?

A) $108

B) $270

C) $324

D) $432

Here's How to Crack It

To find what Don spent on car rental, take 30% of $360: (0.30)($360) = $108. Notice that this number is (A). Partial answers often appear on the SAT. To find the correct answer, we need to multiply by four, because Don shared with three other people, so (4)($108) = $432, and the correct answer is (D). The most common mistake on this question is to multiply by three, which would lead you to pick (C). Watch out for traps; they're everywhere!

———————————○———————————

Notice that the last few problems were accompanied by calculator symbols. That means they are likely to be found in Section 4, where calculator use is permitted. To get you acclimated to test conditions as you work through this book, use the calculator only on those questions that have the appropriate calculator symbol. The next one doesn't have a calculator symbol, so make sure to work through it with your pencil as your only tool.

———————————○———————————

14

$$x^2 + y^2 = 360$$

$$y = -3x$$

If (x, y) is a solution to the system of equations above, what is the value of y^2 ?

A) −18

B) 6

C) 36

D) 324

Here's How to Crack It

First of all, you can eliminate (A) before doing any work—a squared term cannot give you a negative value unless you are dealing with imaginary numbers. One way to solve this is to square both sides of the second equation, so it becomes $y^2 = 9x^2$. Be careful when squaring this term to make sure you get the correct coefficient. You could solve this equation for y^2, but you get a messy fraction. You are less likely to make an error if you

Designed To Do You Wrong

Notice that (A) gives a value for y and (B) gives a possible value for x. The wrong answers don't come out of nowhere—they are answers you'd get if you miscalculated or solved for the wrong quantity.

plug the value for y^2 into the first equation to get $x^2 + 9x^2 = 360$, or $10x^2 = 360$. Therefore, $x^2 = 36$. Don't pick (C) just yet, though! Remember to RTFQ! You are solving for y^2, and $36 + y^2 = 360$, so $y^2 = 324$. The correct answer is (D).

9

If j is any integer such that $4 < \sqrt{j} < 9$, what is the difference between the largest and smallest possible values of j ?

A)   1

B)   3

C)   63

D)   65

Here's How to Crack It

First, square each element of the inequality to get $16 < j < 81$. You may be tempted to simply subtract here: $81 - 16 = 65$. But j is an integer that is *between* these values, so the largest and smallest values for j are 80 and 17, respectively. Therefore, $80 - 17 = 63$, and the correct answer is (C). If you didn't square the inequality, you may have picked (B). If you took the positive square root of the inequality, you may have chosen (A).

TIME MANAGEMENT

You might be wondering at this point how you are supposed to incorporate this advice. Slow down! Use your pencil more! You may think that these techniques will leave you with less precious time for those difficult Math questions. However, consider how little time it will actually take to cross off incorrect answer choices with your pencil. If you eliminate incorrect answer choices immediately as they are identified, the time spent is negligible. Reading the Final Question can also seem more time-consuming than skimming the question quickly and beginning work as soon as possible, but, in reality, reading each question carefully and looking for traps often saves time. Students who do this work each problem more efficiently: they understand the question more quickly and are able to apply smart strategies without losing precious seconds rereading each problem. Time management is certainly important. Following are a few techniques you can use to maximize your time.

Order of Difficulty: It's Personal

Why should a high-scoring student care about the difficulty level of a question on the SAT Math sections? If you've got the math skills to do all—or at least, almost all—of the questions on the SAT Math sections, you may think the best approach for you is to dive straight in and do the questions in order. That's not necessarily the best approach, though.

The questions on the Math sections are presented in a loose Order of Difficulty (OOD), so the easier questions tend to be earlier in a section, and the harder questions tend to be later. However, just because the test writers think a question is easy (or hard) doesn't mean it's easy (or hard) *for you*. It's possible you will find the last question on a section to be surprisingly easy; conversely, you may find one in the middle to be excruciatingly difficult. For what it's worth, we have numbered the math problems that you'll encounter throughout this part of the book to correspond with where they'd approximately appear on the test. There are 38 questions on the calculator portion and 20 on the no-calculator portion, so our numbering should give you a good gauge of how POOD can be of benefit to you.

So, remember to use Personal Order of Difficulty (POOD). To maximize your efficiency, don't linger too long on any one question. Do every question that you understand immediately. If you're not sure how to work a question, or if it just seems like it will be too time-consuming, skip it for now.

Once you have reached the end of the section, go back to the ones you skipped. You will now have more time to decipher their meaning and work through to the answer without worrying about other questions that you haven't gotten to yet. Consider the following scenarios for solving for *x*.

1. $x + 4 > 7$

2. $2x = 8$

3. $x^3 + 3x^2 + 3x + 1 = 0$

4. $\dfrac{x}{4} = \dfrac{3}{5}$

Assume that you have poorly managed your time and you only have two minutes to work these four questions. What would be the advantage of passing over question 3? Perhaps you could solve it if you had enough time. However, compared to the other three questions, it is much more challenging and time-consuming. If you worked questions 1, 2, and 4, you could then use all of the remaining time you had to puzzle out question 3. If you allowed yourself to get bogged down in solving question 3, you might not have any time left to answer question 4.

Using POOD has two major advantages. First, you will be less likely to either skip or have to rush through easier questions because you wasted too much time on hard ones. Second, since this is a timed test, longer or harder problems can cause your anxiety to build, which might affect your performance on other questions. Saving those tough questions for last will allow you to work more smoothly, efficiently, and confidently through the section.

A NOTE ON CALCULATORS

Most common calculators are allowed on Section 4 of the SAT. Some exceptions include

- Laptops
- Calculators with a QWERTY keyboard
- Cell-phone calculators

If you aren't sure whether your calculator is allowed, check the College Board website (www.sat.collegeboard.org and click on "Test Day Checklist").

Your calculator can definitely come in handy for complicated calculations in Section 4; to be efficient on the test, you'll want to make the best use of it. But be careful! Some questions are designed with "calculator traps" in mind—careless errors the test writers know you might make when you just dive into a problem with your calculator.

5

Given the function $f(x) = 5x^2 - x - 7$, what is $f(-4)$?

A) −91

B) −83

C) 69

D) 77

This problem can be solved manually or with the calculator—whichever you prefer! But if you use a calculator, be careful with that (–4). What you punch into your calculator should look something like this:

$$5(-4)^2 - (-4) - 7$$

When working with negative numbers or fractions, make doubly sure that you use parentheses. If you don't, a lot of weird stuff can happen, and unfortunately all of the weird, wrong stuff that can happen is reflected in the wrong answer choices. If you ran this equation and found 77, (D), you got the right answer. If not, go back and figure out where you made your calculator mistake.

Types of Calculators

Throughout the rest of the math chapters, we will discuss how to use your calculator when it is allowed and what to do when you can't use it. We recommend you make sure your calculator is acceptable for use on the test and that it can do the following:

- handle positive, negative, and fractional exponents
- use parentheses
- graph functions
- convert fractions to decimals, and vice versa
- change a linear equation into $y = mx + b$ format

When calculator use is allowed, use it as needed to avoid careless mistakes, but use it wisely. Set up the problem on paper first, and be careful with negative numbers, fractions, and parentheses.

WORKING SMARTER

The techniques and strategies in this book are not that hard to learn, but they will not be second nature to you. Make sure that you focus on putting them into practice. Your goal is to internalize every strategy in this book. When you have internalized a concept, you no longer consciously think about what to do. You simply do it. Think about some of the equations in Example 4 above. Were you able to look at some of them and immediately know what the answer was without consciously thinking about the math? If so, then you have successfully internalized the concepts necessary to manipulate basic equations when solving for x. Test prep is no different!

Successfully incorporating these techniques requires two things: practice and review. Many of the techniques you will learn from these pages may initially seem awkward. You may even ask yourself why you should try something new if you can already solve the problem another way. This is a valid question; however, at its core, it reveals the distinction between a technique and content knowledge. A technique is a transferable skill that you can use on a variety of questions. Content knowledge, while certainly useful, is not necessarily equally applicable to all test questions. Techniques are.

Mastering new skills requires practice. Think about learning a new sport. Your coach explains how to perform an action, such as spiking a volleyball or making a lay-up. You easily comprehend what is being said. "No problem," you think. However, there is a big difference between understanding a concept and having the necessary coordination to complete it. This analogy is comparable to testing techniques. Much of what you read in this book will seem easy, such as using POE. Only practice, however, will make crossing off wrong answers *every time* second nature to you.

The second reason you should try something different is more pragmatic: if you could hit your goal score already, you wouldn't be reading this book! Do not merely skip to the practice questions and try to work them the old way. Even if you think your way is easier, practice the techniques. Remember that working many practice problems will reinforce all the techniques you currently use. This includes bad habits. Practicing math problems without attempting anything new will never improve your score. It is often said that insanity is doing the same thing over and over again but expecting different results. Do not drive yourself crazy with meaningless practice. Apply what you learn in these pages to every single question you work. You will be pleased with the results.

Finally, review your work. Do not simply tally up your points and pat yourself on the back. Every question missed is a learning opportunity. Ask yourself what happened. Did you have the necessary content knowledge? Did you miss an opportunity to use a new technique? Did you rush and miss a keyword? Did you not correctly apply POE? For every problem, you can identify a reason that you missed it. Over time, you will begin to see patterns emerging. For example, you might notice that you tend to rush through all algebra problems and therefore make more careless errors. The beauty of test prep is once you know what you are doing wrong, that problem will vanish. You will be on guard against making the same mistakes in the future.

Summary

- Be on the lookout for trap answers on the SAT and eliminate them when you find them.

- Read each question carefully to understand what it is asking you to do.

- Slow down and use your pencil to avoid careless errors.

- Use your Personal Order of Difficulty to ensure efficiency. Save for last questions that you don't understand or that seem time-consuming.

- When calculator use is allowed, make sure you are still setting the problem up on paper first. Only use the calculator as a last step, when it is necessary to avoid calculation errors.

- Practice all the new strategies in this book until you can use them well. Review your work to learn from any mistakes that you make.

Chapter 16
Algebra, Coordinate Geometry, and Functions

INTRODUCTION

This chapter will focus on the fundamental question types of the SAT Math sections. While there are many legitimate shortcuts that can be made and will be discussed below, ultimately you will simply need to solve many of the questions on the SAT. This chapter will begin with a discussion of the more advanced algebra concepts that appear throughout the SAT. Next, we will discuss functions and the many ways that they can be presented on the SAT. Finally, the chapter will include some drills where you can hone the skills you learned from this chapter.

SAT ALGEBRA

If you are aiming for a top score on the SAT Math sections, you're likely already a pro at algebra. However, SAT algebra is not the same as school algebra. As we discussed already, it is important to Read the Final Question to avoid careless mistakes. In the following questions, we'll look at a few ways in which the SAT makes algebra more complicated than it may be in school.

SOLVING

Some questions on the SAT will require you to use algebraic manipulation to solve equations. Operations done to one side of the equation need to also be performed on the other side of the equation. You have probably done this a lot in math class, so we will focus on some of the strange ways College Board might present solving questions.

Let's look an example of a typical "isolate the variable" question.

6

The electric field inside a spherical shell can be calculated using the equation $E = \dfrac{kqr}{R^3}$, which relates the variables of electric field (E), charge (q), distance from the center of the sphere to the charge (r), and radius of the sphere (R) to one another and to a constant (k). Which of the following expressions best describes how to find the charge (q) that is necessary to create an electric field in a given system?

A) $q = \dfrac{Ekr}{R^3}$

B) $q = \dfrac{ER^3}{kr}$

C) $q = \dfrac{kr}{ER^3}$

D) $q = \dfrac{Ekr}{kR^3}$

Here's How to Crack It

Don't waste time figuring out what all these variables mean. Read the Final Question to see that it asks you to rewrite the expression in terms of charge (the variable q). In order to isolate q on one side of the equation, start by multiplying both sides of the equation by the denominator on the right side: $ER^3 = kqr$. Next, divide both sides of the equation by k and r: $q = \dfrac{ER^3}{kr}$, which matches (B).

SYSTEMS OF EQUATIONS AND INEQUALITIES

The SAT presents systems of equations and inequalities in tricky ways. You will need to be able to recognize what the problems are actually asking for, and use that knowledge to find the best approach for solving the equation.

Let's look at a problem that asks you to work with a system of inequalities.

17

Which of the following accurately defines all possible values of $a - b$ if $5 \leq a \leq 17$ and $9 \leq b \leq 35$?

A) $-30 \leq a - b \leq 8$

B) $-18 \leq a - b \leq -4$

C) $-8 \leq a - b \leq 30$

D) $13 \leq a - b \leq 18$

Here's How to Crack It

If a problem asked you to find all the possible values of $a + b$, you could simply stack and add the inequalities. However, when a problem asks you to subtract, multiply, or divide inequalities, you need to test *each end* of the possible ranges against one another. For example, the low end of the a range (5) minus the low end of the b range (9) is −4, while the low end of the a range (5) minus the high end of the b range (35) is −30. Also, the high end of the a range (17) minus the low end of the b range (9) is 8, while the high end of the a range (17) minus the high end of the b range (35) is −18. Use the highest and lowest numbers you calculated as the ends of the range for $a - b$: $-30 \leq a - b \leq 8$, which matches (A).

Your work for this problem might look like this:

a	b	$a - b$
5	9	−4
5	35	−30
17	9	8
17	35	−18

When a problem presents simultaneous equations, be sure to note what the question is asking for (RTFQ) and find the fastest way to get there.

Equations are like balanced scales, so you can add them together or subtract one from the other. Sometimes, though, you will have to manipulate one or both equations first to get the desired outcome. Let's look at such a question.

19

$$-4a + 2b = 10$$
$$8a + 3b = 29$$

If (a, b) is the solution to the system of equations shown above, what is the value of a ?

A) 0

B) 1

C) 4

D) 7

Here's How to Crack It

You can use various methods to solve a question like this: you could solve one equation for a, then substitute the value into the other equation. Alternatively, you can look for a way to change the equations so that they will stack and add to eliminate a variable. In this case, you could multiply the first equation by 2, then stack and add the equations, like this:

$$\begin{array}{r} -8a + 4b = 20 \\ +\ \ 8a + 3b = 29 \\ \hline 7b = 49 \end{array}$$

Now solve to find that $b = 7$, and substitute that value into one of the original equations: $8a + 3(7) = 29$, so $8a + 21 = 29$, $8a = 8$, and $a = 1$, (B).

Another way College Board will test simultaneous equations is to reference the number of solutions a system has. For instance, if a system of linear equations has *infinite solutions*, then the equations are identical (they represent the same line). On the other hand, if a system of linear equations has *no solutions*, then the lines represented are parallel (they have equal slopes).

Let's look at some examples.

7

$$\frac{y-5}{4} = x$$
$$kx - 3y = -15$$

If the system of equations above has infinitely many solutions, what is the value of the constant k ?

A) 1

B) 4

C) 12

D) 16

Here's How to Crack It

Since the problem specifies that the system of equations has *infinitely many solutions*, the equations represent the same line and are essentially identical. Start by putting both equations into the slope-intercept form: $\frac{y-5}{4} = x$ becomes $y = 4x + 5$, while $kx - 3y = -15$ becomes $y = \frac{k}{3}x + 5$. Since these equations must be identical, $\frac{k}{3}$ must equal 4, so $k = 12$, which matches (C).

Now let's try a question in which a system of equations has *no solution*.

10

$$\frac{1}{3}x - \frac{7}{9}y = 2$$

$$36 - tx = -14y$$

Consider the system of linear equations above, in which t is a constant. If the system has no solutions, what is the value of t?

A) −6

B) $\dfrac{3}{14}$

C) $\dfrac{3}{7}$

D) 6

Here's How to Crack It

Since the problem states that the system has *no solutions,* the equations represent parallel lines (lines with the same slope but different y-intercepts). Start by putting both equations into the slope-intercept form. Clear the fractions in the first equation by multiplying both sides by 9: $\frac{1}{3}x - \frac{7}{9}y = 2$ becomes $3x - 7y = 18$, or $y = \frac{3}{7}x - \frac{18}{7}$. The second equation becomes $y = \frac{t}{14}x - \frac{36}{14}$. Since these equations have the same slope, $\frac{t}{14}$ must equal $\frac{3}{7}$, so $t = 6$, which matches (D).

Another kind of system of equations question may give you a line and an equation that is not linear and ask you for the number of solutions. Here's one to try.

19

$$y = 3x + 2$$
$$y = 4x^2 - 4x + 3$$

How many values of (x, y) satisfy the system of equations above?

A) 0

B) 1

C) 2

D) Infinitely many

Here's How to Crack It

Because the first equation is a line and the second is a quadratic, it is impossible for the two to be equal. This means there cannot be infinitely many solutions to the system of equations; eliminate (D). Next, to determine the number of solutions, begin by combining the equations. Substitute $3x + 2$ for y in the second equation: $3x + 2 = 4x^2 - 4x + 3$. Because this is a quadratic, set it equal to 0 by subtracting $3x + 2$ from both sides: $0 = 4x^2 - 7x + 1$. This doesn't factor nicely, so the easiest way to determine the number of solutions is to consider the *discriminant*. When a quadratic equation is in the form $0 = ax^2 + bx + c$, as this one is, the discriminant is the value of $b^2 - 4ac$. If the discriminant is positive, there are two real solutions. If it is negative, there are no (real) solutions, and if it is equal to 0, then there is one real solution. In this quadratic, $a = 4$, $b = -7$, and $c = 1$. Put these values into the discriminant: $(-7)^2 - 4(4)(1) = 49 - 16 = 33$. This is positive, so there are two real solutions; choose (C).

COMPLEX NUMBERS

Occasionally, a mathematical operation will require taking a square root of a negative number. With real numbers, that isn't possible—no real number can be squared to get a negative number. This is where i comes in. The i stands for "imaginary," to distinguish it from "real" numbers, and it equals $\sqrt{-1}$. When i is squared, the result is –1. "Complex numbers" combine real and imaginary numbers in the form $a + bi$, where a is real, and bi is imaginary.

- The imaginary number $i = \sqrt{-1}$.
- Treat i just like a variable, except that $i^2 = -1$.
- $a + bi$ is a complex number, where a is the real component of the number, and bi is the imaginary component of the number.
- Many calculators have an i button and an $a + bi$ mode, which can come in handy if a question on complex numbers comes up in the section of the test that allows calculators.

Let's look at a problem that puts all of these concepts together.

11

Which of the following imaginary or complex numbers is equivalent to $\dfrac{2-3i}{6+4i}$? (Note: $i = \sqrt{-1}$)

A) $-\dfrac{1}{2}i$

B) $\dfrac{1}{3}+i$

C) $-\dfrac{13i}{10}$

D) $\dfrac{6}{5}-\dfrac{13i}{10}$

Here's How to Crack It

Start by getting rid of i in the denominator of the equation. To do so, multiply the expression by $\dfrac{6-4i}{6-4i}$. This works because $6 - 4i$ is the *conjugate* of $6 + 4i$. A *conjugate* is formed by changing the sign of the second term of the binomial. Since $(a + b)(a - b) = a^2 - b^2$, you can do the same thing here to clear i from the denominator: $(6 + 4i)(6 - 4i) = (36 - 16i^2)$. And since $i^2 = -1$, the denominator simplifies to $36 + 16$, which equals 52. You will need to use FOIL to find the new numerator: $(2 - 3i)(6 - 4i) = 12 - 8i - 18i + 12i^2$, which simplifies to $12 - 26i + 12(-1)$, then $12 - 26i - 12$, or simply $-26i$. Therefore, to put it all together, $\left(\dfrac{2-3i}{6+4i}\right)\left(\dfrac{6-4i}{6-4i}\right) = -\dfrac{26i}{52}$, which simplifies to $-\dfrac{i}{2}$, (A).

TRY IT EXERCISE 1

Try these questions on your own. Only use your calculator when it is allowed. See Chapter 20 for complete answers and explanations.

2

The acceleration rate, a, of a panther is based on the change in velocity, ΔV, in meters per second, and the duration of the time interval at which each of the velocity measurements was taken, ΔT. If $a = \dfrac{V_2 - V_1}{T_2 - T_1}$, which of the following expresses the duration of the time interval in terms of a and V?

A) $T = \dfrac{V_2 - V_1}{a_2 - a_1}$

B) $T_2 - T_1 = \dfrac{V_2 - V_1}{a}$

C) $T = \dfrac{V_2 - V_1}{a}$

D) $T_2 - T_1 = \dfrac{V_2 - V_1}{a_2 - a_1}$

10

For $i = \sqrt{-1}$, what is the product of $(5 + 2i)$ and $(-3 - 4i)$?

A) $-23 - 26i$

B) $-23 - 14i$

C) $-7 - 26i$

D) $-7 - 34i$

31

$$x^2 < 4$$
$$0 < y^3 < 25$$

If x and y are integers that satisfy the above inequalities, how many distinct possible values are there for $x + y$?

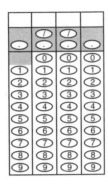

For further practice, go online to your Student Tools and complete the Chapter 16 Fundamentals Drill and Inequalities Drill.

COORDINATE GEOMETRY

If you need additional help in Coordinate Geometry, try our book *SAT Prep*.

Many questions on the SAT test your knowledge of graphs in the *xy*-plane. You will see questions that ask about the graph of an equation, graphs that ask you to find the equation, and much more. If you are reading this book, you likely know the basics of linear coordinate geometry such as the midpoint formula and the distance formula. Below are some of the more advanced facts you need to know about coordinate geometry on the SAT.

Advanced Coordinate Geometry Facts

- A parabola is a graph of a quadratic equation in the *xy*-coordinate plane. The general form of the equation is $y = ax^2 + bx + c$.
- Parabolas are symmetrical around an axis of symmetry and have a single vertex on the axis of symmetry.

- If a is positive, the graph opens upward. If a is negative, the graph opens downward. When a is positive, increasing its value makes a parabola steeper; if a is negative, decreasing its value also makes a parabola steeper. It may be helpful to think of a as analogous to slope.
- Changing the value of b shifts the parabola's axis of symmetry left or right, in the *opposite* direction. So, a negative value for b means that the axis of symmetry is positive, and vice versa.
- c is the y-intercept of the parabola. For example, if $c = 2$, the coordinates of the y-intercept are $(0, 2)$.
- The y-coordinate of any point can be found by putting the x-value into the standard equation and solving for y.
- Parabolas also can be written using the vertex form of the equation: $y = a(x - h)^2 + k$, where a, h, and k are constants.
- The vertex of the parabola in this form is (h, k).

14

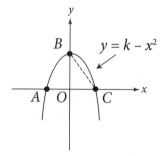

The figure above shows the graph of the parabola $y = k - x^2$, where k is a constant. If the coordinates of point A are $(-2, 0)$, what is the length of line segment BC?

A) $\sqrt{5}$

B) $2\sqrt{5}$

C) 6

D) $5\sqrt{2}$

Here's How to Crack It

The parabola $y = k - x^2$ is centered on the y-axis, so if the coordinates of A are $(-2, 0)$, the coordinates of C must be $(2, 0)$. Whenever you have a point on a graph, you can plug it into the equation to find a missing piece. So, plug in $(2, 0)$ to find k: $0 = k - 2^2$, therefore $k = 4$. This tells that the coordinates of B are $(0, 4)$. To find the length of BC, you don't need the distance formula: just draw a right triangle and use the Pythagorean Theorem. The legs of the triangle are 2 and 4, so $2^2 + 4^2 = (BC)^2$, and $BC = \sqrt{20} = 2\sqrt{5}$. The correct answer is (B).

In the *vertex form* of a parabola, which is written as $y = a(x - h)^2 + k$, the value of a also determines the direction and width of the parabola. A question may ask you to convert from the standard form of a parabola to the vertex form, or vice versa. Here's an example.

27

$$g(x) = (x + 5)(x - 3)$$

Which of the following is an equivalent form of the function g that would be most useful in determining the vertex of the parabola formed when function g is graphed in the xy-plane?

A) $g(x) = (x + 1)^2 - 14$

B) $g(x) = (x + 1)^2 - 16$

C) $g(x) = x^2 + 2x - 15$

D) $g(x) = x(x + 2) - 15$

Here's How to Crack It

The question asks you to convert the equation into the vertex form of the parabola. Before you start, eliminate (C) and (D) because they do not match the vertex form $a(x - h)^2 + k$. To convert the function to vertex form, FOIL the factors together: $g(x) = (x + 5)(x - 3) = x^2 - 3x + 5x - 15 = x^2 + 2x - 15$. Next, you need to "complete the square" in order to convert to the vertex form. Since the vertex form requires the element $(x - h)^2$, add in a constant that will allow you to factor out a squared binomial. In this case, you would need $x^2 + 2x + 1$ to be present so that you can factor it into $(x + 1)^2$. Therefore, rewrite the function by adding a 1 and subtracting a 1: $g(x) = x^2 + 2x + 1 - 1 - 15$. Now you can factor out the squared binomial: $g(x) = (x + 1)^2 - 1 - 15$, which simplifies to $(x + 1)^2 - 16$, (B).

You may also need to complete the square on questions that involve the equation of a circle. Remember that the equation of a circle is $(x - h)^2 + (y - k)^2 = r^2$, where (h, k) is the center of the circle, and r is the radius.

Let's look at an example.

14

$$x^2 - 6x + y^2 - 8y = 0$$

If (h, k) is center of the circle described by the equation above when graphed in the xy-plane, what is the value of h ?

A) 2

B) 3

C) 4

D) 5

Here's How to Crack It

Start by working with the x-terms. Find the coefficient on the x (-6), divide it in half (-3), and square it (9). Add that value to both sides of the equation to get $x^2 - 6x + 9 + y^2 - 8y = 9$. You can convert the x-terms into the square form to get $(x - 3)^2 + y^2 - 8y = 9$. The question asks only for the value of h, which is the x-coordinate of the center when the circle equation is in the form $(x - h)^2 + (y - k)^2 = r^2$. You already have the x-terms in that form, so $h = 3$, which is (B).

If you needed to find the center or the radius of the circle, you would complete the square on the y-terms in the same way: $-8 \div 2 = -4$, and $(-4)^2 = 16$, so the equation becomes $(x-3)^2 + y^2 - 8y + 16 = 9 + 16$ or $(x-3)^2 + (y-4)^2 = 25$. The center is $(3, 4)$ and the radius is 5.

REFLECTION AND TRANSFORMATION FACTS

- Rotation means turning a line or function around a point called the center of rotation.
- Reflecting a line or a function means creating a mirror image of the graph or function around the line of reflection.
- Lines reflected across the x-axis have slopes that are negatives of each other (*not* negative reciprocals) and y-intercepts that are negatives of each other.
- Lines reflected across the y-axis have slopes that are negatives of each other but the same y-intercept.
- A translation moves a figure without reflecting or rotating it. See the following examples.

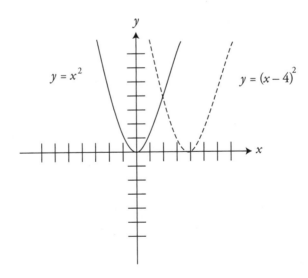

In this example, the graph is translated to the right by adjusting the x-coordinate value. If a number is inside the parentheses with the x-value, then the graph shifts the number of units opposite the direction of the sign.

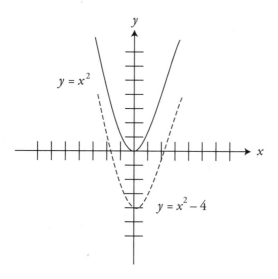

In the example above, the graph is translated down 4 units. Notice that a translation on the y-axis is outside the parentheses, and the shift matches the value of the sign.

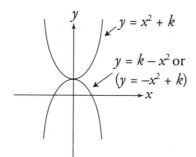

Putting a negative sign in front of x^2 flips the parabola upside down.

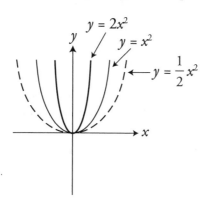

Multiplying x by a constant greater than 1 makes the graph steeper. Conversely, a constant between 0 and 1 makes the graph less steep.

FUNCTIONS

There are two types of functions that you will see on the SAT. The first type is very similar to coordinate geometry and often overlaps significantly with the material discussed earlier. These are often called linear functions. Essentially, a function acts like a machine. A function produces a y-value whenever you put in an x-value. A function can have multiple x-values for a single y-value, but a function can never have multiple y-values for a single x-value. In other words, a function can move up and down in the xy-plane, but it can never double back on itself.

Function notation is slightly different from coordinate geometry notation. The y-value is usually written as $f(x)$. In other words, $f(x) = y$. The value (x) represents all the possible x-values for the function. If there are multiple functions on a graph, then they are usually denoted using an alphabetical pattern: $f(x)$, $g(x)$, $h(x)$.... As long as you are comfortable following directions, functions should not pose too many issues for you. Consider the following example.

Example 1:

The function $f(x)$ is defined by $f(x) = 3x^2 - 1$.
If p is a positive integer, and $4f(p) = 428$, then
what is the value of p ?

Begin by simplifying to the basic function by dividing both sides by 4, so $f(p) = 107$. Next, since $f(p) = f(x)$ with a value of p, substitute the given equation for $f(p)$: $3p^2 - 1 = 107$. Now, solve for p: $3p^2 = 108$, $p^2 = 36$, so $p = 6$.

Function questions on the SAT may also require you to process information from charts and graphs. Since $f(x)$ represents the y-coordinate and x represents the x-coordinate, functions can also be understood as a form of point notation. In the following two examples, consider how function notation can be used to represent coordinate graphs.

Example 2:

> If $f(x)$ is a linear function such that $f(1) = 5$ and
> $f(-1) = 9$, then what is the slope of the graph of
> $y = f(x)$?

As mentioned in an earlier question, don't get confused by the terminology. A linear function is just a line. Since $f(x) = y$, $f(1) = 5$ can be read as "the function $f(x)$ has a y-value of 5 when x is 1." In other words, this is just the point $(1, 5)$. The second pair can be read in the same way: "the function $f(x)$ has a y-value of 9 when x is -1," which is the point $(-1, 9)$. With two points on a line, use the slope formula to find that $m = -2$.

Harder functions may require you to interpret graphical data to find an x- or y- value. Consider the following example.

Example 3:

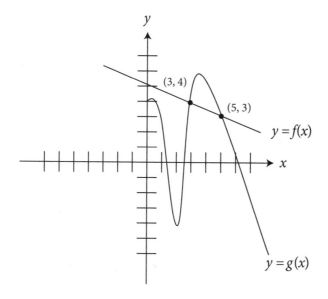

> The figure above shows the graphs of the functions
> $y = f(x)$ and $y = g(x)$. Which of the following describes all
> the values of x for which $g(x) \geq f(x)$?

This question is asking you to find all of the values for x for which the line $g(x)$ is above (greater than) the line $f(x)$. The values range from 3 to 5 or $3 < x < 5$. Trap answers on the SAT would include the y-values or would confuse greater than and less than.

Sometimes a question will present you with information about a graph of a function and ask you to make conclusions about the function based on the graph. Here's an example of this type of question.

13

If the function *g* has four distinct zeros, which of the following could represent the complete graph of *g* in the *xy*-plane?

A)
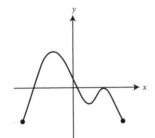

B)
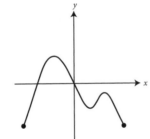

C)
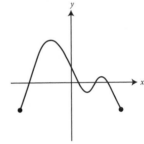

D)
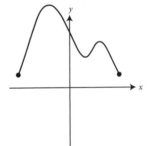

Here's How to Crack It

Zeros are the places where the line and the x-axis meet. If the graph has four distinct zeros, it crosses the x-axis in four places. Only the function in (C) does this.

The zeros of a function may also be tested in a word problem, such as the following example.

10

Which of the following represents all zeros of the function

$$f(x) = -\frac{1}{4}x^5 + \frac{3}{4}x^3 + x \ ?$$

A) 2 only

B) –2 only

C) –2, 2

D) –2, 0, –2

Here's How to Crack It

To find the zeros of a function, you must set it equal to zero and solve. Since this function has a power of 5 in it, some factoring will be required.

$$f(x) = -\frac{1}{4}x^5 + \frac{3}{4}x^3 + x$$

$$f(x) = -\frac{1}{4}(x^5 - 3x^3 - 4x)$$

$$f(x) = -\frac{1}{4}x(x^4 - 3x^2 - 4)$$

$$f(x) = -\frac{1}{4}x(x^2 - 4)(x^2 + 1)$$

$$f(x) = -\frac{1}{4}x(x - 2)(x + 2)(x^2 + 1)$$

Therefore, the real zeros are at $x = 0$, $x = 2$, and $x = -2$. The factor $x^2 + 1$ has no real solutions to it. The correct answer is (D).

TRY IT EXERCISE 2

Attempt these questions, either with or without your calculator as shown, then check your answers in Chapter 20.

10

Which of the following represents a polynomial function with roots of $\{-\dfrac{1}{2}, 3, \text{ and } 3\}$?

A) $f(x) = 2x^3 - 11x^2 + 12x + 9$

B) $f(x) = 2x^3 + 11x^2 + 12x - 9$

C) $f(x) = 3x^2 - 11x + 9$

D) $f(x) = 3x^2 + 11x + 9$

16

Which of the following represents the equation of a quadratic function with vertex $(3, 4)$ that passes through the point $(1, 2)$?

A) $y = -2x^2 + 3x - \dfrac{1}{2}$

B) $y = -\dfrac{1}{2}x^2 + 3x - \dfrac{1}{2}$

C) $y = 2x^2 - 3x - \dfrac{1}{2}$

D) $y = -\dfrac{1}{2}x^2 - 3x - \dfrac{1}{2}$

15

The function $f(x)$ is defined by $f(x) = x^3 - 6x^2 + 11x - 6$. Line $g(x)$ intersects $f(x)$ at the x-coordinate that is the even solution to $f(x)$ and passes through the point $(0, 6)$. If $h(x)$ is a line perpendicular to $g(x)$, then what is the equation of $h(x)$, if $h(x)$ also passes through $(0, 6)$?

A) $h(x) = -\dfrac{1}{3}x + 6$

B) $h(x) = 3x + 6$

C) $h(x) = \dfrac{1}{3}x + 6$

D) $h(x) = -3x + 6$

33

If (h, k) is the vertex of the parabola defined by $f(x) = -x^2 + 6x - 8$, what is the value of $h + k$?

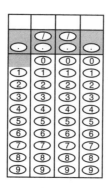

For further practice, go online to your Student Tools and complete the Chapter 16 Coordinate Geometry Drill and Functions Drill.

Summary

- ○ Solving Equations and Inequalities
  - If a question asks you to solve for an unknown value in an equation or inequality, simply manipulate the equation and isolate the variable.
    - ○ When working with inequalities, you must flip the inequality sign when multiplying or dividing by a negative number.
  - If you are given multiple equations and asked to find the value of an expression, try stacking and either adding or subtracting the equations.
    - ○ Still can't get the expression you need? Try multiplying or dividing the resulting equation to get the desired expression.

- ○ Imaginary and Complex Numbers
  - You will encounter imaginary numbers on the SAT; when you think about it, this is crazy!
  - Imaginary numbers result from taking the square root of a negative number.
  - $i = \sqrt{-1}$, $i^2 = -1$, and $i^4 = 1$
  - $a + bi$ is a complex number, of which a is real and bi is imaginary.
  - Don't forget to use the i button and the $a + bi$ mode on your calculator!

- ○ Coordinate Geometry
  - Is there a figure? If not, draw one! Is the provided figure not to scale? Redraw it!
  - Parabolas
    - ○ The general form of a parabola is $y = ax^2 + bx + c$.
    - ○ The vertex form of a parabola with a vertex (h, k) is $y = a(x - h)^2 + k$.
  - Plugging in points from the graphs can be helpful on coordinate geometry problems!

- Functions
  - When working with functions, plug in an *x*-value to find *f*(*x*), or the *y*-value, or vice-versa.
    - When graphing, the solution of a function would be graphed as (*x*, *f*(*x*)).
  - If a question asks about the number of zeroes in a function, simply find the total number of *x*-intercepts.
  - When solving rotation, translation, and reflection questions, sketch the movement on your figure.
    - Rotations should rotate around a point.
    - Reflections provide a mirror image.
    - Translations move the graph up if the number is inside the parentheses, or over if the number is outside the parentheses.

- As always, make sure you use the global techniques of POE to eliminate obviously incorrect answers!

Chapter 17
Alternative
Approaches

INTRODUCTION

Scoring a 750 or higher on the SAT Math sections requires near perfection. Hardly a single problem can be skipped or answered incorrectly. One of the major challenges is developing the necessary flexibility to deal with every type of problem that the SAT might throw at you. Memorizing the many different equations and formulas needed is one way of beating these problems. While there are formulas you'll want to memorize, there are literally hundreds of formulas and concepts that *might* be helpful on the SAT once in a great while.

Additionally, you must ask yourself what you will do if you can't remember the correct formula for a problem. If you are ever stumped on the SAT, you may not hit the score you want.

As a result, it is vital that you develop alternative strategies for dealing with challenging questions. A successful alternative strategy should do several things: 1) it should guarantee the correct answer; 2) it should be as fast as or faster than applying the "correct" algebraic formula; and 3) it should be applicable to numerous situations.

This chapter will cover two alternative techniques for approaching challenging questions: Plugging In and Ballparking.

PLUGGING IN

Speed and accuracy are a vital combination for acing the Math sections of the SAT. If you had only thirty seconds left on one of the Math sections, which of the following two questions would you rather have?

1. A customer walks into a convenience store to purchase two candy bars valued at 50 cents apiece. If he pays with a ten-dollar bill, how much change will he receive?

   A. $6

   B. $7

   C. $8

   D. $9

2. A customer walks into a convenience store to purchase b bars of candy valued at c cents apiece. If he pays d dollars, which of the following expressions represents his change, in dollars?

A. $d - bc$

B. $bc - d$

C. $\dfrac{bc}{100} - d$

D. $d - \dfrac{bc}{100}$

Without a doubt, you would rather do the first problem, but why? The two problems are nearly identical! They cover the same topic and require the same math. What aspect of these problems makes number two so much more challenging? The answer, of course, is the presence of variables. Even if you're really good at algebra, numbers are easier to work with. As a result, the first problem is very straightforward, despite the need to convert from cents to dollars in order to solve for the change. Algebra, on the other hand, is not as intuitive.

By the way, did you get (D) for both questions? If not, come back and try the second one after you've completed this section!

Fortunately, it is possible to eliminate the need to use algebra on many SAT questions. This strategy is called Plugging In. Consider the following problem.

15

Which of the following is equivalent to the expression $\dfrac{3x+3}{\sqrt{x+1}}$?

A) $3x + 3$

B) $\sqrt{x+1}$

C) $3\sqrt{x-1}$

D) $3\sqrt{x+1}$

Here's How to Crack It

Instead of considering each choice and determining whether it is equivalent to $\dfrac{3x+3}{\sqrt{x+1}}$, try Plugging In. Begin by choosing a value for the variable, x. Because you need to take the square root of $x + 1$, choose a value which makes $x + 1$ a perfect square. Try $x = 8$. Make $x = 8$ in the original expression: $\dfrac{3(8)+3}{\sqrt{8+1}} = \dfrac{24+3}{\sqrt{9}} = \dfrac{27}{3} = 9$. Since 9 is the value of the expression in the question, what must be true of the correct answer? The correct answer must also equal 9 when $x = 8$. This is the *target*; circle it on your paper. Now, make $x = 8$ in each answer choice and eliminate what doesn't equal the target value, 9:

A) $3(8) + 3 = 24 + 3 = 27$ This doesn't match your target; eliminate it.

B) $\sqrt{8+1} = \sqrt{9} = 3$ This doesn't match your target; eliminate it.

C) $3\sqrt{8-1} = 3\sqrt{7}$ This doesn't match your target; eliminate it.

D) $3\sqrt{8+1} = 3\sqrt{9} = 3(3) = 9$ This is the only choice that matches your target; it must be the correct answer.

Consider the speed at which it is possible to move through this problem. Since arithmetic is so much more intuitive than algebra, most of these answers were probably obviously incorrect as soon as you plugged in. Also, ask yourself which method is more error prone: using knowledge of algebraic principles and number theory in your head, or doing some basic arithmetic on paper?

Plugging In can be used for any and every question that has variables in the answer choices. Just follow these steps:

1. Choose a number for the variables in the problem.
2. Solve the problem using arithmetic. Circle the solution: this is your *target* number.
3. Plug in the numbers you substituted for variables into each answer choice.
4. The answer choice that matches your target is the correct answer. Be sure to check all four answers.

Now try another.

27

If $x - 6 = r$, what does $x^2 - 36$ equal in terms of r?

A) $(r + 6)^2$

B) $(r - 6)^2$

C) $r^2 + 12r$

D) $r^2 + 6r$

Here's How to Crack It

Here there are a couple of variables and a few tricky steps in the algebra, but Plugging In makes the problem much more straightforward. The first step is to choose values for the variables. Since there are two variables that are related, plug in numbers that make the math as simple as possible. Let's say $x = 8$. Then $8 - 6 = 2$, so $r = 2$. Now solve the problem: $8^2 - 36 = 28$, so 28 is the target. Now, plug in $r = 2$ into each of the answer choices; the correct answer will equal 28.

A) $(2 + 6)^2 = 8^2 = 64$ This doesn't match your target; eliminate it.

B) $(2 - 6)^2 = (-4)^2 = 16$ This doesn't match your target; eliminate it.

C) $2^2 + 12(2) = 4 + 24 = 28$ This matches your target, but check all four choices!

D) $2^2 + 6(2) = 4 + 12 = 16$ This doesn't match your target; eliminate it.

Therefore, the answer is (C).

When plugging in, be careful which numbers you choose, especially when calculator use is not allowed. Take a look at the next problem, and consider what would happen if you plug in $b = 1$.

14

If $a = b^2$ and $b = m^{\frac{1}{3}}$, what is a^3 in terms of m?

A) $\sqrt[3]{\dfrac{1}{m}}$

B) m^2

C) $\sqrt[3]{m}$

D) m^3

Here's How to Crack It

If $b = 1$, then $b^2 = 1$. This means that $a = 1$, and therefore $m^{\frac{1}{3}} = \sqrt[3]{m} = 1$ and $m = 1$. So if you plug in using 1, then your target is also 1. Now try the answer choices.

A) $\sqrt[3]{\dfrac{1}{1}}$ This matches your target.

B) $1^2 = 1$ This matches your target.

C) $\sqrt[3]{1} = 1$ This matches your target.

D) $1^3 = 1$ This matches your target.

By plugging in the number 1 for your value, no answer choices were eliminated. In basic terms, avoid numbers that either have unusual properties (such as 0 or 1), or that might make the math more challenging. The acronym **FROZEN** is useful for remembering which numbers to avoid:

F = fractions
R = repeating the same value (such as x and y are both 2)
O = one
Z = zero
E = extreme (numbers that are very large or that are very small)
N = negatives

Let's try this question again. We'll avoid the **FROZEN** numbers and pick values that make the math as simple as possible. In this question, it's easiest to start by working backwards. Since you are taking the third root of m, pick a number that is the cube of an integer, such as 8. If $m = 8$, then $b = 2$ and $a = 2^2 = 4$. The question asks for a^3, so your target is $4^3 = 64$. Now try the answer choices.

A) $\sqrt[3]{\dfrac{1}{8}} = \dfrac{1}{2}$ This doesn't match your target, so eliminate it.

B) $8^2 = 64$ This matches your target, but check all four answers!

C) $\sqrt[3]{8} = 2$ This doesn't match your target, so eliminate it.

D) $8^3 = 512$ This doesn't match your target, so eliminate it.

Therefore, the answer is (B).

As you can see, Plugging In is a powerful technique for improving both speed and accuracy on challenging problems.

Let's look at one more very challenging algebra problem that is made comparatively simple through the use of Plugging In.

30

If $x > 4$, what is the remainder when polynomial $x^4 + x^3 - 14x + 6$ is divided by the binomial $x - 2$?

A) 0

B) 1

C) 2

D) 3

Here's How to Crack It

You may or may not have run across synthetic division or polynomial division in your math classes. However, even if you have, Plugging In works great here. The question is asking for the remainder when one big, ugly thing is divided by a somewhat less ugly thing. Plug in for x to turn this into an arithmetic problem. Because you're dividing by $x - 2$ (and you have your lovely calculator available), make $x = 12$. That way, you end up dividing by 10 and can simply look at the last digit of the answer after you plug in $x = 12$ for the remainder. If $x = 12$, then the polynomial is $12^4 + 12^3 - 14(12) + 6 = 20,736 + 1,728 - 168 + 6 = 22,302$. When you divide 22,302 by $(12 - 2) = 10$, you are simply moving the decimal place over one spot to the left, giving you 2,230.2. The 2 to the right of the decimal place would be your remainder (because you're dividing by 10), so the answer is (C).

Plugging In More than Once

We have discussed checking each answer choice when plugging in. Why do you need to do that? In some cases, you pick a set of "magic numbers" that makes more than one answer choice work (like making $b = 1$ in question 14 above). There are other problems that are set up in such a way that it's likely that you'll need to plug in more than once. Let's look at an example.

9

If $x < y$ then which of the following must be true?

A) $x < 0$

B) $y > 0$

C) $x - y < 0$

D) $x^2 < y^2$

Here's How to Crack It

As with all Plugging In questions, begin by choosing easy numbers that satisfy the rules of question. For example, $x = 2$ and $y = 3$. Now check each of the answers.

A)	$2 < 0$	Since your x and y satisfy the equation, this is not true, so eliminate it.
B)	$3 > 0$	This is currently true.
C)	$2 - 3 < 0$	This is currently true.
D)	$4 < 9$	This is currently true.

Even though the values you chose for x and y were valid, you were only able to eliminate one answer choice. This is not unusual when plugging in "normal" values for x and y. Remember the FROZEN numbers that we said to avoid? The phrase "must be" includes all possible situations as defined by the equation. Therefore, if $x < y$, the correct answer will be valid even if you plug in a fraction, a repeating number, a one, a zero, an extreme, or a negative. Choose one of the FROZEN numbers and plug in again. FROZEN numbers can even be mixed and matched: for example, a negative fraction. A quick reminder though: you must choose two values that work in the original problem. For example, in this situation, you cannot make x greater than (or equal to) y.

Try Plugging In again, using a negative value for x and zero for y: so $x = -2$ and $y = 0$. Since (A) has been eliminated already, check only the remaining answers:

A)   Already eliminated

B) $0 > 0$ Not true, so eliminate it.

C) $-2 - 0 < 0$ Still true; keep moving.

D) $(-2)^2 < (0)^2$ Not true, so eliminate it.

Therefore, the answer must be (C).

———————————————————

Of course, not every problem on the SAT will look like the problems you just did. However, in many cases, Plugging In is still an effective technique. Let's look at some other situations in which Plugging In works wonders, even if using this technique isn't always immediately obvious.

Plugging In on Grid-Ins

As you just saw, checking each answer choice when Plugging In is very important. But what happens when there are no answer choices? Plugging In works well on Grid-In questions when the values are relative to one another. Let's see an example.

16

If $\dfrac{a}{b-2} = \dfrac{3}{4}$ and $\dfrac{b}{c} = \dfrac{2}{3}$, what is the value of $c - 2a$?

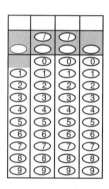

Here's How to Crack It

Let's pick some numbers. If $a = 3$, then $b - 2 = 4$, so $b = 6$. Then, $\dfrac{6}{c} = \dfrac{2}{3}$, so $c = 9$.
Now let's find the answer: the question asks for the value of $c - 2a$, so $9 - 2(3) = 3$.
It's that easy!

Look for relationships between numbers on Grid-In questions; if you spot them, you might have a great opportunity to use Plugging In to make the question a snap!

Interpreting Variables, Constants, and Expressions

Some SAT problems will ask for you to interpret the meaning of part of an equation, inequality, or expression. These problems can seem daunting at first, but approaching the problems systematically and using Plugging In when appropriate will make these questions approachable.

13

Aaron is training for a marathon. He plans to run a total of 5 times each week. Four runs each week (the "short runs") will be the same distance, and each week Aaron will increase the distance of the short runs by a constant amount. The fifth run (the "long run") will increase each week by a constant percentage. Aaron models his total distance, d, in kilometers, w weeks since the beginning of his training plan using the equation $d = 4(5 + 0.5w) + 8(1.1^w)$. What does 0.5 represent in the equation?

A) The increase in total distance each week

B) The number of weeks until Aaron's marathon

C) The increase in distance of each short run each week

D) The increase in distance of each long run each week

Here's How to Crack It

To approach these questions, start by Reading the Final Question and underlining what the question is asking about: the "0.5" in the equation. Next, label what you know in the equation. The variable d represents total distance, and w is the number of weeks since the beginning of training, so the equation is the same as *total distance* = 4(5 + 0.5*weeks*) + 8(1.1^*weeks*). Next, work some Process of Elimination. To begin with, 0.5 is multiplied by *week*, so it doesn't make sense that it represents the number of weeks until the marathon; eliminate (B). The remaining choices discuss distance, which makes sense because the right side of the equation adds up to distance on the left side of the equation. Next, plug in some numbers to see what happens with different values. You don't have your calculator here, so you want be creative. Normally when Plugging In you want to avoid 0 and 1, but here your goal is to understand how the equation works, not to find an algebraic answer choice. So see what happens at $w = 0$ and $w = 1$. When $w = 0$, then $d = 4(5 + 0.5(0)) + 8(1.1^0) = 4(5) + 8(1) = 28$ total kilometers, and when $w = 1$, then

$d = 4(5 + 0.5(1)) + 8(1.1^1) = 4(5.5) + 8(1.1) = 22 + 8.8 = 30.8$ total kilometers. Between week 0 and week 1, the total distance increased $30.8 - 28 = 2.8$ kilometers, not 0.5, so (A) doesn't fit; eliminate it. Next, compare the remaining answer choices. Both talk about the increase in the distance of runs. The question says that the short runs increase by a constant distance each week, whereas the long runs increase by a constant percent. As we'll discuss a bit more in the Word Problems chapter, the formula for linear growth includes multiplication, whereas compounded percent growth involves exponents. The 0.5 is multiplied by w and the other part of the right side of the equation has the exponent. This means that 0.5 must be the increase in short-run distance; choose (C).

These questions can get quite challenging, so if you're serious about getting an elite score on the SAT, be sure to master the approach:

Interpreting Expressions

1. RTFQ: underline what the question is asking about.
2. Label what you know.
3. POE any choice that doesn't make sense.
4. Plug-and-Play: plug in for the variables to see what's happening.
5. Compare answer choices and POE until one choice remains.

For these questions, creative use of Plugging In can give you an insight into what's going on in an algebraic expression.

Plugging In with Graphs and Charts

Process of Elimination and Plugging In can also be useful when the SAT asks you to make inferences from data or graphs. Let's look at an example.

Questions 18 and 19 refer to the following information.

Population densities of emerald ash borer

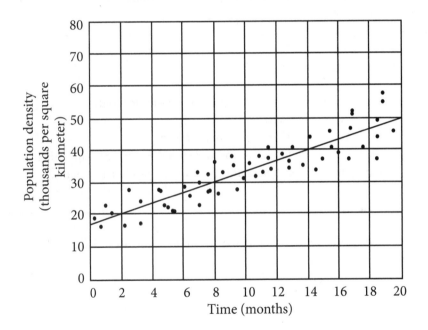

The scatterplot above shows the population densities of emerald ash borer, *Agrilus planipennis*, an invasive insect species which threatens North American ash species. The scatterplot shows the population densities, *p*, of different locations *m* months after the discovery of emerald ash borers in that location.

18

Which of the following inferences is best supported by the scatterplot above?

A) On average, the population density of a given location increases by 33% each month.

B) At the site with the lowest population density, 17 emerald ash borers per square kilometer were found.

C) A site is expected to have 50,000 ash borers per square kilometer 20 months after the discovery of ash borers.

D) At a given location, the population of ash borers is expected to stop increasing and stabilize eventually.

Here's How to Crack It

Whenever you are confronted with a chart or graph, always read the axes. Here, the vertical axis is "Population density (thousands per square kilometer)" and the horizontal axis is "Time (months)." Next, because the question wants the best-supported inference, go right to Process of Elimination. For (A), you can plug in using the graph. The line of best fit goes through the points (2, 20) and (8, 30). You can determine the average percent increase per month over that interval by finding the average increase and seeing what percent that is of the first point. The population density increased by $80 - 20 = 60,000$ per square kilometer over $8 - 2 = 6$ months, making an average increase of $\dfrac{60,000}{6} = 10,000$ per month. This is an increase of $\dfrac{20,000 - 10,000}{20,000} \times 100 = 50\%$, not 33%. Eliminate (A). Choice (B) ignores that the vertical axis is in *thousands* per square kilometer; the lowest point would be 17,000, not 17, insects per square kilometer; eliminate (B). For (C), at 20 months, the line of best fit is at 50, which represents 50,000 insects per square kilometer (remember the units!), so keep (C). While (D) may be true, the scatterplot only shows an increase, so the data doesn't support a leveling off of the population; eliminate (D) and choose (C).

As you just saw, many SAT problems that feature charts, graphs, or other visual representations of data are great opportunities to plug in. In fact, in many cases, the key to Plugging In on these problems is to use the numbers given in the graphic, rather than do all the hard work that the test-writers want you to do. Let's look at another question based on the same scatterplot.

19

Which of the following equations represents the line of best fit of the scatterplot above?

A) $p = 0.33m + 17$

B) $p = 1.67m + 17$

C) $p = 0.33^m$

D) $p = 17m + 0.33$

Here's How to Crack It

You can spend a lot of time analyzing the entire line, but your job isn't to come up with the equation for the line of best fit on your own; instead, you only need to pick from one of the four provided choices. Pick a point on the graph: at 2 months, the population density is 20,000 insects per square kilometer. Make $m = 2$ in each answer choice and eliminate any in which p isn't close to 20. Only (B) is anywhere close (rounding makes (B) 20.33, which is much closer than the other choices).

Ultimately, Plugging In is a great tool in your toolbox. It can increase both speed and accuracy, especially on challenging questions. In order to achieve your goal score, you must have a method for approaching every question on the SAT, and Plugging In is often the fastest and safest way to go. Plugging In can also give you a way into a question that seems confusing or daunting. Look for opportunities to plug in any time you see variables in the answer choices or relationships between numbers or when you feel an urge to solve algebra equations.

Here are a few Plugging In questions for you to try. Be sure to only use your calculator on those questions with a calculator symbol next to them! Read the explanations when you are finished to ensure that you are using the Plugging In technique correctly. Then review the questions from the previous chapter to see if Plugging In could be used on any of them to make your work easier or faster.

TRY IT EXERCISE 1

See Chapter 20 for answers and explanations. Only use your calculator when permitted.

12

The weight of a certain shipment of apples may not deviate from 50 pounds by more than 5 pounds. If W is the weight, in pounds, of the shipment, which of the following represents all possible values of W?

A) $|W - 5| \leq 50$

B) $|W - 50| \leq 5$

C) $|W + 50| \leq 5$

D) $|W - 5| \geq 50$

18

The wholesale price of a boat is x dollars. At an auction, the boat sells for y percent more than the wholesale price. Don later purchases the boat at z percent below the auction price. Which of the following expressions represents the price, in dollars, that Don paid for the boat?

A) $x\left(1 + \dfrac{y}{100}\right)\left(1 - \dfrac{z}{100}\right)$

B) $x\left(1 + \dfrac{y}{100}\right)\left(1 + \dfrac{z}{100}\right)$

C) $x\left(\dfrac{xy}{100}\right)$

D) $x\left(\dfrac{xy}{100} + \dfrac{xz}{100}\right)$

20

Which of the following expressions is equivalent to $3^{2x} \times 27^{\frac{1}{2}x}$?

A) 3^x

B) $3^{\frac{7}{2}x}$

C) $3^{\frac{9}{2}x}$

D) $3^{\frac{13}{2}x}$

27

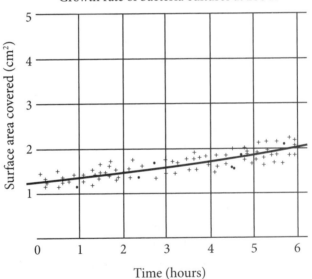

Growth rate of bacteria cultures at 280 K

The scatterplot above shows the surface area A, in cm², of standard petri dishes covered by bacteria grown at 280 Kelvin h hours after being placed in the temperature-controlled refrigerator. Which of the following best describes the curve of best fit?

A) $A = 1.1^h + 1.25$

B) $A = 0.9^h + 1.25$

C) $A = 1.122^h$

D) $A = 1.1^h + 0.25$

15

Which of the following is equal to the expression

$$\frac{x^5 - 2x^4 - 13x^3 + 14x^2 + 24x}{x+3}, \text{ for all values of } x \neq -3 ?$$

A) $x^4 + x^3 - 10x^2 - 16x - 24 - \dfrac{72}{x+3}$

B) $x^4 + 5x^3 + 2x^2 - 8x$

C) $x^4 + x^3 + 16x^2 + 62x + 164 - \dfrac{492}{x+3}$

D) $x^4 - 5x^3 + 2x^2 + 8x$

For further practice, go online to your Student Tools
and complete the Chapter 17 Plugging In Drill.

BALLPARKING

The other technique that can increase your accuracy and speed on the SAT is Ballparking. Rather than working a multiple-choice question all the way to the exact answer, you can sometimes get right to the only answer in the ballpark by using Process of Elimination on answers that aren't anywhere close to what the right answer has to be.

One place where Ballparking is especially helpful is on the No Calculator section of the Math. Let's look at some examples of situations where Ballparking is much faster than doing long calculations.

8

If $\dfrac{x}{11} - \dfrac{3}{11} = 79$, what is the value of $x - 3$?

A)   82

B)   237

C)   869

D) 2,607

Here's How to Crack It

Start by Reading the Final Question. You need to find $x - 3$, which is straightforward once you realize that multiplying both sides by 11 will clear the fractions on the left side of the equation and give you $x - 3 = 79 \times 11$. So you reach for your favorite calculator…but then remember this is the No Calculator section! Fret not! Look at the answer choices: they are very far apart indeed. Round 79 up to 80 and 11 down to 10. The answer has to be somewhere near $80 \times 10 = 800$. Only (C) is anywhere near 800, so it must be the answer.

When you don't have access to your calculator, Ballparking can save tons of time and let you avoid tedious, arduous, wearisome calculations. However, even when you *can* use your calculator, sometimes it's still faster to use Ballparking rather than grabbing your calculator and punching some numbers.

19

Number of participants in Grand Prix Tournaments
by location, 2014 and 2015

	2014	2015
Montreal	2,978	3,213
Quebec City	1,782	1,702
Toronto	3,098	3,982
Vancouver	2,321	2,355

The two-way table above shows the number of participants in Grand Prix Tournaments in four Canadian cities in 2014 and 2015. Which city had the greatest ratio of participants in 2014 to participants in 2015?

A) Montreal

B) Quebec City

C) Toronto

D) Vancouver

Here's How to Crack It

If you want to compare ratios, convert to fractions. Here, you want to express each city as $\dfrac{\text{participants in 2014}}{\text{participants in 2015}}$. Write the fraction for each city next to its answer choice:

A) Montreal $\dfrac{2{,}978}{3{,}213}$

B) Quebec City $\dfrac{1{,}782}{1{,}702}$

C) Toronto $\dfrac{3{,}098}{3{,}982}$

D) Vancouver $\dfrac{2{,}321}{2{,}355}$

You might now be tempted to grab your calculator and turn each fraction into a decimal, but only Quebec City has a numerator greater than the denominator, so Quebec City's ratio must be greater than 1, whereas the other three choices will have ratios less than 1. Now you know that Quebec City, (B), is the answer *without* having to punch all these numbers into your calculator!

Sometimes questions want you to explicitly use Ballparking. Here's an example.

28

Growth rate of bacteria cultures at 280 K

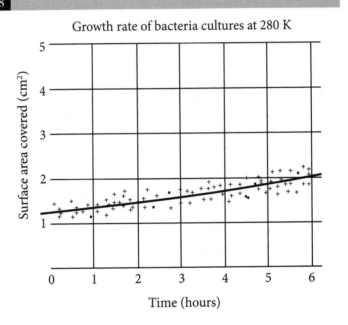

The scatterplot above shows the surface area A, in cm², of standard petri dishes covered by bacteria grown at 280 Kelvin h hours after being placed in the temperature-controlled refrigerator. Which of the following is closest to the projected surface area covered at 8 hours?

A) 2 cm²

B) 3 cm²

C) 4 cm²

D) 5 cm²

Here's How to Crack It

First, the curve is already at 2 cm² at 6 hours, so 2 cm² doesn't make sense for 8 hours; eliminate (A). Next, 8 hours isn't on the chart. So take your pencil and extend the curve and the vertical axis.

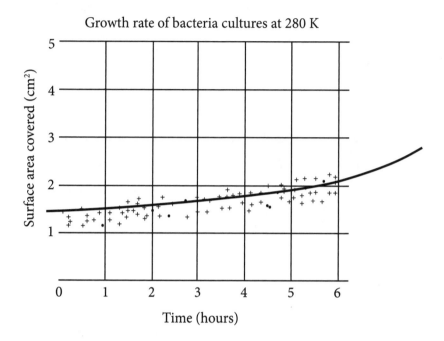

Growth rate of bacteria cultures at 280 K

The curve ends up a bit short of 3 cm². Choices (C) and (D) are far too high, so the best option is (B).

TRY IT EXERCISE 2

Here are a few questions to try Ballparking on. Use the technique, even if you know how to do the question "for real." Changing the way you approach the SAT is the key to changing your score! Oh, and don't forget to leave your calculator to the side for any question without a calculator symbol! Answers can be found in Chapter 20.

9

On a backpacking trip, Jane started by walking north at a rate of 6 kilometers per hour for $\frac{3}{8}$ of her total walking time. She then walked east at a rate of 3 kilometers per hour for the rest of the time. The distance that Jane covered while walking north was what fraction of the total distance she walked?

A) $\frac{1}{3}$

B) $\frac{3}{8}$

C) $\frac{5}{11}$

D) $\frac{6}{11}$

13

If $7(x^2 - 3) = 679$, what is the value of $x^2 + 3$?

A)   10

B)   103

C)   685

D) 4,759

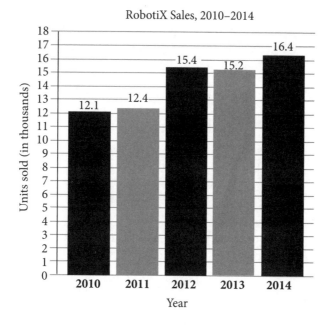

The figure above shows the total sales per year at RobotiX from 2010 through 2014. Which year had the greatest percent increase in units sold over the previous year?

A) 2011

B) 2012

C) 2013

D) 2014

15

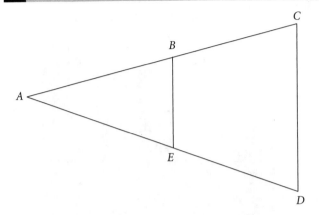

In the figure above, *BE* ∥ *CD*, *E* is the midpoint of *AD*, and *BE* = 3. What is the value of *CD* ?

A) 1.5

B) 3

C) 4

D) 6

Summary

o Using alternative techniques is the key to nailing the SAT Math.
  - Alternative techniques must be accurate and faster than doing the question "the right way."
  - Alternative techniques are tools for your toolbox. They do NOT completely replace knowing the math for every question!

o Plugging In turns many crazy algebra problems into straightforward arithmetic questions.

o Steps to Plugging In:
  - Assign values for the variables.
  - Solve the problem using numbers. Find the answer to the question. This is the Target Value. Circle it!
  - Using your assigned values, plug in the numbers into each answer choice.
  - The answer choice that matches your target is the correct answer. Be sure to check all four choices!

o Questions that ask you to interpret expressions are also great opportunities to Plug In:
  - RTFQ: underline what the question is asking about.
  - Label what you know.
  - POE any choice that doesn't make sense.
  - Plug-and-Play: plug in for the variables to see what's happening.
  - Compare answer choices and POE until one choice remains.

- o For charts, graphs, and other sorts of data, look to plug in data points into answer choices, rather than coming up with algebraic expressions of the information. Your job is to pick the right answer choice, NOT to do all the hard statistical analysis yourself!

- o Ballparking is another great alternative technique.
  - Avoid long calculations on the no calculator section by using POE on any answer choice not in the ballpark.
  - Try Ballparking rather than using your calculator on data analysis questions.
  - Look to ballpark when the SAT gives you a figure in a Geometry question.

Chapter 18
Word Problems
and Other Hot
Topics

INTRODUCTION

On the SAT, word problems can present some special difficulties. The test writers love these problems because there are many ways that they can lead you into traps. This chapter presents the most effective strategies for avoiding these traps, and it covers the topics that are most likely to trip you up on hard problems.

USE BITE-SIZED PIECES

The first step in conquering word problems is to break the question into bite-sized pieces. After you Read the Final Question (RTFQ), go back to the beginning. As soon as you find something simple to do, do it! Let's use the question below as an example.

6

In a particular bowl of candy-coated chocolates, there are twice as many red pieces as brown ones, three times as many green pieces as brown ones, and half as many yellow pieces as green ones. If there are a total of 75 candy-coated chocolates in the bowl, how many of them are not yellow?

A) 10

B) 15

C) 55

D) 60

Here's How to Crack It

Remember to Read the Final Question (RTFQ) first, and underline what the question is asking for. Now go back to the beginning and take it one bite-sized piece at a time.

> In a particular bowl of candy-coated chocolates, there are twice as many red pieces as brown ones…

You could tackle this piece of information by saying that red = $2x$ and brown = x. Now tackle the next bite-sized piece.

> …three times as many green pieces as brown ones…

Since brown was x, green must be $3x$. Move on to another bite-sized piece.

...and half as many yellow pieces as green ones.

Since green was $3x$, yellow must be $\frac{1}{2}(3x) = 1.5x$. Move on to another bite-sized piece.

If there are a total of 75 candy-coated chocolates in the bowl...

Since 75 is the number of red, brown, green, and yellow pieces, you can say that $2x + x + 3x + 1.5x = 75$. So $7\frac{1}{2}x = 75$, and thus $x = 10$. Do not go to the answer choices yet! Very likely, 10 is there and is a wrong answer. Instead, you should re-read the Final Question so that you know what the question is actually asking for.

... how many of them are not yellow?

Notice that the question is <u>not</u> asking for x, but rather for $2x + x + 3x$, which equals $6x$, or 60. The correct answer is (D).

Using bite-sized pieces will help you break problems into a series of simple, manageable steps, improving both your accuracy and efficiency.

Start with the Most Straightforward Piece

The example above was relatively simple because it presented the pieces in a logical order. But this won't always happen on harder SAT questions. Two of the test writers' favorite tricks are to make you do unnecessary work and to mix up the logical order, hiding the most useful information in the middle or near the end of the problem. Take a look at the next example.

7

Which of the following expressions is equivalent to $(2a^2b^3c^4d^5)^3$?

A) $8a^6b^6c^{12}d^{15}$

B) $8a^6b^6c^7d^{15}$

C) $8a^6b^9c^{12}d^{15}$

D) $8a^6b^9c^7d^{15}$

Here's How to Crack It

Is it helpful to calculate $(2a^2)^3$? What about $(d^5)^3$? In this case, a quick scan of the answer choices tells you that this would be a waste of time. But what happens if you calculate just $(b^3)^3$? That lets you quickly get rid of two wrong answer choices, (A) and (B). When you compare the remaining ones, you only have to calculate $(c^4)^3$ to get rid of another wrong answer choice, (D), and select the correct answer, (C). What if, instead, you started by calculating $(c^4)^3$? Again, you can quickly get rid of two wrong answer choices, (B) and (D), and then you would only have to calculate $(b^3)^3$ to get rid of another wrong answer choice, (A), and select the correct answer, (C). Always use Process of Elimination as you work the problem, or POE-as-you-go. Don't waste time working all the way through it.

Let's practice using bite-sized pieces with a word problem, eliminating after each piece.

4

Anthony is joining a *tae kwon do* class that charges a monthly membership fee of $19.99. A tax of 7% is applied to the monthly membership fee, and an additional graduation fee of $15 is charged each time he moves up a belt level. If Anthony moves up 2 belt levels in n months, which of the following represents his total charge, in dollars, for that period of membership?

A) $1.07(19.99n + 30)$

B) $1.07(19.99n) + 30$

C) $1.07n(19.99 + 2n)$

D) $1.07n(19.99) + 2n$

Here's How to Crack It

The first two lines of the word problem tell you that the base fee is $19.99 plus 7% tax for each month. All four answer choices start off with exactly that information (1.07 times 19.99 times n), so starting with this initial information will waste your time. The middle part of the word problem tells you that he moves up two belt levels, which means an extra $30. You can eliminate (C) and (D) at this point, since $2n$ would be 4, which isn't in the question. Since there is no mention of a tax being applied to that $30, you can also eliminate (A), and now you can select the only remaining option, (B).

To summarize: break the problem into bite-sized pieces, and start with the most straightforward piece, which is not necessarily the first piece of the problem.

PLUG IN THE ANSWERS (PITA)

In the previous chapter, we saw how useful it can be to Plug In whenever there are variables in the answer choices. A closely related technique is Plugging In the Answers (PITA for short). When the answers contain numbers rather than variables, see if you can Plug In the Answers! Let's look at an example.

10

A cargo ship currently holds two-thirds of its maximum capacity by weight. If seven tons of cargo were added to the ship, it would hold 75% of its maximum capacity. What is the maximum capacity, in tons, of the ship?

A) 48

B) 60

C) 84

D) 96

To Plug In the Answers, follow these simple steps:

1. Label the answer choices to avoid careless mistakes and trap answers.
2. If the question asks for the greatest or smallest value, start there. Otherwise, start with one of the answers in the middle.
3. Work the steps, using Bite-Sized Pieces.
4. Eliminate answers that are too big or small.
5. When one of the answers works—STOP.

Here's How to Crack It

First, label the answer choices. In this case, the answers represent the maximum capacity of the ship, so write something like "max" over the answer choices. Since the question is asking for the greatest value ("maximum"!), start with (D) and work through the problem in bite-sized pieces. We need to find two-thirds of 96, which is 63. Then we need to add 7 more tons, so we have 70. Finally, we ask whether 70 is 75% of 96. That is false, so (D) is incorrect. Here's what your work should look like so far:

A cargo ship currently holds two-thirds of its maximum capacity by weight. If seven tons of cargo were added to the ship, it would hold three-fourths of its maximum capacity. What is the maximum capacity, in tons, of the ship?

Max.	2/3	+ 7	= 75% ?
A) 48			
B) 60			
C) 84			
~~D) 96~~	63	70	No

Does it matter which answer we try next? Remember that we're looking for a maximum! So let's try (C). Two-thirds of 84 is 56. Add 7 more tons and we have 63. Is 63 equal to 75% of 84? Yes, it is, so (C) is the correct answer. Here's what your work should look like now:

A cargo ship currently holds two-thirds of its maximum capacity by weight. If seven tons of cargo were added to the ship, it would hold three-fourths of its maximum capacity. What is the maximum capacity, in tons, of the ship?

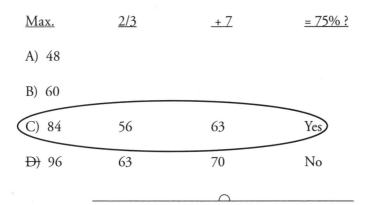

Max.	2/3	+ 7	= 75% ?
A) 48			
B) 60			
C) 84	56	63	Yes
~~D) 96~~	63	70	No

Remember how you have to check all the answers when you plug in your own number? Well, when you Plug In the Answers, you don't need to check all four answers! There is only one correct answer, so stop as soon as you find it.

Let's try a more difficult problem.

15

During the 93 days of summer, the number of tourists at a certain resort can be modeled by the function $n(d) = \frac{1}{5} d^2 - 14d + c$, where c is a constant and $n(d)$ represents the number of visitors on day number d for $1 \leq d \leq 93$. The number of visitors on day number 20 was equal to the number of visitors on what number day?

A) 40

B) 50

C) 60

D) 70

Here's How to Crack It

This problem is tougher than the last, but it can be beaten by the same approach. Start by labeling the answers; they represent the number of a day (for example, the 40th day, the 50th day, etc.). Now work the problem in bite-sized pieces. First, we need to know the number of visitors on the 20th day, so plug 20 into the function: $n(20) = \frac{1}{5}(20)^2 - 14(20) + c$. This simplifies to $-200 + c$. What's c? We don't know, so we can either just leave it or else plug in our own number for c. Either way will work. Say we leave it; the total we are looking for is $-200 + c$.

Now tackle the answer choices, starting with one of the answers in the middle. Say we start with (B). Plug 50 into the function: $n(50) = \frac{1}{5}(50)^2 - 14(50) + c$. This simplifies to $-200 + c$. Success! Choice (B) is the correct answer, and you are done working this problem! How does that feel?

As you can see, if the question is not asking for a greatest or least value, it pays to start with either (B) or (C). If your first choice is not the correct answer, you can usually tell which direction you should go: to the lower or to the higher number.

However, you should always remember there is an exception to this rule. As we've seen, when a question asks for the *least* value (or for the *greatest* value), you should start with the smallest (or the largest) answer choice. Sometimes, the fact that the test-writers are doing this can be difficult to see. Let's try an example.

8

Linda has four children: Adam, Baron, Karin, and Darren. Each child was born exactly three years apart. In 2015, their combined ages were 34 years. What was the age in years of the youngest child in 2012?

A) 1

B) 2

C) 3

D) 4

Here's How to Crack It

Again, start by labeling the answer choices. They represent the age of the youngest child in 2012. Since the problem asks for the age of the youngest child, you start working in bite-sized pieces with (A), the smallest number. The next column could contain the sum of the ages of the four children in 2012, which in this case is $1 + 4 + 7 + 10 = 22$. The final column should contain the sum of the ages of the four children in 2015. This is 3 years later, so you want to add 3 years for each child, or 12 years all together. In this case, that would be $22 + 12 = 34$. Finally, you ask whether your calculation equals 34. Since it does, you select (A), and you are done!

As you can see, PITA is a very useful strategy: it can save you time and bail you out when you don't know how to solve a question. Remember, when you PITA, do the following:

1. Label the answer choices.
2. If the question asks for the greatest or smallest value, start there. Otherwise, start with one of the answers in the middle.
3. Work the steps, using Bite-Sized Pieces.
4. Eliminate answers that are too big or small.
5. When one of the answer works—STOP.

To practice Plugging In the Answers, try the drill below. Then go back though the previous chapters and see if Plugging In the Answers would increase your speed on any of the questions you've already solved.

TRY IT EXERCISE 1

See Chapter 20 for complete answers and explanations. Only use your calculator when you are allowed to do so.

11

A physics student was conducting experiments to determine the correct equation to describe the trajectory of a ball that was thrown straight up into the air from a height of five feet above the ground with an initial velocity of 3 feet per second. If the height of the ball is given by the equation $h = 5 + 3t - 2t^2$, where h = height in feet and t = time in seconds, at which of the following values for t will the ball have the greatest height?

A) 0.75

B) 1

C) 1.5

D) 2.5

18

Mrs. Johnson earns $60 more per week than Mr. Johnson. If three-fifths of Mrs. Johnson's weekly salary is equal to two-thirds of Mr. Johnson's weekly salary, how much do the Johnsons earn together in one week?

A) $540

B) $780

C) $960

D) $1,140

13

If a and c are positive integers such that $\frac{2}{5}a = b$ and $b = \frac{3c^2}{4}$, what is the least possible value of a ?

A) 30

B) 36

C) 42

D) 48

For further practice, go online to your Student Tools and complete the Chapter 18 PITA Drill.

HOT TOPICS

You may not yet realize it, but the SAT is pretty predicable. The test writers like to recycle the same old topics, year after year. Below are some of the SAT's greatest hits, with some helpful strategies to get you through these questions.

Percents

With percent questions, it's often helpful to translate English to math. The following terms come up frequently, so make sure you know how to translate them.

English	Math
percent (%)	divide by 100
of	multiply
is, are	equals, costs
what, what number, some number	x (or any variable)

Let's try an example.

8

A study found that 10% of Americans have a diagnosable personality disorder. If only 5% of people with personality disorders seek psychological treatment, and there are 320 million Americans, how many Americans with personality disorders (in millions) seek psychological treatment?

A) 1.6

B) 3.2

C) 6.4

D) 7.2

Here's How to Crack It

Remember to use Bite-Sized Pieces and translate. The phrase "10% of Americans" can be translated as $\frac{10}{100}$ (320 million) = 32 million. The phrase "5% of people with personality disorders" can now be translated as 5% of 32 million, or $\frac{5}{100}$ (32 million) = 1.6 million. The correct answer is (A).

Arithmetic concepts are often tested with charts and tables. The test writers hide the data you need in the graphic, so you have to pull the right numbers out. Let's try an example.

5

The following bar-graph shows the densities of several pure metals, measured in grams per cubic centimeter.

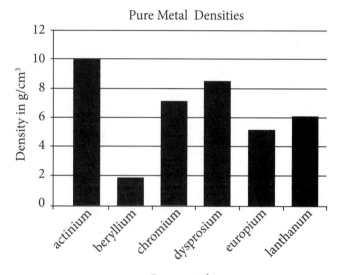

The density of beryllium is approximately what percentage of the density of actinium?

A)   5

B)   10

C)   20

D) 500

Here's How to Crack It

Plug in the numbers from the chart: the density of beryllium is approximately 2 g/cm³, and the density of actinium is approximately 10 g/cm³. So you can read the question in this way:

2 is approximately what percentage of 10?

Now translate the English into math: $2 = \dfrac{x}{100} \times 10$, which reduces to $2 = \dfrac{x}{10}$, so $x = 20$, which is (C).

Mean, Median, and Mode

Average (also called "arithmetic mean") is one of the SAT's favorite subjects. Whenever you are facing an average question, think $T = AN$.

> Use $T = AN$ for average questions.
>
> T is the Total.
>
> A is the average.
>
> N is the number of things.

In any average calculation, three components are involved: the total, the number of things, and the average. Any time you have two of the components, you can easily find the third by plugging the known information into the equation $T = AN$ and solving it for the unknown piece. Let's look at a sample question.

3

The average (arithmetic mean) weight of five gold bars is 9 pounds. After two more bars are added, the average weight increases to 11 pounds. What is the average weight, in pounds, of the two bars that were added?

A) 13

B) 14

C) 15

D) 16

Here's How to Crack It

Start with the first (bite-sized) sentence. The average is 9, and the number of things is 5, so plug those into the equation. It becomes $T = (9)(5) = 45$. Now do the same for the next sentence. The average is 11, and there are 7 things, so $T = (11)(7) = 77$. Finally, to tackle the last sentence, use the equation once again. The total is $77 - 45 = 32$, and there are 2 things, so $32 = (A)(2)$. Divide both sides by 2 to get $16 = A$, and the correct answer is (D).

Along with average, the SAT likes to throw in the related concepts of median and mode. Just remember that median is the middle number of an ordered list, and mode is the number (or numbers) that occurs most often in an ordered list. Try a question.

24

[1, 3, 9, 10, 17]

A list of five numbers is shown above. A new list of seven numbers is to be formed from the list above by repeating one number, using the remaining numbers once each, and adding one additional number. If the mean and median of the new list is 9, which of the following CANNOT be the mode?

A)   3

B)   9

C)   10

D)   17

Here's How to Crack It

This is a tough question, so you need to be organized. You know that the mean (average) of the new list of 7 numbers is 9, so fill in the $T = AN$ equation. This becomes $T = (9)(7) = 63$.

Since the original total is $1 + 3 + 9 + 10 + 17 = 40$, and the new total has to be 63 in order for the mean to be 9, the repeated number plus the new number must equal 23.

You also know that the median is 9, so draw 7 spots and put 9 in the middle.

__   __   __   9   __   __   __

Now, PITA! Start with (B). If the mode is 9, that means the repeated number must be 9. We need to add 23, so the new number is $23 - 9 = 14$. Fill in your list:

1   3   9   9   10   14   17

The median is still 9, so (B) checks out, which means it's <u>NOT</u> the answer.

Which answer should we try next? It's hard to tell, so if you're not sure, pick a direction and go! Let's try (C). If the mode is 10, that's the number we repeat, so the new number is 23 – 10 = 13. Now fill in the list again.

<u>1</u>   <u>3</u>   <u>9</u>   <u>10</u>   <u>10</u>   <u>13</u>   <u>17</u>

This time, the median is 10, but since the question states that the median is 9, 10 cannot be the mode, and the correct answer is (C).

One of the keys to mean, median, and mode questions is to stay organized. Using the equation $T = AN$ and writing everything down will help you to avoid overlooking important pieces of the puzzle.

Mean, Median, and Mode are the three big statistical concepts you can expect to see on the SAT. Since mean, median, and mode measure the middle (MMM MM!), they are called measures of central tendency. In addition to knowing about the middle of your data, sometimes you want to know about how far the data are spread, or how evenly they are spread. The next two concepts help you do just that.

Range and Standard Deviation

Range is a simple concept: the distance from the lowest to the highest number. Standard deviation is a less simple concept, but in a nutshell, it measures the evenness of your data. Let's illustrate both concepts with a concrete example.

Say you poll twenty people in a fast food restaurant on a given day and time. You find that the wealthiest person there makes $400,000 per year, the poorest person there makes $10,000 per year, and everybody else is somewhere in between. Based on this information alone, you can calculate the range of incomes: $400,000 – $10,000 = $390,000. This number does give you some information about the people in the restaurant that day, but not much.

To know more, you would want to know the mean, median, and/or mode. Let's say you figure out that the mean income of your twenty people is $70,000 per year. This information answers some questions, but leaves others open. Maybe eighteen people make around $55,000 per year, and just two make much less or much more. In that case, most of the people make about the same income: that means that your data have low variability, and so you would have a small standard deviation. But maybe five people make between $10,000 and $30,000; another five make between $30,000 and $60,000;

another five make between $60,000 and $70,000; another four make between $75,000 and $100,000, and just one makes $400,000. In that case, people have very different incomes: that means that your data have high variability, so you would have a higher standard deviation.

Luckily, you will never have to calculate a standard deviation for the SAT! Let's see how the SAT might test your knowledge of range and standard deviation.

15

A billionaire visiting a fast food restaurant decides to give $20,000 to everyone in the restaurant. What effect does this gift have on the mean and standard deviation of the patrons' incomes for that year?

A) It would increase the mean and the standard deviation.

B) It would increase the mean but have no effect on the standard deviation.

C) It would decrease the mean and the standard deviation.

D) It would decrease the mean but have no effect on the standard deviation.

Here's How to Crack It

Since standard deviation is a measure of how spread-out or even the data is, the only things that change it are changes to individual data points. If data points are removed or added, or if some increase or decrease while others stay the same, the standard deviation will be affected. In this case, the income of all patrons in the restaurant changed, and the income changed by the same amount for everyone. The standard deviation would therefore be the same, so eliminate (A) and (C). Everyone would have more money this year, so the average or mean income would increase, making (B) the right answer.

Sampling Error

Some SAT Math questions will feel more like the questions you'd find on a science test. They may give you the data from an experiment and ask questions about it. If you encounter questions that ask about the sampling error of a study, identify the variables and determine whether the conclusion is supported by the experiment or study. When considering the validity of study, check to ensure that the study was conducted on an unbiased sample that is representative of the target population, the conclusion is supported by the data, and the conclusion is based solely on the acquired data.

1

VRT is a company interested in testing out a new virtual reality device to determine whether or not the device will be popular among suburban moms. VRT decides to do product testing at four soccer tournaments around the country, requesting that all interested individuals take part in a live demonstration in each stadium's lobby. After conducting the testing, VRT collected the data, finding that 65% of the suburban moms who participated were interested in purchasing the virtual reality device. Based on this finding, would VRT be justified in claiming that the majority of suburban moms would likely purchase the new virtual reality device?

A) Yes; the majority of suburban moms who participated in the live demonstration indicated that they would likely purchase the new virtual reality device.

B) Yes; VRT's study used a representative sample of the target population, indicating that the conclusion is accurate.

C) No; while 65% of the suburban moms who participated in the study indicated that they would likely purchase the virtual reality device, the sample failed to accurately represent the target population.

D) No; the majority of suburban moms indicated that they would not purchase the new virtual reality device.

Here's How to Crack It

When you encounter questions that ask about the validity of a conclusion, you want to examine the information provided, eliminating answer choices that fail to support the data. In this scenario, VRT wished to determine whether or not suburban moms would be interested in purchasing the new virtual reality device. However, the sample that VRT used was not representative of the target population. Indeed, VRT only went to four locations nationwide that were holding soccer tournaments. Not only did VRT limit the sample by only gathering data from four locations, but VRT also failed to account for the fact that not all suburban moms have children who play soccer. To make matters worse, VRT requested that individuals test the product in the lobby, meaning that only those who were interested in the product would attend the demonstration. Accordingly, VRT would not be justified in claiming that the majority of suburban moms would likely purchase the new virtual reality device as the sample was not representative of the target population; choose (C).

Unit Conversion

The SAT can also test proportions with questions about unit conversions and scale drawings. Try this one.

33

In tabletop gaming, 28 mm scale figurines are at a 1:64 scale to their real-world equivalents. The above minotaur figurine is 43 millimeters (mm) tall. If this figurine uses 28 mm scale, then how tall would the equivalent real-world minotaur be, rounded to the nearest foot? (Note: 1 foot = 304.8 millimeters)

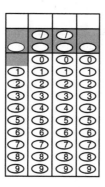

Here's How to Crack It

Use proportions to convert the units to feet. First, figure out how many millimeters tall the real-world minotaur would be by setting up a proportion:

$$\frac{1}{64} = \frac{43\,\text{mm}}{x\,\text{mm}}$$

Solve for x by cross-multiplying: $x = (43)(64) = 2{,}752$ mm. Next, set up another proportion using the conversion factors. Remember to label your units and have the same units in the numerators and denominators of each fraction:

$$\frac{1\,\text{foot}}{304.8\,\text{mm}} = \frac{x\,\text{feet}}{2{,}752\,\text{mm}}$$

Cross-multiply to get $304.8x = 2{,}752$. Divide both sides by 304.8 and you get $x = 9.03$, which rounds to 9 feet.

PROBABILITY

Here's the basic definition of probability:

$$\text{Probability} = \frac{\text{number of desired options}}{\text{number of possible options}}$$

Let's try a question.

1

Blood Type	Number of Americans
A+	108,800,000
A–	19,200,000
B+	32,000,000
B–	6,400,000
AB+	12,800,000
AB–	3,200,000
O+	118,400,000
O–	19,200,000

The chart above shows the number of Americans living in the United States that have a particular blood type. Based on the information provided, what is the probability that a randomly selected American in the United States will have neither an A or O blood type?

A) 5%

B) 17%

C) 57%

D) 83%

Here's How to Crack It

In order to determine the probability that a randomly selected American in the United States will have neither an A nor O blood type, you must first find the total population. Add the individual populations to find that the total population is 108,800,000 + 19,200,000 + 32,000,000 + 6,400,000 + 12,800,000 + 3,200,000 + 118,400,000 + 19,200,000 = 320,000,000. Next, you have to find the total population of Americans living in the United States that have neither A nor O blood types. Add the B+, B–, AB+, and AB– populations together to find this total to be 32,000,000 + 6,400,000 + 12,800,000 + 3,200,000 = 54,400,000. Finally, you can determine the probability that a randomly selected American in the United States will have neither an A or O blood type by dividing the population that has neither A nor O blood types by the total population of Americans living in the United States; $\dfrac{54,400,000}{320,000,000} = 17\%$. Select (B).

SEQUENCES

Like several of the topics in this chapter, the most important thing to do with SAT sequences is to organize them. If a question asks you about the first six terms of a sequence, make slots for each term and label them, like this:

1st	2nd	3rd	4th	5th	6th
___	___	___	___	___	___

It also helps to look for patterns that will make the question easier to manage. Let's try an example.

9

$$\frac{1}{j}, \frac{1}{2}, \frac{j}{4}, \ldots$$

In the sequence shown above, the first term is $\frac{1}{j}$ for all values of j greater than 2. Each term after the first is equal to the preceding term multiplied by a constant. Which of the following, in terms of j, is equal to the sixth term of the sequence?

A) $\dfrac{j^2}{16}$

B) $\dfrac{j^3}{16}$

C) $\dfrac{j^3}{32}$

D) $\dfrac{j^4}{32}$

Here's How to Crack It

Did the phrase "in terms of" ring a bell? If you thought to plug in, that was a smart choice! Since $j > 2$, let's see what happens if we plug in $j = 3$. Then, the first three terms are $\frac{1}{3}, \frac{1}{2}$, and $\frac{3}{4}$. It's not easy to spot the relationship between these numbers. Is each term really the preceding term multiplied by a constant? It's hard to tell, so let's plug in another number that makes the math easier. If $j = 4$, then the first three terms are $\frac{1}{4}, \frac{1}{2}$, and 1. Now we can see the relationship. Each term is double the previous term! Armed with this knowledge, you should make a diagram for the first six terms:

1st	2nd	3rd	4th	5th	6th
$\frac{1}{4}$	$\frac{1}{2}$	1	2	4	8

The sixth term is 8, so that's our target. Now plug $j = 4$ into the answers, and pick the one that equals 8; it's (D).

GROWTH AND DECAY

Sequences reflect numbers changing in a pattern over time. If a population increases by a set factor or percent over time, it is said to be growing exponentially. Things like compound interest, the spread of viruses, or population growth of bacterium might show this sort of growth. Similarly, if it shrinks by a set factor or percent, it is showing exponential decay. The amount of radiation in an isotope or the drug concentration in a person's body decrease in this way over time. Unlike growth at a constant rate, which involves multiplication and a linear graph, exponential growth involves exponents, hence the name.

> When the growth is a **percent** of the total population, the formula for exponential growth or decay is
>
> $$\textit{final amount} = \textit{original amount}\ (1 \pm \textit{rate})^{\textit{number of changes}}$$
>
> When the growth is a **multiple** of the total population, the formula for exponential growth or decay is
>
> $$\textit{final amount} = \textit{original amount}\ (\textit{multiplier})^{\textit{number of changes}}$$

Use this knowledge to make the next question easier.

1

Researchers at Cat-In-A-Tube are working on technology that infuses kittens with glow cells that allow cats to glow in the dark. After much work, the researchers have created glow cells that reproduce at a rate of 32% each day. If the researchers start with two glow cells, what is the minimum number of days before the researchers have 550 glow cells?

A) 20

B) 21

C) 22

D) 23

Here's How to Crack It

In order to determine the minimum number of days before the researchers have 550 glow cells, it is helpful to know the formula for growth: *final amount = original amount* $\times$ $(1 + rate)^n$, where n = the number of changes. Here, you are told that the researchers start with two glow cells and that the population grows at a rate of 32% each day. Accordingly, the growth equation will be $550 = 2(1.32)^n$. Since the question provides numerical answer choices in ascending order, and asks you to find the minimum number of days to have 550 glow cells, you can use PITA to tackle this question! If you start with (B), the number of glow cells after 21 days will be $550 = 2(1.32)^{21}$; $550 = 2(340.45)$; $550 = 680.90$. Since the question asks you to find the minimum number of days it takes to create 550 glow cells, you can now eliminate (C) and (D). Next, check (A). Here, the number of glow cells after 20 days will be $550 = 2(1.32)^{20}$; $550 = 2(257.92)$; $550 = 515.83$. Since you have not reached the minimum number of glow cells, eliminate (A) and select (B).

EQUATIONS

Although Plugging In and PITA are extremely valuable strategies, once in a while you just have to write equations and solve. This often happens near the end of the grid-in section. When you're faced with this situation, translate the word problem carefully, and pay close attention to what the problem is asking for. Let's try an example.

33

Two rival cell-phone companies have different rate structures. Company X charges a flat rate of $0.15 per minute. Company Y charges $0.25 per minute for the first five minutes, and $0.10 for each minute after the first five. If a call costs the same amount with either plan, how long, in minutes, does that call last?

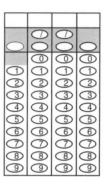

Here's How to Crack It

Let's break this down into bite-sized pieces. We'll say that x equals the number of minutes. A call with the company X costs $0.15x$. A call with company Y costs—be careful here—$5(0.25) + 0.1(x - 5)$. The two calls cost the same amount, so set them equal to each other and solve; you should get $x = 15$, so the correct answer is 15.

Sometimes a question will require two variables, so you'll need to write two equations. Try the next question.

17

On Saturday, Abeke participated in a long-distance race. After the race, he learned that 11 more runners finished before him than finished after him. He also learned that the total number of runners who finished the race was four times the number of runners who finished after him. How many runners finished the race before Abeke did?

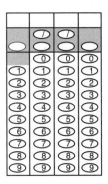

Here's How to Crack It

When we first discussed bite-sized pieces, we said that the test writers will often hide the most useful information near the end of a problem. That's definitely the case here. The second sentence is much easier to handle than the first, so let's deal with it first. But even before that, draw a map or picture of the problem. The total is four times the number who finished after Abeke. Let's say the total is t, and the number who finished after Abeke is x. Therefore, $t = 4x$. Now let's translate the first sentence. If x runners finished after Abeke, then $x + 11$ finished before him, and the total number is $x + (x + 11) + 1$ (we have to count Abeke), which simplifies to $2x + 12$. Now we can write a second equation: $t = 2x + 12$. From the first equation, substitute $4x$ for t in the second equation, so now you have $4x = 2x + 12$. Solve this to get $x = 6$.

Wait! Stop! Don't forget to RTFQ! The question asks how many runners finished *before* Abeke, which is $x + 11$, so the correct answer is $6 + 11 = 17$. No matter how pleased you are when you've solved a question, don't forget to READ THE FINAL QUESTION.

TRY IT EXERCISE 2

▼

Questions 27 and 28 refer to the following information.

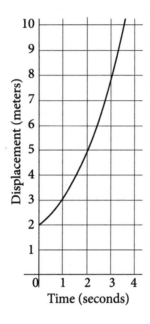

When acceleration is constant, change in displacement is directly proportional to time and proportional to the square of time. This is expressed by the Merton rule: $x = x_0 + v_o t + \frac{1}{2}at^2$, where x is the final displacement, x_0 is the initial displacement, v_0 is the initial velocity, a is acceleration, and t is time in seconds. The graph above shows the displacement of an object under constant acceleration.

27

Which of the following expresses t in terms of x, x_0, v_0, and a?

A) $t = \dfrac{-v_0 \pm \sqrt{(v_0)^2 - 2a(x_0 - x)}}{a}$

B) $t = \dfrac{-v_0 \pm \sqrt{(v_0)^2 - 4a(x_0 - x)}}{2a}$

C) $t = \dfrac{-v_0 \pm \sqrt{(v_0)^2 - 2a(x_0 - x)}}{(x_0 - x)}$

D) $t = \dfrac{-v_0 \pm \sqrt{(v_0)^2 - 4a(x_0 - x)}}{2(x_0 - x)}$

28

According to the graph and equation above, what is the value of a if the initial velocity is 0.5 m/s ?

A) 0.25

B) 0.5

C) 1.0

D) 2.0

For further practice, go online to your Student Tools and complete the Chapter 18 Word Problems Drill.

Summary

○ Don't choke when you see long word problems. Instead, break down the question into manageable, bite-sized pieces and RTFQ.

○ When you see word problems with numbers in the answer choices that are in either ascending or descending order, use PITA. When you find the right answer, pick it and move on!

○ When dealing with percent questions, translate the English words into math terms.

○ Remember that Mean, Median, and Mode measure the middle (MMM MM).
  • Mean is the average; use the equation $T = AN$ to keep yourself organized.
  • Median is the number in the middle of a set; make sure you put your numbers in order.
  • Mode is the most frequently occurring number in a set.

○ You won't have to calculate a standard deviation on the SAT, but you should know that standard deviation indicates how data is distributed across a given range.

○ When asked about sampling error, ensure that the data collection was done properly, the sample is representative of the target population, and the conclusion is based on the data.

○ When converting between different units, create a proportion.

○ Probability can be thought of as $\dfrac{\textit{what you want}}{\textit{total number of possibilities}}$.

- If a question asks you to find the probability that one event *and* another event will occur, multiply the individual probabilities together.
- If a question asks you to find the probability that one event *or* another event occurs, add the individual probabilities together.

○ When working with sequences, organize and label the terms in the sequence. It'll make your life much easier.

○ Growth and Decay
- For questions about exponential growth or decay when growth is a percent of the total population, use the formula *final amount = original amount* $(1 \pm \textit{rate})^{\textit{number of changes}}$.
- For questions about exponential growth or decay when growth is a multiple of the total population, use the formula *final amount = original amount* $(\textit{multiplier})^{\textit{number of changes}}$.

○ When working with equations, isolate the variable in question.

○ Make sure that you only use your calculator when you are allowed to do so!

Chapter 19
Plane Geometry

INTRODUCTION

Plane geometry makes up a small part of the SAT—at most, you will see six plane geometry questions over the entire test. Beating tough geometry problems is all about putting together puzzle pieces. Many students struggle with geometry because, unlike algebra, they cannot see the end result as easily. If this is you, try to think of geometry as a puzzle. First, you find the corner pieces. Next, you build the edges. Finally, you finish the interior. Geometry is the same way. There are three steps to beating any geometry problem.

- If there's no figure, draw your own; if a figure is noted as not drawn to scale, re-draw it.
- Write any information from the problem directly on the figure.
- Write down any formulas you need, and add in any information from the problem.

Always start by drawing the figure if one is not provided. Next, label the figure with all the information that you know. Last, always write down any formulas you need. These steps are comparable to finding the corner and edge pieces of a puzzle. Once these are in place, you will often be able to see what the next step is. Consider the following.

17

A square is inscribed in a circle with a circumference of 8π. What is the area of the square?

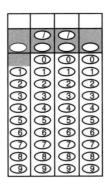

Here's How to Crack It

At first glance this may seem to be a very challenging problem. Don't panic. Instead, begin by drawing the figure:

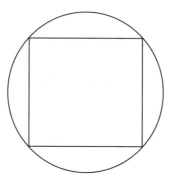

Now, label the figure. The only information that the problem provides is the circumference of the circle, which is 8π. Now, write down formulas. The problem asks for the area of the square. The formula for the area of a square is $A = s^2$, where A is the area of the square and s is the length of each side. To solve this problem, you need to somehow find the length of one of the sides of the square. Next, since the problem provided the circumference, write that down as well: $C = \pi d$ (or $C = 2\pi r$). Put the information from the problem into this equation to find that $8\pi = \pi d$, so the diameter is 8. Now, add this information to the figure. A diameter is any line segment that extends from one edge of a circle to another while passing through the center of a circle. Be sure to add the information to the figure in a way that helps with the square:

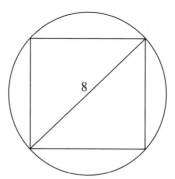

As you can see from this figure, the diameter of the circle is the same distance as the diagonal of the square. Whenever a square is bisected, two special right triangles are formed with angle measures of 45°-45°-90°. The side lengths of this triangle are fixed as well into the following ratio: $s:s:s\sqrt{2}$, where s are the legs of the triangle and $s\sqrt{2}$ is the hypotenuse. Use this ratio to solve for s: $s\sqrt{2} = 8$, so $s = \dfrac{8}{\sqrt{2}}$. Congratulations, you have finally found the last piece of the puzzle you needed. At the beginning of this example, you determined that in order to find the area of the square, you needed the length of the sides. Finish the problem by solving for the area of the square: $s^2 = \left(\dfrac{8}{\sqrt{2}}\right)^2 = \dfrac{64}{2} = 32$. The answer is 32.

To review, three basic techniques are needed to beat every geometry question. A figure is necessary; the SAT will sometimes provide the figure and sometimes force you to create your own. Secondly, label all of the information that the problem gives you about the figure. The labeling process should continue throughout the problem. As you discover more information about the problem, be sure to continue labeling your figure. Finally, many challenging geometry questions appear unsolvable at first glance. To avoid the panic that this feeling may cause, write down formulas for every measurement mentioned in the problem. Writing down the formulas will ensure that you do not make math errors, will give you a goal, will give you some starting math to do, and will often lead you directly to the solution.

Since formulas are so important, make sure you know all your geometry facts cold. Do the following Try It Exercises, and if you find that you are rusty on any geometry definitions and rules, make sure to look those up and maybe even make some flashcards. And make sure to keep the following in mind.

SAT GEOMETRY FACTS

- On the SAT, if something looks like a straight line, it is actually straight.
- On the SAT, if a line appears to pass through a point, then it does actually pass through that point.
- On the SAT, the following special right triangles commonly appear: 3-4-5; 6-8-10; 5-12-13.
- The reference box at the beginning of the Math sections provides the formulas and facts for many basic geometry shapes already mentioned. Make sure you know which ones are there.
- If a questions asks for the volume of a shape not listed in the reference box, the test will provide the formula to you in the question.

Reference Information

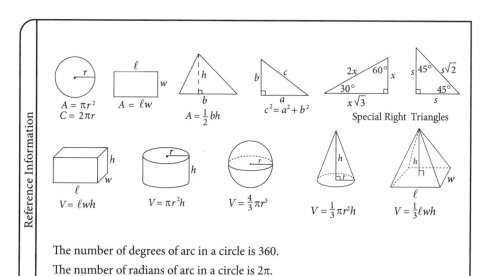

The number of degrees of arc in a circle is 360.

The number of radians of arc in a circle is 2π.

The sum of the measures in degrees of the angles of a triangle is 180.

TRY IT EXERCISE 1—ANGLES AND LINES

After you try these questions, go to Chapter 20 to check your answers. Remember to leave that calculator alone on questions with no calculator symbol.

3

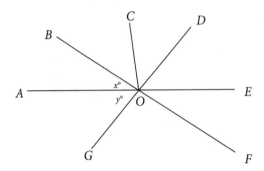

Note: Figure not drawn to scale.

In the figure above, lines *AE*, *BF*, and *DG* all intersect at vertex *O*. If $x + y = 70°$ and if line *CO* bisects angle *BOD*, then what is the measure of angle *BOC* ?

A) 20°

B) 40°

C) 55°

D) 75°

4

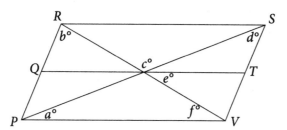

In the figure above, $RS \parallel QT \parallel PV$. Which of the following must equal 180°?

A) $a + b + c$

B) $a + c + e$

C) $b + c + d$

D) $c + e + f$

6

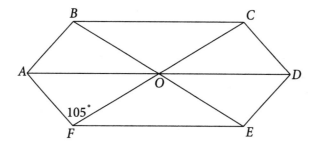

In the figure above, $BC \parallel AD \parallel FE$, and lines AD, BE, and CF all intersect at point O. If $BA \perp AF$, and $BE = CF$, then what is the measure of BOC?

A) 75

B) 90

C) 105

D) 120

TRY IT EXERCISE 2—TRIANGLES

Work these questions, with or without your calculator as indicated, then check the answers in Chapter 20.

1

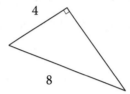

What is the area of the triangle above?

A) $8\sqrt{3}$

B) 16

C) $16\sqrt{3}$

D) 32

8

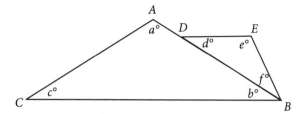

Note: Figure not drawn to scale.

In the figure above, point D is on side $\overline{AB}$ of $\triangle ABC$.
If $b = f = 30$, $a = 100$, $d = 50$, $\overline{AD} = \dfrac{1}{3}\overline{AB}$, and $\overline{BE} = \dfrac{1}{2}\overline{AB}$,
which of the following is equal to $\overline{BC}$?

A) $2\overline{AD}$

B) $2\overline{AB}$

C) $4\overline{AD}$

D) $\overline{AB}\sqrt{2}$

20

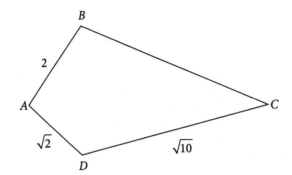

In the figure above, line segments *AC* and *BD* are perpendicular and intersect at point *O* (not shown). If *AO* = *DO*, then what is the ratio of the area of triangle *ACD* to the area of triangle *ABC* ?

A) 1 to $\sqrt{3}$

B) 1 to 2

C) 1 to 3

D) $\sqrt{3}$ to 1

TRY IT EXERCISE 3—RIGHT TRIANGLE TRIGONOMETRY

After you try these questions, go to Chapter 20 to check your answers. Remember to leave that calculator alone on questions with no calculator symbol.

11

In right triangle ABC (not shown), if $\sin CAB = \dfrac{7}{25}$, and the perimeter of triangle ABC is 14, which of the following is closest to the length of BC?

A) 1.75

B) 6

C) 6.25

D) 7

12

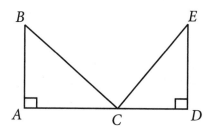

In the triangles shown above, if $BC \perp CE$, which of the following statements must be true?

A) $AC = ED$

B) $\dfrac{AB}{AC} = \dfrac{DE}{CD}$

C) $\dfrac{AB}{BC} = \dfrac{CD}{CE}$

D) $\dfrac{BC}{AC} = \dfrac{CE}{CD}$

15

Sam is standing at the edge of the roof of a building looking straight ahead. He then directs his gaze downward 63° and sees a pothole 10 meters from the base of the building. If Sam's eye level is 1.2 meters above the rooftop, which of the following is closest to the height of the building?

A) 5.13 meters

B) 18.43 meters

C) 19.63 meters

D) 20.83 meters

TRY IT EXERCISE 4—CIRCLES

Work these questions, either with or without your calculator as you see fit, then check the answers in Chapter 20.

7

A homeowner is buying a circular rug for a square room that has an area of 144 square feet. If the homeowner wants the rug to be centered in the room with 1 foot of space between the edge of the rug and any wall, which of the following is closest to the largest possible area of the circular rug, in square feet?

A) 25

B) 80

C) 100

D) 115

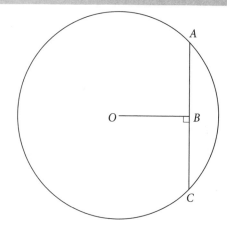

In the figure above, A and C are points on the circumference of circle O. If the area of the circle is 64π and the measure of minor arc AC is 4π, then what is the length of line segment BO?

A) 4

B) $4\sqrt{2}$

C) 8

D) $8\sqrt{2}$

19

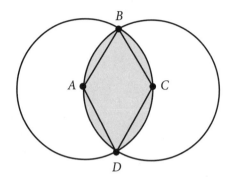

In the figure above, *A* and *C* are the centers of the circles and *B* and *D* are the points of intersection. If the perimeter of the shaded region is 40°, what is the perimeter of quadrilateral *ABCD* ?

A)   40

B)   60

C)   80

D) 120

TRY IT EXERCISE 5—CIRCLE TRIGONOMETRY

After you try these questions, go to Chapter 20 to check your answers. Remember to leave that calculator alone on questions with no calculator symbol.

6

Points *A* and *C* are two points on a circle with center *O*. If the circle has a circumference of 16π and the radian measure of angle *AOC* is $\dfrac{5\pi}{4}$, what is the length of minor arc *AC* ?

A) 4π

B) 5π

C) 10π

D) 12π

21

Given that $\dfrac{7\pi}{6} < x < \dfrac{5\pi}{3}$, where x is in radians, which of the following could be the value of $\sin x$?

A) $-\dfrac{\sqrt{3}}{2}$

B) $\dfrac{-1}{2}$

C) $\dfrac{1}{2}$

D) $\dfrac{\sqrt{3}}{2}$

28

If $\tan \theta$ is $\dfrac{1}{\sqrt{3}}$ and θ is in radians, which of the following could be the value of $\theta + \dfrac{\pi}{2}$?

A) $\dfrac{-\pi}{6}$

B) $\dfrac{5\pi}{4}$

C) $\dfrac{7\pi}{6}$

D) $\dfrac{5\pi}{3}$

TRY IT EXERCISE 6—THREE DIMENSIONAL FIGURES

Work these questions, either with or without your calculator as indicated, then check the answers in Chapter 20. Don't forget to look at the reference box to find the formula you need, even if you think you know it already.

13

A right circular cone and a right circular cylinder have equal heights and the volume of the cylinder is twice that of the cone. What is the radius of the cylinder if the base radius of the cone is 3 cm and the volume of the cone is 18π cm^3 ?

A) $\sqrt{2}$

B) 2

C) $2\sqrt{3}$

D) $\sqrt{6}$

26

A cube with a volume of 64 cubic inches is inscribed in a sphere so that all vertices of the cube touch the sphere. What is the volume, in cubic inches, of the sphere?

A) $16\pi\sqrt{3}$

B) $32\pi\sqrt{3}$

C) $64\pi\sqrt{3}$

D) $128\pi\sqrt{3}$

17

The radius of right circular cylinder A is half of that of right circular cylinder B. Cylinder A has a volume of 100π cubic centimeters and a height of 4 centimeters. If the volume of cylinder B is 200π cubic centimeters, what is the height of cylinder B ?

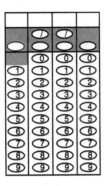

BALLPARKING AND GEOMETRY

Ballparking is also a great technique on Geometry questions. Most of the time, the figures College Board provides are drawn to scale. (The exceptions are when the question says, "Note: Figure not drawn to scale" under the figure.) When the figure is drawn to scale, you can Ballpark to eliminate answers that don't fit with the figure, and sometimes narrow the answers down to just one without a ton of extra work.

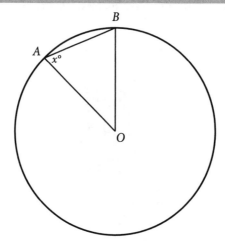

28

In the figure above, O is the center of the circle and $x = 67.5°$. If the area of the circle is 64π, then what is the area of triangle ABO ?

A) 12

B) $16\sqrt{2}$

C) 12π

D) $32\sqrt{2}$

Here's How to Crack It

This is a tricky question. If you're not sure how to solve it, or you think you might not have time, consider Ballparking instead. Also, you can use Ballparking to eliminate trap answers before beginning to actually solve a problem.

The first step of Ballparking is to generate a rough estimate of what value you are looking for. The figure is drawn to scale, so carve up the circle into multiple triangles of the same size as the one in the problem. Use your pencil to extend the lines of triangle ABO into diameters. Then keep adding lines until you have filled up the circle.

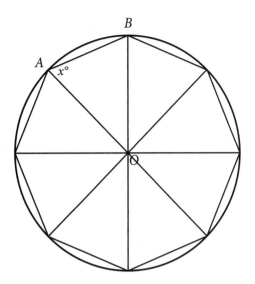

Eight triangles of similar shape fit inside the circle; therefore, the area of the triangle is going to be a little less than $\frac{1}{8}$ of the area of the circle. Since the area of the circle is 64π, then the area of the triangle is going to be just less than 8π. Continue Ballparking by rounding the value of π to 3. Therefore, you need an answer choice whose value is just below $8 \times 3 = 24$. Now look at the answers and use POE aggressively:

A)   12   This is too small, eliminate it.

B) $16\sqrt{2}$ $\sqrt{2}$ is about 1.4, so this is about 22.4. It's close, so keep it!

C) 12π This is too large, so eliminate it.

D) $32\sqrt{2}$ This is too large, so eliminate it.

Therefore, the answer is (B).

Now that you know how to Ballpark on geometry questions, be on the lookout for opportunities to do it going forward.

Summary

- On geometry problems, remember to do these three steps:
  - Draw a figure if there isn't one, or redraw it if it's not to scale.
  - Label all information from the problem in the figure.
  - Write down any equations you need.

- Once you've done these things just take things one puzzle piece at a time!

- Keep in mind that Plugging In is a useful tool in geometry problems too. Just make sure you follow the rules of geometry with any numbers you pick.

- Ballparking can be a useful tool on geometry questions to save time and help you avoid careless errors.

- Review your geometry facts as needed to make sure you can handle any geometry question the SAT can throw at you.

Chapter 20
Math Exercises:
Answers and
Explanations

CHAPTER 16: ALGEBRA, COORDINATE GEOMETRY, AND FUNCTIONS

Try It Exercise 1

2. **B**   While this question may look complicated, it is really just a matter of algebraic manipulation to isolate the requested variables. By crossing out the phrase "in terms of a and V," you know that you need to find the duration of the time interval, ΔT, which is expressed as $T_2 - T_1$ in the provided equation, $a = \dfrac{V_2 - V_1}{T_2 - T_1}$. Accordingly, you can eliminate (A) and (C) because they are simply looking at T, not ΔT expressed as $T_2 - T_1$. Next, manipulate the equation, $a = \dfrac{V_2 - V_1}{T_2 - T_1}$ by multiplying both sides of the equation by $T_2 - T_1$ to find that $a(T_2 - T_1) = V_2 - V_1$. Finally, isolate $T_2 - T_1$ by dividing both sides of the equation by a to find that $T_2 - T_1 = \dfrac{V_2 - V_1}{a}$. Accordingly, eliminate (D) and select (B).

10. **C**   Treat the imaginary number i just like any other variable, except that whenever i^2 appears, replace it with -1. Start by using FOIL to multiply the complex numbers: $(5 + 2i) \times (-3 - 4i) = -15 - 20i - 6i - 8i^2$, which simplifies to $-15 - 26i - 8i^2$. Now, replace i^2 with -1: $-15 - 26i - 8(-1) = -15 - 26i + 8$, which simplifies to $-7 - 26i$, (C).

31. **4**   This question deals with the basic properties of integers as they are squared or cubed. Any squared value will be positive, so x can be either negative or positive. On the other hand, y can only be positive, since its cube is positive (a cubed negative number will always result in a negative). Remember to RTFQ! The question asks for distinct values of $x + y$. Start by writing down all possible values for x and y. Since x^2 is less than 4, the only possible values for x are -1, -1, 0, and 1. Since y^3 is less than 25 but greater than zero, the possible values for y are 1 and 2. Since there are three values for x and two for y, you might assume the answer is $3 \times 2 = 6$. But like most easy short cuts on the SAT, this is a trap. Write it out!

Sum the values systematically:

$-1 + 1 = 0$

$-1 + 2 = 1$

$0 + 1 = 1$

$0 + 2 = 2$

$1 + 1 = 2$

$1 + 2 = 3$

Since the distinct values of $x + y$ are 0, 1, 2, and 3, the answer is 4.

Try It Exercise 2

10. **A** When given a polynomial and asked for the solutions, you need to factor the polynomial, set each factor equal to 0, then solve each one. Here, you are given the roots, or the values of x that satisfy the equation, so you need to work backward. If $x = -\frac{1}{2}$, then one factor of the polynomial is $(x + \frac{1}{2})$. If $x = 3$, then another factor is $(x - 3)$. There are two 3s in the list of roots, so the final factor is also $(x - 3)$. Now that you have the factors, multiply them together to get the polynomial. The first factor is awkward to work with, so multiply the equation $x + \frac{1}{2} = 0$ by 2 to get $2x + 1 = 0$. Now the function is $f(x) = (2x + 1)(x - 3)(x - 3)$.

$$= (2x + 1)(x^2 - 6x + 9)$$

$$= 2x^3 - 12x^2 + 18x + x^2 - 6x + 9$$

$$= 2x^3 - 11x^2 + 12x + 9$$

The correct answer is (A).

16. **B** Recall that the vertex form of a parabola is $y = a(x - h)^2 + k$. Plug in the vertex and the given point to find the value of a.

$$2 = a(1 - 3)^2 + 4$$

$$2 = a(-2)^2 + 4$$

$$2 = 4a + 4$$

$$-2 = 4a$$

$$-\frac{1}{2} = a$$

Now, plug your value of a into the vertex form and expand it out. Watch the signs!

$$y = -\frac{1}{2}(x-3)^2 + 4$$

$$y = -\frac{1}{2}(x^2 - 6x + 9) + 4$$

$$y = -\frac{1}{2}x^2 + 3x - \frac{9}{2} + 4$$

$$y = -\frac{1}{2}x^2 + 3x - \frac{1}{2}$$

The correct answer is (B).

15. **C** If only calculator use was allowed on this one! You could graph $f(x)$ and find the even solution immediately. To begin solving this one, you must first factor $f(x)$. The first factor is not obvious, so this requires a little guess and check on your part. You must first look to the coefficient of the x^3 term, 1, and the y-intercept term, −6. Determine the factors of both:

Factors of −6:   ±1, ±2, ±3, ±6

Factors of 1:   ±1

Determine a value to try as a factor by dividing factors of 6 by the factors of 1. Let's check the first one, 1/1, or just 1. If 1 were a solution, then that would mean that $(x - 1)$ would be a factor of the polynomial. Test it out by dividing $f(x)$ by $(x - 1)$:

$$
\require{enclose}
\begin{array}{r}
x^2 - 5x + 6 \\[-1pt]
x-1 \enclose{longdiv}{x^3 - 6x^2 + 11x - 6} \\[-1pt]
\underline{-(x^3 -x^2)} \\[-1pt]
-5x^2 + 11x \\[-1pt]
\underline{-(-5x^2 + 5x)} \\[-1pt]
6x - 6 \\[-1pt]
\underline{-(6x - 6)} \\[-1pt]
0
\end{array}
$$

Success! A good rule of thumb when you must guess a factor is to start small. It works out that way more often than not. What this tells us is that $f(x)$ factors to $(x - 1)(x^2 - 5x + 6)$. Now factor the rest of the expression so you can figure out the even x-value of the solutions.

$$(x - 1)(x^2 - 5x + 6) = (x - 1)(x - 2)(x - 3)$$

This means that your solutions are at $x = 1$, 2, and 3. The only even solution is $x = 2$, which equates to the coordinate $(2, 0)$. Now take the coordinate in conjunction with what you know regarding $g(x)$. You also know it passes through $(0, 6)$, and with two points, you can determine the slope of the line.

$$m_g = \frac{rise}{run} = \frac{6 - 0}{0 - 2} = \frac{6}{-2} = -3$$

To start working on $h(x)$, recall that the question said it is perpendicular to $g(x)$, so you must find the slope by calculating the negative reciprocal.

$$m_h = \frac{1}{3}$$

To find the equation of $h(x)$, you just need the y-intercept, or the point where $x = 0$. The question gave you the point $(0, 6)$, so you already have that information. Therefore, the equation is $h(x) = \frac{1}{3}x + 6$. The correct answer is (C).

33.   **4**   Begin by completing the square to write the function in the vertex form of a parabola. Watch the signs!

$$f(x) = -x^2 + 6x - 8$$

$$= -(x^2 - 6x) - 8$$

$$= -(x^2 - 6x + 9 - 9) - 8$$

$$= -(x^2 - 6x + 9) - (-9) - 8$$

$$= -(x^2 - 6x + 9) + 9 - 8$$

$$= -(x - 3)^2 + 1$$

Therefore, the vertex is at $(3, 1)$, and $h = 3$ and $k = 1$. Therefore, $h + k = 4$.

CHAPTER 17: ALTERNATIVE APPROACHES

Try It Exercise 1

12. **B** Plug in! The weight of the shipment must be within 5 pounds of 50 pounds, so start with $W = 50$. Because you're looking for the choice that describes all possible values of W, the correct answer must be true when $W = 50$. Choices (C) and (D) are false for $W = 50$, so eliminate them. Next, you want to plug in again. If you try $W = 55$, both (A) and (B) are true; the same is the case for $W = 45$. What you want to try is a number *outside* the range; make $W = 44$ and eliminate answer choices that are *true* with that value. If $W = 44$, (A) is still true; eliminate (A) and choose (B).

18. **A** Don't panic with labor-intensive problems such as this. Instead, get rid of the algebra by Plugging In. Also, don't worry about making the numbers realistic. Set the price of the boat as $x = 100$ since this number works well with percentages. Make the markup at auction $y = 20$ and the discount $z = 10$. Now use these numbers to find the price of the boat. Since the markup is 20%, the auction price of the boat is $120. Don later purchased the boat for 10% off. 10% of $120 is $12, so the final purchase price is $108. This is the target number. Now plug those numbers into a calculator: (A) is the only one that matches your target. The answer is (A).

20. **B** Challenging exponent questions are among some of the fastest questions on the SAT when you use Plugging In. Set $x = 2$ and run the numbers through the calculator: $3^4 \times 27^1 = 2,187$. This is the target. Now, plug in $x = 2$ to the answers. Only (B) matches this target.

27. **D** Plug in, using points from the curve. Look for places where it is easy to determine where the curve is. At $h = 6$, $A = 2$. Plug in $h = 6$ and eliminate any choice that does not make $A = 2$. This eliminates (A) and (B). Try another point. At $h = 0$, $A = 1.25$. Choice (C) does not work for this value; eliminate (C) and choose (D).

15. **D** Use Plugging In, and pick an easy number, since calculator use is not allowed. Make $x = 2$. The question then becomes

$$\frac{(2)^5 - 2(2)^4 - 13(2)^3 + 14(2)^2 + 24(2)}{2 + 3} = \frac{32 - 2(16) - 13(8) + 14(4) + 48}{5}$$

$$= \frac{32 - 32 - 104 + 56 + 48}{5} = \frac{0}{5} = 0 \,.$$

This is your target; circle it. Make $x = 2$ in each choice and eliminate any choice that does not equal 0. (Note: you can eliminate (A) and (C) without solving entirely because the fractions at the end will leave a decimal, making it impossible for those two answers to equal 0 when $x = 2$.) The only choice that works is (D).

Try It Exercise 2

9. **D** Jane spends a little less than half her time walking a *lot* faster, so it stands to reason that she would cover more than half the total distance at the faster speed. Another way to look at this is that if she spent half as much time walking at 6 kph as she did walking 3 kph, the two speeds would balance out, and she would cover the same distance at both speeds. But if that were the case, she would spend $\frac{1}{3}$ of her time walking at the faster speed. Since she spends more than $\frac{1}{3}$ of her time walking fast, she will cover more than half the distance at the faster speed. Notice that only (D) is a fraction greater than $\frac{1}{2}$, so (D) is the only possible answer.

If you want to solve this question exactly, you can use the formula *rate* $\times$ *time* = *distance*. Let's say her total time is x. At the beginning, her distance is $6 \times \frac{3}{8}x = \frac{18}{8}x$. For the second part, her distance is $3 \times \frac{5}{8}x = \frac{15}{8}x$. Therefore, her total distance is $\frac{18}{8}x = \frac{15}{8}x = \frac{33}{8}x$. To find the answer, divide $\frac{18}{8}x$ by $\frac{33}{8}x$ to get $\frac{6}{11}$.

Alternatively, you could plug in on this problem. Suppose Jane's total walking time is 6 hours. First, she walks 3 hours at 6 kph for a distance of $3 \times 6 = 18$ kilometers. Next, she walks 5 hours at 3 kph for a distance of $5 \times 3 = 15$ kilometers. Her total distance was $18 + 15 = 33$; the northbound part of the trip was $\frac{18}{33} = \frac{6}{11}$.

Either Plugging In or Ballparking works great here; the worst strategy is the one you learned in math class. Remember, the goal is to get the question right by the easiest method.

13. **B**   The answer choices are really far apart, and you're not allowed a calculator, so this is a great opportunity to use Ballparking. Round 679 up to 700: $7(x^2 - 3) = 700$. Divide both sides by 7: $x^2 - 3 = 100$. To get to $x^2 + 3$, add 6 to both sides and you get $x^2 + 3 = 106$. This is really close to 103, and really far from every other answer choice, so choose (B).

22. **B**   Ballpark! First, eliminate (C) because 2013 was a decrease, not an increase, over 2012's sales. 2011 is only a tiny increase over 2010, whereas 2012 is a huge jump from 2011; (A) is definitely not as big of an increase as (B), so eliminate (A). 2012 is $15.4 - 12.4 = 3,000$ units more than 2011, whereas 2014 is only $16.4 - 15.2 = 1,200$ units more than 2013. Furthermore, the percent change formula means you will be dividing 2012 by a smaller number (12,400) than what you'll be dividing 2014 by (15,200), so 2012 will clearly be the greater percent increase; choose (B).

15. **D**   Can you Ballpark on geometry questions? The figure is drawn to scale, so definitely try Ballparking. CD is definitely longer than BE, so eliminate (A) and (B). CD is more likely to be twice BE than only be a little more than BE, so (D) makes more sense given the diagram provided.

Alternatively, this question is testing similar triangles. Both triangle ABE and triangle ACD share angle A. Because BE and CD are parallel, the other corresponding angles are also congruent, so the triangles are similar. If E is the midpoint of AD, then $AE = \frac{1}{2}AD$, so $BE = \frac{1}{2}CD$. If $BE = 3$, then $3 = \frac{1}{2}CD$, making $CD = 6$.

CHAPTER 18: WORD PROBLEMS AND OTHER HOT TOPICS

Try It Exercise 1

11.   **A**   This is a great question to use Plugging In the Answers. Each answer represents a possible value of t, so plug them in for t in the equation and see which gives you the greatest height. Calculator use is allowed, so it should be fairly painless. Usually, you would start in the middle when using PITA, but this is a quadratic function, or an upside-down parabola. Therefore, the values for h will go up, then back down, so try all the given values of t in the answer choices. For (A), if $t = 0.75$, $h = 5 + 3(0.75) - 2(0.75)^2 = 6.125$. Follow the same steps to find that at $t = 1$, $h = 6$; at $t = 1.5$, $h = 5$; and at $t = 2.5$, $h = 0$. The greatest height, 6.125, occurred when $t = 0.75$, so the correct answer is (A).

18.   **D**   In this question, you may need to mix a bit of basic algebra with Plugging In the Answers. Start with (B). If the Johnsons earn \$780, you need to find what each of them earns. Let's say Mr. Johnson's earnings are x. Then, Mrs. Johnson's are $x + 60$, so $2x + 60 = 780$ and $x = 360$. Therefore, Mr. Johnson earns \$360, and Mrs. Johnson earns \$420. Now, does $\frac{3}{5}(420) = \frac{2}{3}(360)$? No, so (B) is incorrect. Keep trying until you get to (D). If the Johnson's earn \$1,140, then $2x + 60 = 1,140$ and $x = 540$, so Mr. Johnson earns \$540 and Mrs. Johnson earns \$600. Now check again: does $\frac{3}{5}(600) = \frac{2}{3}(540)$? Yes, so the correct answer is (D).

13.   **A**   Since this question is asking for the *least* possible value, start with (A). If $a = 30$, then $\frac{2}{5}(30) = 12 = b$, and $12 = \frac{3c^2}{4}$, so $c^2 = 16$, and c (which must be positive) is 4. The question specifies that a and c must be positive integers, and they are, so (A) works, and there is no need to check any other answers.

Try It Exercise 2

27. **A** The answer choices are a clue for this question: the form of the answers is similar

to the quadratic formula. There's also both a t and a t^2 in the original equation,

which means the equation is quadratic with regards to t. Start by rearranging

the equation into standard form with t as x. This means you want the form to be

$0 = at^2 + bt + c$. Subtract x from both sides: $0 = x_0 + v_o t + \dfrac{1}{2} at^2 - x$. Rearrange to

have the t terms in descending order by degree: $0 = \dfrac{1}{2} at^2 + v_o t + x_0 - x$. This means

the a term is $\dfrac{1}{2} a$, the b term is v_o, and the c term is $x_0 - x$ (neither of these terms are

multiplied by t, so they must be c). Insert these values into the quadratic formula:

$t = \dfrac{-v_0 \pm \sqrt{\left(v_0\right)^2 - 4\left(\frac{1}{2} a\right)\left(x_0 - x\right)}}{2\left(\frac{1}{2} a\right)}$. This isn't quite any answer choice, but you can

eliminate (C) and (D) because the wrong terms are in the denominator. Simplify by

multiplying the $\left(\dfrac{1}{2} a\right)$ terms by the coefficients to get $t = \dfrac{-v_0 \pm \sqrt{\left(v_0\right)^2 - 2a\left(x_0 - x\right)}}{a}$,

which is (A).

28. **C** There are a ton of unknowns in the equation. You need to use points from the graph

to solve for the different unknowns. Start with $t = 0$. At $t = 0$, displacement, x, is 2.

This makes the equation $2 = x_0 + 0.5(0) + \frac{1}{2} a(0)$, which simplifies to $2 = x_0$. Now, pick another point where t is not 0 and make $x_0 = 2$. At $t = 2$, $x = 5$. Input into the equation: $5 = 2 + 0.5(2) + \frac{1}{2} a(2)^2$. Simplify: $5 = 2 + 1 + 2a$, then $5 = 3 + 2a$, so $2 = 2a$, and $a = 1$, (C).

CHAPTER 19: PLANE GEOMETRY

Try It Exercise 1—Angles and Lines

3. **C** There are several ways to solve this one. Here is an efficient way. Line BF has 180 degrees. Since $x + y = 70$ degrees, then angle GOF must be 110 degrees. Since opposite angles are congruent, angle BOD is also 110 degrees. Finally, since line CO bisects this angle, angle BOC is half this size, or 55 degrees. The answer is (C).

4. **B** To tackle this problem efficiently, try penciling in every angle that's equal. Like this:

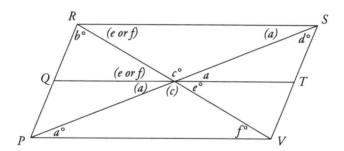

Note that angles e and f are also equal, as indicated above. Now you can clearly see that a, c, and either e or f make up straight line QT. Therefore, the correct answer is (B).

6. **D** This one is tricky. Draw in lines BF and CE. Since lines BE and CF are equal lengths, $BCEF$ must be a rectangle. The diagonals of a rectangle intersect at their midpoints, so point O is actually the midpoint of BE and CF. Therefore, $BO = FO = CO = EO$. Since AD intersects point O and is parallel to BC and EF, it must bisect $\angle BOF$, so angles BOA and FOA must be congruent, which also means that angles BAO and

FAO are also congruent. Since ∠*BAF* is 90°, angles *BAO* and *FAO* must be 45° each. There are 180° in a triangle, so angles *BOA* and *FOA* are each 30°. Finally, there are 180 degrees in a line, so ∠*BOA* + ∠*FOA* + ∠*BOC* = 180°, and ∠*BOC* = 180° − 30° − 30° = 120°, (D).

Try It Exercise 2—Triangles

1. **A** Don't let the diagram throw you. The base of a triangle is always perpendicular to its height. The long way to solve this is to use the Pythagorean Theorem to find the length of the third side: $4^2 + b^2 = 8^2$, so $b^2 = 48$ and $b = 4\sqrt{3}$. Now, put this into the area formula for a triangle: $\frac{1}{2}(4)(4\sqrt{3}) = 8\sqrt{3}$.

   The faster way to solve is to recognize that this is a 30-60-90 right triangle. Since two sides of a right triangle determine the third side, any right triangle in which the hypotenuse is twice one of the legs *must* be a 30-60-90 right triangle. If you recognize this, it can save you some time on calculations. Either way, the answer is (A).

8. **C** Remember the three steps for Geometry:

   1 – Draw the figure

   2 – Label the info

   3 – Write the formula(s)

   Step 1 – They've given you a figure, so you don't need to draw anything.

   Step 2 – Write in the information they've given you: $b = f = 30$, $a = 100$, $d = 50$. If you continue to determine all of the angle measurements, you'll find that these are two similar triangles.

   Step 3 – Write the formula(s). There aren't actually any formulas that you need to solve this question (apart from the basic formulas for the sum of angles in a triangle and for similar triangles).

   Once you recognize the similar triangles, the next step is to plug in for the unknown lengths of the sides they've given in the question: $\overline{AD} = \frac{1}{3}\overline{AB}$. Plug in 2 for $\overline{AD}$, which means that $\overline{AB}$ is 6, $\overline{BD}$ is 4, and $\overline{BE}$ is 3. Next, use a proportion to determine

$\overline{BC}$: $\dfrac{\overline{AB}}{\overline{BE}} = \dfrac{\overline{BC}}{\overline{BD}}$ or $\dfrac{6}{3} = \dfrac{\overline{BC}}{4}$. So $\overline{BC} = 8$. That's the target. Now go back to the answers and plug in the appropriate side lengths to determine which answer choices match 8, and only (C) does.

20.   **A**   Start by drawing line segments *AC* and *BD*, and label their intersection as *O*. Since *AO* and *DO* are the same lengths, $\angle AOD$ is a 45-45-90 right triangle (*any* right triangle with two legs that are the same is automatically a 45-45-90). Since the hypotenuse is $\sqrt{2}$, $AO = DO = 1$. See the figure below:

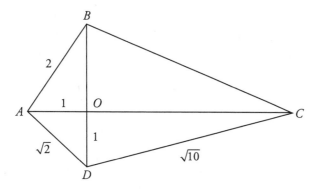

As mentioned two questions ago, any right triangle in which the hypotenuse is twice one of the legs must be a 30-60-90 right triangle, so *BO* is $\sqrt{3}$. Now, use the Pythagorean Theorem to find the length of *OC*, which is 3. Next, use the area formula of a triangle to find the area of triangles *ABC and ACD*. Area of *ABC* = $\dfrac{1}{2}(\sqrt{3})(4) = 2\sqrt{3}$ and area of *ACD* = $\dfrac{1}{2}$ (1)(4) = 2. Finally, set this into a ratio, being careful to match the order asked in the question: area of *ACD* to area of *ABC*, so 2 to $2\sqrt{3}$, which reduces to 1 to $\sqrt{3}$. The correct answer is (A).

Try It Exercise 3—Right Triangle Trigonometry

11.   **A**   Begin by sketching a right triangle and labeling the points *A*, *B*, and *C*. It does not matter which vertices you label as which as long as *CAB* is not your right angle. No matter how you draw the figure, the side opposite from *CAB* is *BC*, so side *BC*

corresponds to 7, whereas the hypotenuse corresponds to 25. If you are not familiar with the 7-24-25, you can use the Pythagorean Theorem to figure out that the third side must correspond to 24. Now, add up these three values to get a total of 56. Since you know that the perimeter of ABC is actually 14, you can set up a proportion: $\frac{14}{56} = \frac{BC}{7}$. Therefore, the value of BC is 1.75.

12. **C** The question tells you that $BC \perp CE$, so mark angle BCE as a right angle in your figure. Now you should be able to see that angles BCA and DCE are complementary angles and therefore the sine of one is equal to the cosine of the other. Choice (C) reflects this relationship. Both (B) and (D) mismatch corresponding sides, and note that (A) is wrong because the triangles are similar, but not necessarily congruent.

15. **B** Start by sketching and labeling the figure as shown below:

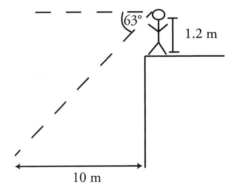

(Note: Make sure you read carefully to determine where the 63° angle is!)

Now you can figure out that angle opposite to the 10 meters is complementary to 63°, so it must be 27°. Since you want to determine the adjacent side, you should use tangent. Set up your equation: $\tan 27° = \frac{10}{adjacent}$. Using a calculator, you can determine that the adjacent side, the vertical height of the sketched triangle, is 19.63 meters. Be careful though, this is the height from Sam's eye-level to the ground, but

the problem tells us that his eye-level is 1.2 meters high, so the building must be
19.63 – 1.2 = 18.43 meters tall.

Try It Exercise 4—Circles

7. **B**   Begin by drawing the figure described. The room is square and has an area of
144 ft². Since the area of a square is s^2, then each side of the room measures 12 ft.
Next, draw the circular rug in the center of the room. Be sure to leave 1 foot of
space between the rug and each wall. The figure should now appear similar to the
one below:

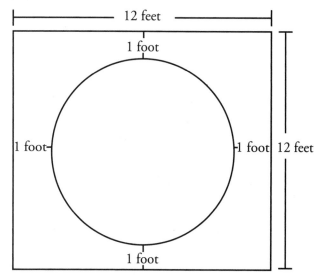

Since there is 1 foot of space on each side, the diameter of the rug must be 10 ft and
the radius 5 ft. The area of a circle is $A = \pi r^2$, so $A = 5^2\pi$ or 25π. This translates to
an actual value of about 78.5 square feet, but you're looking for the closest answer,
which is (B).

15. **B**   Begin by drawing lines *AO* and *CO* in order to highlight the minor arc distance
better. Since the problem mentions the area of the circle, write down the formula
$A = \pi r^2 = 64\pi$. Therefore, $r = 8$, which is the distance of *AO* and *CO*. The problem

mentions an arc length, so calculate the circumference: $C = 2\pi r = 16\pi$. Now, use a proportion to find the measure of central angle AOC: $\dfrac{x}{360°} = \dfrac{4\pi}{16\pi}$, where x is the central angle measure. Central angle AOC is 90°, which is bisected by line segment BO. Therefore, there are two 45-45-90 triangles. The hypotenuse AO is 8, so use the properties of a 45-45-90 triangle to find that BO is $\dfrac{8}{\sqrt{2}} = 4\sqrt{2}$. The answer is (B).

19. **D** This is a tricky problem. However, always begin by labeling what is known. Any line from the center of a circle to a point on the circle is a radius. Therefore, in order to find the perimeter of $ABCD$, you need to find the radii of circles A and C. First, draw line segment AC. Since A and C are the centers of the circle, but also lie on the circumference of the other circle, these two circles must be identical.

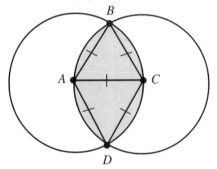

All radii are equal, so the shaded region is formed from two equilateral triangles. Work with only one of the two circles. Start by halving the perimeter to 20π. Since there are two equilateral triangles, $\angle BAD$ must be 120°, or one-third of the full circle. Knowing this, you can set up a proportion to find the radius: $\dfrac{\text{inscribed angle}}{360} = \dfrac{\text{arc}}{\text{circumference}}$, so $\dfrac{120}{360} = \dfrac{20\pi}{2\pi r}$. When you solve for r, you get $r = 30$. Multiply by 4 to get the perimeter, which is 120. The answer is (D).

Try It Exercise 5—Circle Trigonometry

6. **C** Solving arc length with radian measures is pretty straightforward: just use the formula $S = r\theta$. Since the circumference is 16π, the diameter must be 16, and the radius is 8. All you have to do is multiply $\frac{5\pi}{4}$ by 8 to get an arc length of 10π.

21. **A** Start by considering the sign of the answer. If $\frac{7\pi}{6} < x < \frac{5\pi}{3}$, then x is in either the third or fourth quadrant, and since sine values are y-value on the unit circle, all of these values will be negative. Eliminate (C) and (D). Now, it gets a little trickier. You may notice that $\sin\frac{7\pi}{6}$ is (B) and $\sin\frac{5\pi}{3}$ is (A). However, since the inequality excludes both of these values, you need to figure out whether (A) or (B) occurs somewhere else within this range of x-values. A sin value of $\frac{-1}{2}$ occurs twice on the unit circle: $\frac{7\pi}{6}$ and $\frac{11\pi}{6}$, and a sin value of $\frac{-\sqrt{3}}{2}$ occurs at $\frac{4\pi}{3}$ and $\frac{5\pi}{3}$. Only $\frac{4\pi}{3}$ is included within the given range, so (A) is correct.

28. **D** Take this one step at a time. Since the tan q is positive, it must be in the first or third quadrant. Therefore, $q + \frac{\pi}{2}$ must be in the second or fourth quadrant. You can therefore eliminate (B) and (C). Now, you can plug in either of the remaining answers. Starting with (A), if $q + \frac{\pi}{2} = \frac{-\pi}{6}$, then $q = \frac{-2\pi}{3}$. Use your calculator to check tan $\frac{-2\pi}{3}$. It's not $\frac{1}{\sqrt{3}}$, so eliminate (A); the answer must be (D).

Try It Exercise 6—Three Dimensional Figures

13. **D** The first thing you should solve for is the height of the cone using the formula from the reference box: $V = \frac{1}{3}\pi r^2 h$. You get $18\pi = \frac{1}{3}\pi(3)^2 h$, so $18\pi = 3\pi h$. Therefore, $h = 6$. Now draw and label the cylinder using this information. The volume of the

cylinder is twice that of the cone, or 36π, and the formula for the volume of a cylinder is $V = \pi r^2 h$. Thus, $36\pi = \pi r^2(6)$, $r^2 = 6$, and $r = \sqrt{6}$. The answer is (D).

26. **B**   You are given the volume of the cube, so start there. $V = s^3$, so $64 = s^3$ and $s = 4$. The longest diagonal of the cube will be the diameter of the sphere, so find the diagonal using the "super-Pythagorean" formula: $a^2 + b^2 + c^2 = d^2$. Since this is a cube, all the sides are the same, so $4^2 + 4^2 + 4^2 = d^2$, and $d = \sqrt{48} = 4\sqrt{3}$ (if you don't want to simplify roots, you can just convert to decimals on your calculator). Divide by two to find the radius, which is $2\sqrt{3}$. Now plug that into the formula given in the reference box for the volume of a sphere: $V = \dfrac{4}{3}\pi r^3 = \dfrac{4}{3}\pi(2\sqrt{3})^3 = 32\pi\sqrt{3}$.

17. **2**   Begin by drawing the figure, labeling it, and writing down the volume formula for a right circular cylinder: $V = \pi r^2 h$. Now, put the information from the problem into the formula: $100\pi = \pi r^2(4)$ and solve for r; you should get $r = 5$. Now draw and label cylinder B. The radius of B is twice that of A, so $r = 10$. Now, put this information into the volume formula and solve for the height: $200\pi = \pi 10^2 h$, so $h = 2$.

Chapter 21
Math Drill 1: No Calculator Section

The following is a brief sampling of math problems on a variety of topics as they would appear on the No Calculator section of the test. The instructions for that section are included, so that you can get used to them now and save time on test day. There is no answer sheet for the multiple-choice questions—just work out your answers and circle the right answer choices. For grid-ins, read the instructions carefully and mark your answers in the provided grids. Make sure to leave your calculator alone as you work these problems!

For questions **1-15**, solve each problem, choose the best answer from the choices provided, and fill in the corresponding circle on your answer sheet. For questions **16-20**, solve the problem and enter your answer in the grid on the answer sheet. Please refer to the directions before question 16 on how to enter your answers in the grid. You may use any available space in your test booklet for scratch work.

NOTES

1. The use of a calculator **is not permitted**.
2. All variables and expressions used represent real numbers unless otherwise indicated.
3. Figures provided in this test are drawn to scale unless otherwise indicated.
4. All figures lie in a plane unless otherwise indicated.
5. Unless otherwise indicated, the domain of a given function f is the set of all real numbers x for which $f(x)$ is a real number.

REFERENCE

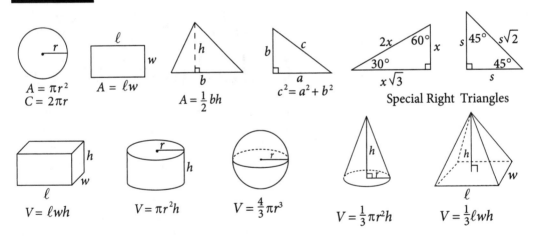

$A = \pi r^2$
$C = 2\pi r$

$A = \ell w$

$A = \frac{1}{2} bh$

$c^2 = a^2 + b^2$

Special Right Triangles

$V = \ell w h$

$V = \pi r^2 h$

$V = \frac{4}{3}\pi r^3$

$V = \frac{1}{3}\pi r^2 h$

$V = \frac{1}{3}\ell w h$

The number of degrees of arc in a circle is 360.
The number of radians of arc in a circle is 2π.
The sum of the measures in degrees of the angles of a triangle is 180.

2.

If $n \geq m$, which of the following must be true?

A) $m - n > 1$

B) $n - m \leq 1$

C) $m + n \geq 0$

D) $m - n \leq 0$

4

If $\dfrac{5}{\sqrt{10}}h = \dfrac{3}{\sqrt{2}}$, then what is the value of h ?

A) $\dfrac{3}{\sqrt{2}}$

B) $\dfrac{5}{\sqrt{2}}$

C) $\dfrac{3}{\sqrt{5}}$

D) $\dfrac{3}{5}$

5

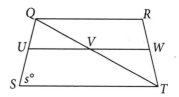

Note: Figure not drawn to scale.

In the figure above, $\overline{QR} \parallel \overline{UW} \parallel \overline{ST}$ and $\overline{QV} = \overline{UV}$. If the measure of $\angle QVW$ is 122°, what is the value of s ?

A) 29

B) 58

C) 61

D) 116

7

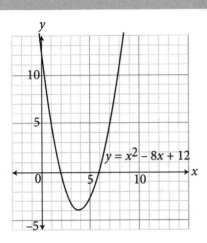

$y = x^2 - 8x + 12$

Which of the following equations, when graphed in the *xy*-plane above would create a system of equations with solutions at points (3, –3) and (8, 12) ?

A) $3x - y = 12$

B) $-3x + y = 12$

C) $x - 3y = 12$

D) $-x + 3y = 12$

8

Which of the following expressions is equivalent to $4^{2y}\, 8^y$?

A) 2^{3y}

B) 2^{5y}

C) 2^{7y}

D) 4^{3y}

11

A palm tree is planted in a pot. The monthly growth rate of the tree can be modeled as $y = 0.15x + 14$, where x represents the number of months since the tree was planted, and y is the total height of the tree, in inches. Which of the following statements is true?

A) The tree grows 14 inches per month.

B) The tree was 14 inches tall when it was planted in the pot.

C) The diameter of the pot is 14 inches.

D) The conversion factor for finding the height in centimeters is 14.

12

$$BMI = \frac{w}{h^2} \times 703$$

A physician wants to determine if her patient is at a healthy weight for his height. She calculates his Body Mass Index (BMI) using the equation above, where w is the patient's weight in pounds and h is his height in inches. If the patient is 70 inches tall, which inequality best represents the approximate weights that would suggest that the patient has a BMI greater than 25 ?

A) $w > 175$

B) $w < 175$

C) $w > 150$

D) $w < 150$

14

$$3x - 19y = 17y + 6$$
$$x = 6y + 3$$

Based on the system of equations above, what is the value of the quotient $\frac{x}{y}$?

A) $\dfrac{1}{6}$

B) $\dfrac{2}{3}$

C) 4

D) 24

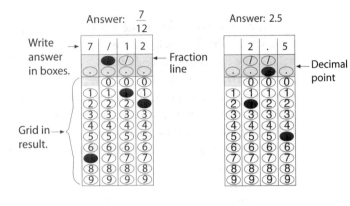
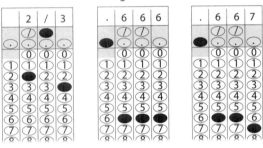
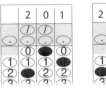

16

Let the function f be defined by

$f(x) = \dfrac{\left(x^2 - x\right)}{x}$, where x is an integer

and $x \neq 0$. If $10 < f(y) < 14$, what is one

possible value of y ?

18

If $\dfrac{1}{z} + \dfrac{4z + 2}{z^2 + 11z} = \dfrac{12z - 24}{z^2 + 11z}$, what is the

value of z ?

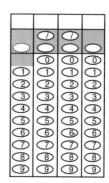

Chapter 22
Math Drill 2: Calculator Permitted Section

The following is a small selection of math problems on a range of concepts as they would appear on the Calculator Permitted section of the test. The instructions for that section are included, so that you can become familiar with them now and save time on test day. There is no answer sheet for the multiple-choice questions—just work out your answers and circle the right answer choices. For grid-ins, read the instructions carefully and mark your answers in the provided grids. Calculator use is permitted on all of these questions, so use it to avoid making careless mistakes when necessary, but always set up the problem on paper first.

DIRECTIONS

For questions **1-30**, solve each problem, choose the best answer from the choices provided, and fill in the corresponding circle on your answer sheet. For questions **31-38**, solve the problem and enter your answer in the grid on the answer sheet. Please refer to the directions before question 31 on how to enter your answers in the grid. You may use any available space in your test booklet for scratch work.

NOTES

1. The use of a calculator **is permitted**.
2. All variables and expressions used represent real numbers unless otherwise indicated.
3. Figures provided in this test are drawn to scale unless otherwise indicated.
4. All figures lie in a plane unless otherwise indicated.
5. Unless otherwise indicated, the domain of a given function f is the set of all real numbers x for which $f(x)$ is a real number.

REFERENCE

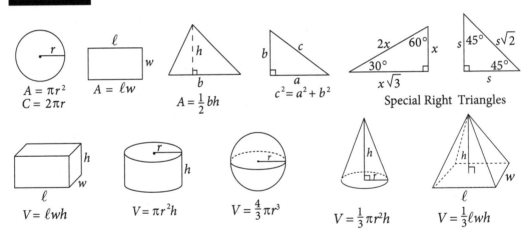

$A = \pi r^2$
$C = 2\pi r$

$A = \ell w$

$A = \frac{1}{2} bh$

$c^2 = a^2 + b^2$

Special Right Triangles

$V = \ell wh$

$V = \pi r^2 h$

$V = \frac{4}{3} \pi r^3$

$V = \frac{1}{3} \pi r^2 h$

$V = \frac{1}{3} \ell wh$

The number of degrees of arc in a circle is 360.
The number of radians of arc in a circle is 2π.
The sum of the measures in degrees of the angles of a triangle is 180.

5

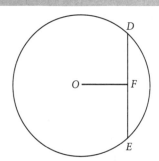

Note: Figure not drawn to scale.

In the figure above, the circle has center O and area 169π. The midpoint of $\overline{DE}$ is F, and $\overline{OF} = 12$. What is the length of $\overline{DE}$?

A) 5

B) 10

C) 13

D) 26

8

A store reduces the price of a pair of shoes by 15 percent. If the sale price is r dollars, which of the following is the closest approximation of the original price, in dollars, of the shoes, in terms of r ?

A) $1.18r$

B) $1.15r$

C) $1.10r$

D) $0.87r$

12

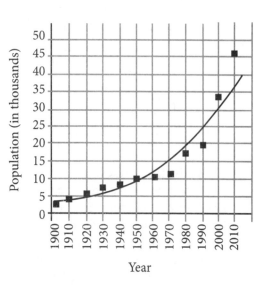

Year

The scatterplot diagram above shows the population of Warren County, Iowa, in thousands of people, since 1900. The curve of best fit shown has a y-intercept of 3,400. Which of the following statements is true about the population of Warren Country, Iowa, given this y-intercept?

A) The median population for Warren County, Iowa, from 1900 to 2000 was 3,400.

B) On average, the population of Warren County, Iowa, increased by 3,400 every 10 years.

C) The population of Warren County, Iowa, in 1900 was exactly 3,400.

D) The population of Warren County, Iowa, in 1990 was approximately 3,400.

15

Driver Age (Years)	Sign Legibility Distance (feet)
15	550
25	512
31	487
35	472
42	443
50	409

A biostatistician is studying the relationship between a driver's age and the driver's visual ability. She finds that the distance from which the driver can read a certain highway sign depends on the driver's age, as shown in the table above. Which of the following best describes the relationship between the age of the driver and the sign legibility?

A) The relationship is approximately exponential, since for every year, the sign legibility distance decreases by approximately 15%.

B) The relationship is approximately exponential, since for every year, the sign legibility decreases by approximately 25%.

C) The relationship is approximately linear, since for every year, the sign legibility distance decreases by approximately 4 feet.

D) The relationship is approximately linear, since for every year, the sign legibility distance decreases by approximately 8 feet.

17

As a result of the rapid growth of cell phone usage in the United States, the number of people using telephone landlines in a certain small town in California is decreasing at a rate of 25% per year. If there are currently 150,000 people using landlines in this particular town, and x represents the number of years, which of the following expressions best represents the trend in the town's landline usage?

A) $150,000(0.25)^x$

B) $150,000(0.25)x$

C) $150,000(0.75)^x$

D) $150,000(0.75)x$

20

$$f(x) = (x^2 - 2x - 35)(x + 5)(x + c)$$

The function f above is a polynomial function where c is a constant. If $(-5, 0)$ and $(3, 0)$ are points on the graph of $f(x)$, what is the product of the zeros of f?

A) -525

B) -105

C) 105

D) 525

23

An athletic trainer coaches only athletes who play football, baseball, and soccer. In a certain month, 3 football players were coached for every 7 baseball players, and 6 soccer players were coached for every football player. If the total number of athletes coached that month was between 375 and 400, how many soccer players were coached?

A) 42

B) 72

C) 98

D) 252

26

Scott takes three times as long to pack 12 boxes as Jean takes to pack 7 boxes. What is the ratio of Scott's average packing rate to Jean's average packing rate?

A) 2:3

B) 4:7

C) 7:4

D) 7:12

DIRECTIONS

For questions 32-33, solve the problem and enter your answer in the grid, as described below, on the answer sheet.

1. Although not required, it is suggested that you write your answer in the boxes at the top of the columns to help you fill in the circles accurately. You will receive credit only if the circles are filled in correctly.

2. Mark no more than one circle in any column.

3. No question has a negative answer.

4. Some problems may have more than one correct answer. In such cases, grid only one answer.

5. **Mixed numbers** such as $3\frac{1}{2}$ must be gridded as 3.5 or 7/2. (If $\boxed{3\ 1\ /\ 2}$ is entered into the grid, it will be interpreted as $\frac{31}{2}$, not as $3\frac{1}{2}$.)

6. **Decimal Answers:** If you obtain a decimal answer with more digits than the grid can accommodate, it may be either rounded or truncated, but it must fill the entire grid.

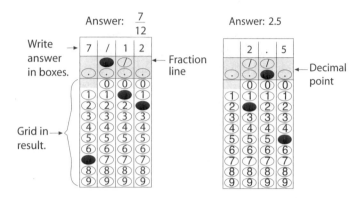

Answer: $\frac{7}{12}$ Answer: 2.5

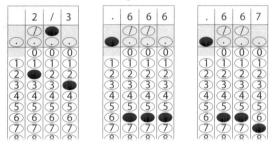

Acceptable ways to grid $\frac{2}{3}$ are:

Answer: 201 – either position is correct

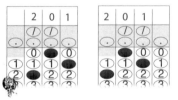

NOTE: You may start your answers in any column, space permitting. Columns you don't need to use should be left blank.

32

The function f is defined by $f(x) = 4x + 3$. If $3 \cdot f(r) = 93$, what is the value of r?

```
          ⊘ ⊘
  ○       ○ ○ ○
    ⓪ ⓪ ⓪
  ① ① ① ①
  ② ② ② ②
  ③ ③ ③ ③
  ④ ④ ④ ④
  ⑤ ⑤ ⑤ ⑤
  ⑥ ⑥ ⑥ ⑥
  ⑦ ⑦ ⑦ ⑦
  ⑧ ⑧ ⑧ ⑧
  ⑨ ⑨ ⑨ ⑨
```

33

A jar contains glass beads of equivalent weights. If 47 glass beads have a total weight of 3.2 ounces, and the maximum capacity of the jar is 4 pounds, how many glass beads can the jar hold? (Note: 16 ounces = 1 pound)

```
          ⊘ ⊘
  ○       ○ ○ ○
    ⓪ ⓪ ⓪
  ① ① ① ①
  ② ② ② ②
  ③ ③ ③ ③
  ④ ④ ④ ④
  ⑤ ⑤ ⑤ ⑤
  ⑥ ⑥ ⑥ ⑥
  ⑦ ⑦ ⑦ ⑦
  ⑧ ⑧ ⑧ ⑧
  ⑨ ⑨ ⑨ ⑨
```

Chapter 23
Math Drills:
Answers and
Explanations

MATH DRILL 1

2. **D**   With variables in the question and variables in the answers, you should plug in on this question. Also, because it asks what MUST BE true, you should be prepared to plug in more than once. So if $m = 2$ and $n = 3$, (A) is $2 - 3 > 1$, which is false, so eliminate it. Choice (B) is $3 - 2 \leq 1$, which is true, so leave it in. Choice (C) equals $2 + 3 \geq 0$, which is true, so leave it in. Choice (D) is $2 - 3 \leq 0$, which is also true. Now choose two different numbers. Pay particular attention to the ways they're trying to trick you: try plugging in the same value for both integers, or try a negative number or zero since there are no restrictions on what kind of values you can plug in. Let's say both m and n equal 0. Choice (B) becomes $0 - 0 \leq 1$, which is true, so leave it. Choice (C) becomes $0 + 0 \geq 0$, which is true again, so leave it. Choice (D) becomes $0 - 0 \leq 0$, which is true as well. Now try negative values, like $m = -6$ and $n = 0$. Choice (B) is false, with $0 - (-6) \leq 1$ or $6 \leq 1$. Eliminate it. Choice (C) says $-6 + 0 \geq 0$, which is not true, so get rid of it. The answer is (D): $-6 - 0 \leq 0$.

4. **C**   Plugging In the Answers could get ugly here, and it might be hard to tell which direction to go if your first try doesn't work. Solve this one instead. Multiply both sides of the equation by $\sqrt{10}$ to get $5h = \dfrac{3\sqrt{10}}{\sqrt{2}}$. The $\sqrt{10}$ on the right side can be rewritten as $\sqrt{2 \times 5}$ or $\sqrt{2} \times \sqrt{5}$. The $\sqrt{2}$ in the numerator and the denominator cancel out, leaving $5h = 3\sqrt{5}$. Divide both sides by 5 to get $h = \dfrac{3\sqrt{5}}{5}$. This doesn't match any of the answers exactly, but (D) can definitely be eliminated. Choice (C) is the closest, so work with that answer to get the root out of the denominator. Multiply the fraction in the answer by $\dfrac{\sqrt{5}}{\sqrt{5}}$, which will not change the value of the answer. The answer becomes $\dfrac{3}{\sqrt{5}} \times \dfrac{\sqrt{5}}{\sqrt{5}} = \dfrac{3\sqrt{5}}{5}$, which is the value you found for h.

5. **C** Any time you see parallel lines, you need to be thinking about the angles they create. Extend the parallel lines so the angles are easier to see. If $\angle QVW$ is 122°, then $\angle QVU$ is 58°. The question also says that $\overline{QV} = \overline{UV}$, so you know that the angles across from those sides are equal; with 180° in a triangle, and 58° already accounted for, that means $\angle VQU$ and $\angle VUQ$ are both 61°. Then, using parallel lines, you can determine that angle s will also be equal to 61°, or (C).

7. **A** When given points that represent the solutions of the system of equations, test those points out in the given equations. If they work in both equations, they are the solutions to the system. Start with point (8, 12) since it doesn't have any negative values to complicate things. The point is clearly on the graph of the parabola, so try it in the answer choices. Plugging it into (A) results in 3(8) − 12 = 12, or 24 − 12 = 12. This is true, so (A) might be the answer. You could check (8, 12) in all the other answer choices to see if any work, or just check (3, −3) in (A). The second option is quicker: (A) becomes 3(3) − (−3) = 12, or 9 + 3 = 12, which is also true, so the answer is (A).

8. **C** Anytime a question asks you to manipulate exponents, remember that exponent rules apply only to the expressions with the same base, so start by converting each expression into the same base. Both 4 and 8 are powers of 2, so you should get $4^{2y} \times 8^{y} = (2^2)^{2y} \times (2^3)^{y} = 2^{4y} \times 2^{3y} = 2^{7y}$, which is (C).

11. **B** Start by labeling the parts of the equation. The question says that y is the height of the tree in inches and x is the number of months since the tree was planted. So the equation is really *height in inches* = 0.15(*months*) + 14. Does this tell you anything about the diameter of the pot, or the height in centimeters? No, so eliminate (C) and (D). Now plug in some numbers to see if (A) or (B) is true. For (A), plug in 1 for x to find that the height after 1 month is 14.15 inches. If $x = 2$ months, the tree is 14.3 inches. The tree did not grow 14 inches, so (A) is false and (B) must be true. When the tree is planted, $x = 0$, so the height is 14 inches.

12. **A** Plugging In could work here, but it might be tricky without a calculator. Instead, set up the inequality and solve it. You want BMI > 25, so plug in what is given into the BMI formula. The inequality becomes $\dfrac{w}{70^2} \times 703 > 25$. This looks a bit ugly to deal with, so round 703 to 700, which will still give you the "approximate" weights.

Also, rewrite 70^2 as 70×70 to make it easier to reduce before solving. Now the inequality is $\dfrac{w}{70 \times 70} \times 700 > 25$. Cancel one of the 70s in the denominator with the 700, leaving 10 in the denominator, or $\dfrac{w}{70} \times 10 > 25$. Now reduce the 10 and the 70 to get $\dfrac{w}{7} > 25$. Finally, multiply both sides by 7 to get $w > 175$.

14. **D** Start by simplifying the first equation by adding $19y$ to both sides to get $3x = 36y + 6$. Looking at the two equations, it doesn't seem possible to get anything into the form $\dfrac{x}{y}$ that the question asks for. It will be necessary to solve for x and y. You could substitute the value of x in the second equation into the first equation or divide the first equation by 3 so they are both written as $x = $ something, then set those two parts equal. Use whichever method is least likely to cause you to make a careless error, especially since you can't use a calculator.

Substitution: put $6y + 3$ in for x in the equation $3x = 36y + 6$ to get $3(6y + 3) = 36y + 6$. This becomes $18y + 9 = 36y + 6$ or $18y = 3$. Therefore, $y = \dfrac{1}{6}$.

Setting the equations equal: dividing the first equation, $3x = 36y + 6$, by 3 results in $x = 12y + 2$. Set this equal to the second equation to get $12y + 2 = 6y + 3$, so $6y = 1$ and $y = \dfrac{1}{6}$.

Regardless of how you arrive at the value for y, plug this value into the simpler second equation to find that $x = 6\left(\dfrac{1}{6}\right) + 3 = 1 + 3 = 4$. Now take the quotient $\dfrac{x}{y} = \dfrac{4}{\frac{1}{6}} = 4 \times 6 = 24$, which is (D).

16. **12, 13, or 14**

You have variables, so use Plugging In. Since you can't use your calculator, start out small with $y = 5$ to see what you get. $25 - 5$ is 20, divided by 5 is 4: that doesn't meet the requirement that the function needs to be larger than 10. Try plugging in 10, which yields 9—closer! Try again with 11, which gives you EXACTLY 10. Be careful, though; the question said the function must be LARGER than 10, so

y cannot be equal to 11. That's enough information, though, to know that some integers larger than 11 will satisfy the condition, so you can answer 12. Actually solving this would show that 13 and 14 also work for y.

18. $\dfrac{37}{7}$ or **5.28** or **5.29**

To add the fractions on the left side of the equation, you need a common denominator. One way to do that is to use the Bowtie Method—multiply the denominator of the first fraction by the numerator of the second fraction to get a new numerator for the second fraction, and multiply the denominator of the second fraction by the numerator of the first fraction to get the new numerator of the first fraction. The denominator of both fractions will be the product of the existing denominators. You can then add the fractions together easily.

In this case, however, that would change the denominator of the second fraction, which already matches that of the fraction on the right side of the equation. Instead, find a way to make the denominator of the first fraction match the other two. The binomial $z^2 + 11$ can be rewritten as $z(z + 11)$, so to get z looking like $z^2 + 11$, multiply the numerator and denominator of the first fraction by $\dfrac{z+11}{z+11}$.

The left side becomes $\dfrac{1(z+11)}{z(z+11)} + \dfrac{4z+2}{z^2+11z} = \dfrac{z+11}{z^2+11z} + \dfrac{4z+2}{z^2+11z} = \dfrac{5z+13}{z^2+11z}$.

Now, since the denominators match on both sides, you know that $5z + 13 = 12z - 24$. Subtract $5z$ from both sides to get $13 = 7z - 24$, then add 24 to both sides to get $37 = 7z$. Finally, divide both sides by 7 to get $z = \dfrac{37}{7}$. On a calculator, this would equal 5.28 or 5.29, so technically, those answers are acceptable as well. Since this is in the No Calculator section, though, stick with the fraction as long as it fits in the grid.

MATH DRILL 2

5. **B** Remember the three steps for Geometry:

1 – Draw the figure

2 – Label the info

3 – Write the formula(s)

Step 1 – A figure is already provided.

Step 2 – Label $\overline{OF}$ = 12, and identify that $\overline{DF}$ and $\overline{EF}$ are congruent.

Step 3 – Write the formula for the area of a circle, since that's what they've provided. $A = \pi r^2$. Solve to find $r = 13$. The radius isn't drawn in, so draw in either $\overline{OD}$ or $\overline{OE}$. You will now see that you have a right triangle with one leg of 12 and a hypotenuse of 13, which should trigger your memory of Special Right Triangles: 5-12-13. That means that both $\overline{DF}$ and $\overline{EF}$ are 5. Be careful as you read the question: it's asking for $\overline{DE}$, which has a length of 10, *not* $\overline{DF}$ or $\overline{EF}$, both of which are 5. The credited response is (B).

8. **A** Start by Ballparking: if r is the sale price of the shoes, the original price must be greater than r. Therefore, (D) is too small. Variables in the question and answers are good indicators to use Plugging In! Since the question deals with percentages, start with $100 for the original price of the shoes. The price is reduced 15%, which means it is now $85, or r. The question is asking for the original price, which makes $100 the target. Plug $85 into the answer choices to find the one that comes closest to $100. Choice (A) is $100.30 and (B) is $97.75. Choice (A) is closer and is therefore the closest approximation.

12. **D** A scatterplot shows distinct data points, one dot for each paired x- and y-coordinate. Process of Elimination can be used to get rid of (A) and (B). The median will be somewhere near the middle of the graph, or specifically the average of the population values of 1950 and 1960, which is around 10,000. The average is harder to calculate, as you'd have add all the population values and divide by 12, the number of data points, but it has nothing to do with the y-intercept of the curve. A line or curve of best fit is often drawn to show the best approximation of the majority of data. It

can be used to get an idea of where new data points might fall on the graph, but it is only an educated guess. The *y*-intercept on the curve of best fit for this graph can estimate the population in 1900, which is $x = 0$ on the graph, but it won't be exact. In fact, you can see that the point for 1900 falls just slightly below the curve of best fit. This makes (D) the correct answer.

15. **C** To determine how much the sign legibility distance is changing as a function of the driver's age, take two sets of data from the chart. Start with an age of 15 years and go to an age of 25 years. This is an increase in age of 10 years. Over that increase in age, sign legibility distance goes from 550 feet to 512 feet. This is a decrease of $550 - 512 = 38$ feet. To find the decrease per year, divide 38 by 10 to get 3.8 or approximately 4 feet per year. This makes (C) look like it might be correct, but try it one more time to make sure the relationship holds. The increase from 35 to 42 years reflects a difference of 7 years, over which sign legibility distance decreases from 472 or 443 feet, which is a difference of 29 feet. Per year, that's $29 \div 7 = 4.12$ feet. Again, this is approximately 4 feet per year, so (C) is correct. If the relationship were exponential, the values for the sign legibility distance would be decreasing at a more rapid rate.

17. **C** There are a couple of different ways to approach this question. You can do some busywork on your calculator and then plug values into the answer choices in order to determine which one matches your data. It would probably be easier to do some quick Process of Elimination with the answer choices. Since the number of people using landlines is decreasing at a rate of 25% per year, this is an exponential relationship, and thus you can eliminate (B) and (D), which are linear equations (no exponent). Choice (A) is a tricky one, since the number 25 is in the question stem, but the correct answer is actually (C). Since the rate is decreasing 25% each year, that means that each year the number of landline users is 75% of what it was the previous year—hence (C).

20. **B** The zeros of a function when graphed in the *xy*-plane are the places where the function crosses the *x*-axis. They may also be referred to as roots, solutions, or *x*-intercepts. No matter what they are called, they are the places where $y = 0$. The question actually gives two such places: $(-5, 0)$ and $(3, 0)$. This tells you that -5 and 3 are two of the zeros of *f*. When finding the solutions or roots of a polynomial, you

factor it and set each binomial equal to zero. The $(x + 5)$ binomial gives you the root -5. Factor the $(x^2 - 2x - 35)$ part of f to see if the other given root, 3, comes from that or from $(x + c)$. Factoring $(x^2 - 2x - 35)$ gives you $(x - 7)(x + 5)$, so the roots of that part are 7 and -5. This means that the root of 3 comes from $(x + c)$, and you now have all the roots. The graph of f crosses the x-axis at -5, 3, and 7. Remember not to count the -5 twice: the graph of a function can only cross the x-axis once at a given value of x. So the product of the zeros is $(-5)(3)(7) = -105$, which is (B).

23. **D** There is a lot going on in this question, so write things down to keep your information organized. The first relationship given is 3 football players for every 7 baseball players. The next piece says there are 6 soccer players for every football player, so if there are 3 football players, there are $3(6) = 18$ soccer players. These are the numbers of each type of players in the ratio, but that doesn't reflect the actual number of players. Add the numbers of each type of player to find that there are $3 + 7 + 18 = 28$ players in a group, and the total number of players must be some multiple of this number. The next piece of information given is that the total actual number of players coached in the month was between 375 and 400, so you'll have to do a bit of Ballparking to determine how many groups of 28 were coached. The number in each group is close to 30, and to get from 30 to at least 375, you'll have to multiply by at least 11 or 12. Try 12, and see what your actual number becomes: $28 \times 12 = 336$. That's not big enough, so try 13 or 14: $28 \times 14 = 392$, which is exactly in the range you're looking for. Now, just use this information to find the number of soccer players, the group the question asks about. If there are 14 groups with 18 soccer players in each group, then $14 \times 18 = 252$ soccer players were coached. The correct answer is (D).

26. **B** One of the ways the SAT makes questions challenging is by combining multiple concepts into one problem. This question is a ratio question, but there's also information missing, and it asks for the ratio of their averages, not their time or actual number of boxes packed. Start by plugging in for the missing information so you can actually work with values. The missing information is the amount of time it takes each of them to pack different numbers of boxes. So, say Jean takes 2 hours to pack 4

boxes; if it takes Scott three times as long to pack his 12 boxes, it takes him 6 hours. Next use the rate equation to determine their individual rates. For work rates, the equation is $W = RT$, in which W is work, R is rate, and T is time. For Scott, this becomes 12 boxes = (R)(6 hours), so $R = 2$ boxes per hour. For Jean, this becomes 7 boxes = (R)(2 hours), so $R = 3.5$ boxes per hour. The last step is to find the ratio of Scott's average to Jean's average. Currently, it looks like 2:3.5, but it's unusual for the SAT to have decimals in average questions, so you'll need to convert that into whole numbers: 4:7, which is (B). Notice that (C) is a trap answer: it reverses the ratio, so read the question carefully!

32. **7**   Start by dividing $3 \times f(r) = 93$ by 3 to get to the value of $f(r)$, 31. Then set the original function equal to 31 and solve:

$f(x) = 4x + 3$

$f(r) = 4r + 3$

$31 = 4r + 3$

$\underline{-3 \qquad -3}$

$\dfrac{28}{4} = \dfrac{4r}{4}$

$7 = r$

33. **940**   Solve this using proportions: $\dfrac{16 \text{ ounces}}{1 \text{ pound}} = \dfrac{x \text{ ounces}}{4 \text{ pounds}}$ will tell you that the capacity of the jar is 64 ounces. Next, set up a proportion of beads to ounces: solve $\dfrac{47 \text{ beads}}{3.2 \text{ ounces}} = \dfrac{x \text{ beads}}{64 \text{ ounces}}$ by cross-multiplying to get $3.2x = 3{,}008$, so $x = 940$ glass beads that the jar can hold.

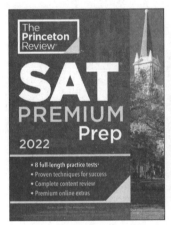

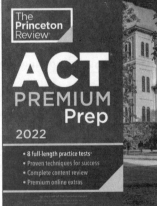